# The American ⅃
## in the
# The Meuse Height⸱
## to the Armistice

This book is dedicated to Eric Mueller, Matthew Young, Todd Rambow and Paul Osman, who keep the history and memory of the US 26th, 29th and 33rd Divisions alive, and to Tom Gudmestad who over the years has provided me with invaluable information in the form of books, photographs, general advice and, dare I say it, friendship.

# The American Expeditionary Forces in the Great War
# The Meuse Heights to the Armistice

Maarten Otte

Pen & Sword
**MILITARY**

AN IMPRINT OF PEN & SWORD BOOKS LTD.
YORKSHIRE - PHILADELPHIA

First published in Great Britain in 2021 and reprinted in 2022 by
Pen & Sword Military
an imprint of
Pen & Sword Books Ltd
Yorkshire – Philadelphia

ISBN 978 1 52679 617 2

Typeset in Times New Roman by
SJmagic DESIGN SERVICES, India

Printed and bound in the UK by
CPI Group (UK), Croydon, CR0 4YY

Pen & Sword Books Ltd incorporates the imprints of
Pen & Sword Archaeology, Atlas, Aviation, Battleground, Discovery,
Family History, History, Maritime, Military, Naval, Politics,
Railways, Select, Social History, Transport, True Crime,
Claymore Press, Frontline Books, Leo Cooper, Praetorian Press,
Remember When, Seaforth Publishing and Wharncliffe.

For a complete list of Pen & Sword titles please contact
PEN & SWORD BOOKS LIMITED
47 Church Street, Barnsley, South Yorkshire, S70 2AS, England
E-mail: enquiries@pen-and-sword.co.uk
Website: www.pen-and-sword.co.uk

# Contents

Series Editor's Introduction ..... vi
Introduction ..... xi
List of Maps ..... xxi

**Chapter 1**    The Americans in the Meuse ..... 1
**Chapter 2**    Summary of Operations, 26 September to
                 31 October ..... 20
                     The 33rd Division
                     The 29th Division
                     The 26th Division
**Chapter 3**    Summary of operations, 3 to 11 November ..... 70
                     The 79th Division
                     The 26th Division
                     The 32nd Division
**Chapter 4**    The 5th Division, 3 to 11 November ..... 95

**The Tours**
**Car Tour 1:**   The 29th and 33rd Divisions' sector ..... 110
**Car Tour 2:**   The 26th and 79th Divisions' sector ..... 137
**Car Tour 3:**   The 5th and 32nd Divisions' sector ..... 159
**Car Tour 4:**   The 5th Division – the Meuse Crossings ..... 182
**Walk 1:**        The 26th and 79th Divisions – Ormont Hill ..... 204
**The Henry Gunther Tour** ..... 214

**Appendices**
1. Order of Battle for operations on the Right Bank,
    First Army, AEF. ..... 230
2. The French divisions employed in operations on the
    Right Bank. ..... 235
3. The composition of an average American infantry division. ..... 237
4. Some statistics. ..... 239
5. The German and KuK outline Order of Battle for the
    Right Bank operations. ..... 242

Advice to travellers ..... 250
Acknowledgements ..... 255
Select bibliography and suggested further reading ..... 256
Selective Index ..... 258

# Series Editor's Introduction

On a sunny day in June 2020, recently – or at least partially – liberated from M Macron's Covid-induced house-arrest, I found myself standing on a concrete bunker, part of a modern water reservoir system, just east of Haraumont and more or less on the Kriemhild Line, part of the so-called Hindenburg system. The views obtained from here to the south and to the west, well across the left bank of the Meuse, are magnificent; for example, Montfaucon, getting on for thirteen kilometres away, is clearly visible. Although the AEF got close to the Kriemhild Line on the Right Bank – or the Meuse Heights – they did not occupy it until after the Armistice.

What was quite apparent from my perch is the view that German artillery observers all along the right bank of the river had over much of the ground across which Pershing's First Army was advancing. After some initial impressive gains on the 26th and 27th September, the Americans were finding it increasingly difficult to make much meaningful progress. The situation was not improved by much until General Liggett took command of the First Army in mid October, Pershing having abandoned his quixotic, untenable attempt to be both Commander in Chief of the AEF and the field commander of the USA's (then) only Army, a huge formation, vastly bigger than any other Army formation on the Western Front.

As Maarten points out (and as was clear to me from my first visit to the area with the Meuse Argonne Offensive as its object), the German artillery on the Meuse Heights, an area known as the Right Bank during the Battle of Verdun 1916, had wonderful fields of fire across the river. A place like Montfaucon, for example, would be well within range of their bigger calibre guns; whilst these guns would be pretty well immune to counter battery fire, protected by the topography, with its ravines, its folds in the ground and good reverse slope positions. Any advance, particularly on the right of the First Army, would have to take place under the gauntlet of this fire. The Germans also had good artillery coverage of the American attack on the left, from the high ground to the north of the Argonne Forest; but that is a different story.

One of the hardest lessons that the German army learnt from the Battle of Verdun came early on in that offensive. If things had gone very well, the problem of the French artillery on the far side of the Meuse, the so-called Left (or west) Bank, might not have been too significant. As things worked out, the initial counter battery fire was quite inadequate and the reinforced array of French artillery on the Left Bank became of such significance that the Germans were left with but little alternative than to extend their offensive to that side of the river as well in early March.

In September and October 1918 the situation was comparable: this time the advance would be on the Left Bank and the Right Bank would be covered by the French XVII Corps (under American command), not by an infantry attack but by what turned out to be a rather pathetic display of counter battery fire. The Germans were initially quite convinced that the American attack would be on their Right Bank positions and that the initial assault across the river was just a diversion: to them it would make more strategic sense. However, it did not take them long to realise that it was no diversion and they reacted accordingly. Their consolation was that the Americans had failed to make massive gains in the opening few days of the Offensive and, like the Germans in February 1916, they were now confronted by accurate, incessant and deadly flanking fire from across the Meuse.

Eventually Pershing had to tackle the problem; some rather more significant attacks in October pushed the Germans back somewhat on the Right Bank, but this was a matter of removing outpost positions, not dealing with the real problem. It was in the dying days of the war that more significant progress was made – by which stage, in any case, the German positions on the Left Bank had more or less collapsed. The Hindenburg Line had not been completely breached in this area by the time of the Armistice. If the Meuse-Argonne Offensive in general is relatively little known about today, not least in the United States itself, the AEF's fighting on the right bank appears as but a footnote to it. Even in Pershing's two volumes of war-time memoirs the total space taken up by it would probably come to less than the equivalent of a single page – and much of that was devoted to the activity of one of his beloved regular army divisions, the 5th. The men of all sides who fought and died here in these twilight days of the war deserve far better.

This is a fascinating battlefield of the First World War to visit. There has been very little intrusive development and there are significant vestiges of the war, as well as physical reminders in the form of earthworks and of concrete structures of various kinds. The country offers a wide range of high ridges, forestry and then the great contrast of the Woevre Plain. It is one of the few parts of the battlefields that German military cemeteries outnumber the allied ones. Maarten's tours, on foot and in a vehicle, are extensive and fascinating. As an aside, I would strongly recommend that anyone making a detailed visit to this (largely) American battlefield reads Christina Holstein's *Verdun 1917: The French Hit Back* in this series, in particular the coverage of the various, often quite successful, endeavours of the French army to eat away at the gains made by the Germans on this side of the river in 1916. It provides a very useful background to the situation that would face the AEF in autumn 1918.

Finally, a note of thanks. I turned up at Maarten and Didi's wonderful bed and breakfast on 14 March 2020 for a planned stay of eight nights or so, during which I would accompany Maarten on the tours and walks in this book. On 17 March, at noon (we got back just in time, the church clock ringing the hour, having done much of Car Tour 4), we went into a very strict lockdown. They were finally able to wave a doubtless heartfelt goodbye to me on 13 June! To you, 'the staff'; and to friends made in Nantillois – especially the Deputy Mayor, Patrick Salaûn, who had the church open for me every Sunday and some days during the week, my enduring thanks. Didi and Maarten have now transferred to more palatial quarters in Montfaucon and I look forward to my next visit; but I shall always have very pleasant memories of my enforced, extended stay in the beautiful rural backwater that is Nantillois.

*Nigel Cave*
Ratcliffe College, October 2021

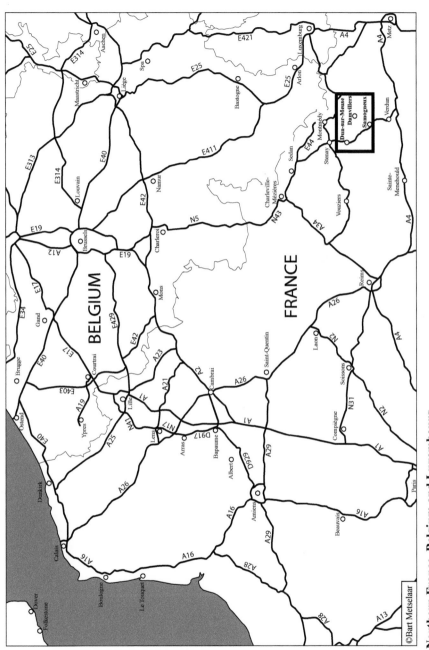

**Northern France, Belgium and Luxembourg.**

©Bart Metselaar

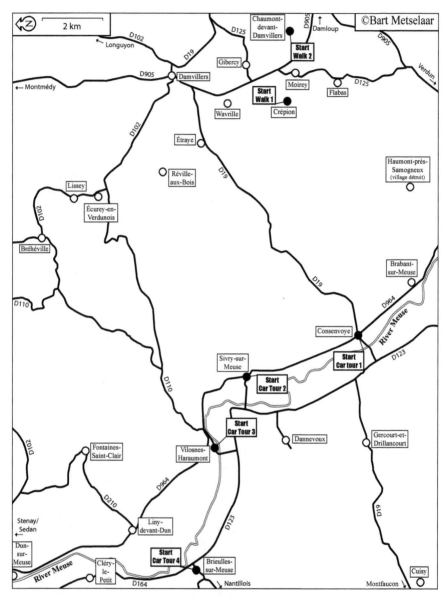

**Starting points of the walks and car tours.**

# Introduction

With the extensive media coverage of the centenary of the First World War, more people have found their way to the American battlefield of the Meuse-Argonne; however, a significant part of the offensive, which took place on the right bank of the Meuse, is still largely neglected even by those interested enough to come to the area. The lack of grand monuments of the AEF, such as the Montfaucon Memorial and the magnificent Meuse-Argonne American Cemetery, is a possible cause; whilst there is an all but total lack of typical tourist infrastructure, such as signposts, cafés or lodgings. This guide aims to fill much of the gap, showing that this part of the battlefield is very well provided with relevant points of interest. It is easy to make a detour to the area from wherever you stay on the left bank or from the cities of Verdun and Stenay.

The book is split into two parts: the first gives an outline of the history of the campaign, generally by chronological order and divisional sector; the second is made up of self-guided tours to the battlefield. The short narratives in chapters 2, 3 and 4 are based on original divisional and regimental histories, gas reports etc. and are supplemented by a thorough investigation of the battlefield by the author. The points of interest in the tour section are easy to find with the aid of GPS coordinates and clear directions, accompanied by excellent, clear maps by Bart Metselaar. Many sites are relatively unknown to the general public and are often hidden in the woods. Therefore, certain points of interest can only be located with the help of a GPS device; the references are given at the start of each tour. Divisions are considered from west to east and from south to north; and in chronological order.

The impact of the First World War on the United States should not be underestimated, even though its role in the conflict is not widely known. In America, it redefined women's rights, race relations, mass production in factories, the nature of jobs, civil liberties and America's role in the world amongst many other things. It was a major step in America's rise to super power status, quite a change when one recalls that a mere fifty years earlier the Civil War (1861-1865) had torn the country in two. From 1915 to 1918 the US, a former colony, came to the aid, first financially and later militarily, of the 'old continent' and the (at the time) dominant powers of 'western civilization'. To achieve its coming of age a high price had to be paid. 1918 alone caused more military American deaths (116,516, of which 53,402 were in combat) than, for example, US involvement in the Vietnam War (58,220), which lasted from 1965 to 1975. The Americans in part owe today's prosperity to those who sacrificed their lives for freedom back in 1918.

After nearly three years of attempts at remaining neutral, with varying degrees of success and whilst in fact tacitly supporting the Allies from the side lines (not least because it was economically very profitable to do so), President Wilson was forced into taking action. He had won re-election – just – in November 1916, at least in part by use of the slogan 'he kept us out of the war'.

**President Woodrow Wilson (1856-1924).**

If some 2,000 Californians had switched their vote, then he would have lost the Electoral College in what turned out to be a far closer election than almost anyone had anticipated. And yet, within only a few weeks of his inauguration for his second term, he asked Congress to declare war on Germany.

The return of a strategy of unrestricted submarine warfare by the Germans on 1 February 1917 and the consequent sinking of neutral US shipping by German submarines made war more likely, despite a strong isolationist wing in Congress and in particular in the Senate.

**President Wilson addresses Congress to call for a declaration of war on Germany, 2 April 1917.**

However, the revelation of the text of the so-called Zimmerman Telegram by the British (all telegraph lines from Europe to North America, the trans Atlantic cable, ran via Great Britain) revealed a German plot to persuade Mexico to wage war on the United States. Whilst these factors might well have been enough to sway the average American, there was also the pressing financial case in favour of an intervention on the side of the Entente powers. Since 1915, the US had lent vast amounts of money to the Allies. Even the Germans were lent about forty million dollars (by some calculations 700 million dollars in 2020 terms); but this was dwarfed by the hundreds of millions lent to the Allies. In short, there was a lot of capital already invested in the Allied cause.

In 1917, because of the war, the American economy became the biggest in the world. In fact, the foundations of America's prosperity – and certainly the strength of those foundations – were laid during the Great War; and it was her coming of age, albeit somewhat hesitant, as an international power, a process which reached its fruition after December 1941 and then in the post Second World War settlement.

At the same time, on the Western Front, things were still stuck in a bloody stalemate. 1916 had not been a particularly good year for either side, although perhaps marginally better for the Allies than 1915 had been; yet the number of casualties was mounting horrendously, with Verdun and the Somme remaining even today bywords for mass slaughter. However, a major Allied offensive was scheduled to commence in early April, around Arras (the British) and what was promised to be a decisive French attack, the Nivelle Offensive, largely centred on the Champagne. To balance this, there had been a revolution in Russia in March, which had overthrown the Tsar and the imperial regime and was replaced by a provisional government that was prepared, however, to continue with the war. It was quite obviously in the interests of American industrialists, bankers and investors to support the allies, for if they lost the war, large parts of the US economy would go bankrupt, and that was just the obvious outcome. Something had to be done.

All of these factors led President 'He kept us out of the war' Wilson to call on a special joint session of Congress to approve a declaration of war on Germany, which duly followed four days later, on 6 April 1917, and the creation of the AEF, the American Expeditionary Forces, under the command of General 'Black Jack' Pershing. Wilson's rigorous pre-war policy of no military involvement in the war in Europe meant that the army of the United States, in particular, was in an (arguably culpable) utterly unprepared state for a massive overseas commitment.

The USA mustered more than 4.7 million servicemen by the end of the war; an astonishing achievement. Of course the AEF contributed to the German defeat in 1918, but the hundreds of thousands of American soldiers that poured into France monthly served as the straw that broke a severely weakened camel's back. The Germans knew that with the American declaration of war, over time the balance of power had definitely swung in the Allies' favour. By launching their Spring Offensive in March 1918, they hoped to beat the French and British armies before the Americans had arrived in overwhelming numbers. By the end of June 1918 several American divisions had

**General John J. Pershing.**

been actively involved in engagements on various parts of the Front, such as in Flanders, Cantigny, the Aisne-Marne, Château Thierry and

**American soldiers embark for France.**

Belleau Wood. The AEF had played its part in first holding the Germans and then in working to push them back. By August 1918 the Germans had simply run out of manpower, certainly manpower enough to face the coordinated attacks of the Allied armies all along the Front. They started a retreat that would end on 11 November 1918 with the Armistice.

Yet in contrast to these vital contributions to this war, the Great War has become a forgotten war for many Americans, despite all the attention during the centenary years. One of the many reasons for this (apart from the fact that a very high proportion of Americans have their origins in the country as immigrants after the war), is that the USA did not suffer in the way that the Europeans and often their colonies or dominions did. The US effectively fought for about six months whereas the British, French and Germans lost a good part of a male generation during over four years of conflict. This is by no means to belittle the American sacrifice; if nowadays the same casualty rate in six months was suffered in another theatre of war somewhere in the world, people would be both absolutely horrified and provide a more than understandable reason for public outrage and mass protest. However, if you contrast 4.7 million draftees to 103 million American citizens in 1917, it means that after the war only a few million American families would have first-hand recollections of the war. Another plausible reason is that the Second World War, besides the Civil War and perhaps Vietnam, is THE war that first comes to the mind of the average American today. D Day, Bloody Omaha, the Battle of the Bulge and even the Hollywood vision of war; these are all etched in the collective American (and European) minds and are a part of our joint legacy. One other factor in this seeming collective amnesia about the war is that for every military fatality of the war, in the period 1917-1919, give or take, ten Americans died of the Spanish flu, thus a considerably greater personal disaster to a much higher proportion of the population of the USA.

The biggest offensive launched by the Americans as an independent Army during the war was the Meuse-Argonne Offensive, which lasted from 26 September 1918 to 11 November 1918. The aim of the offensive was to break through the powerful German Kriemhild defences and then to force a break through in the direction of Sedan, a major railhead and vital for the German supply chain. Geographically and strategically, if such an outcome could be achieved in the Meuse-Argonne area, it would lead, practically inevitably, to the evacuation of northern France by the German army. The only other line of retreat for the Germans ran through and over the Ardennes, difficult and hilly terrain that was not easily passable in winter. If the Americans succeeded, it would greatly speed up the end of the war.

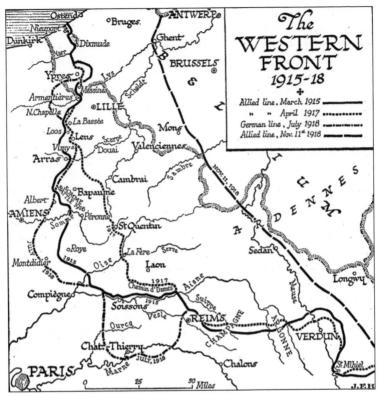

**Map of the Western Front between 1915 and 1918; the Meuse-Argonne is bottom right.**

Given the benefit of hindsight, the Meuse-Argonne Offensive was beset with all kinds of errors. Some of these were the inevitable consequence of a young army, massively expanded in a very short time frame, inexperienced in continental scale warfare, and fighting against a disciplined, generally well led, well-equipped enemy, even though it had been substantially weakened by the efforts in the offensives of spring and early summer 1918 and by the various allied onslaughts since then. The plan of attack, much poor and basic staff work, quite frankly inexcusable jealousy and egotism found amongst some senior commanders, lack of training, arms and equipment, logistical problems and too many failings in leadership at all levels, collectively contributed to an unnecessarily high casualty rate. Over-confidence, especially after such speedy success at St. Mihiel, amongst a significant proportion of the American senior commanders, along with a certain arrogance towards the 'old' allied armies, led all too often to an unwarranted under estimate of the fighting capabilities of the Germans. General Foch, the Allied *Supremo* on the Western Front, pertinently observed that if the Americans would not learn from the French and British they would certainly learn from the Germans. And they did. Despite the litany of criticism above, the AEF faced enormous challenges that go a long way to moderating the force of such criticism. The AEF learnt much during the Offensive; they learnt quickly - indeed they had to learn fast. The real heroes of the Meuse-Argonne Offensive are the ordinary 'Doughboys' who, despite all the mistakes made in the upper echelons, despite their suffering and hardships, despite the fact that many had been plucked from their civilian occupations only months before and of whom the vast majority had only been in France for a very limited time, despite the fact that the great majority lacking anything like adequate training – despite all of this they soldiered on regardless and often did more than reasonably could be expected of them. It is their perseverance and adaptability, along with an abundance of materiel and manpower, that won the war in this part of France.

One of the biggest failures of the planners of the Meuse-Argonne Offensive was to discount – or at least under rate – the large number of German gun batteries that occupied the Meuse Heights (and, albeit of lesser significance, the guns at the northern end of the Argonne Forest, over to the west). Situated on the right bank of the River Meuse, the Heights offered clear views and an excellent field of fire for the German artillery. From these positions they were able to pour fire into the American right flank and beyond, something the German gunners continued to do until the end of October, almost six weeks after the start of the offensive on 26 September. Probably only second to the Spanish Influenza pandemic that raged through Europe at the end of 1918, it was German artillery that caused most of the American casualties. When it was finally recognized that the German artillery on the right bank was largely responsible for the premature breakdown of the first and second phase of the Meuse-Argonne Offensive, only half-hearted measures were taken; the few artillery batteries that were available to support the divisions who would make the attack on the right bank could rarely sustain a barrage longer than thirty minutes simply because of a lack of ammunition. No priority was given to operations on the right bank and, as a consequence, a few divisions equipped with rather inadequate machine guns, rifles and grenades, were to attack eight German and Austrian-Hungarian divisions (weak numerically though they may have been) that were armed with an abundance of machine guns, trench mortars and a vast number of artillery pieces.

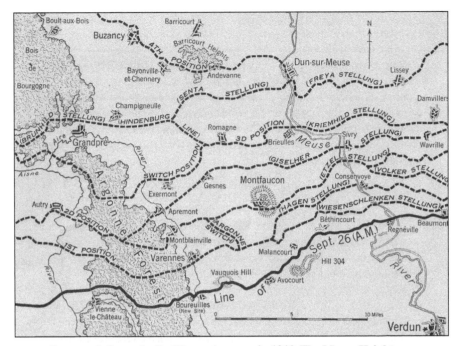

**German defences in the Meuse-Argonne in 1918. The Meuse Heights, on the right bank of the River Meuse, were not under attack until 8 October. After the capture of Consenvoye on that same day, progress more or less came to a standstill; Sivry was only liberated on 6 November. For all that time the Germans were able to use their guns in enfilade.**

Sadly, after this study, I can only come to the conclusion that the American high command's failure to recognize this serious flaw in their plans (i.e. not attacking the right bank in concert with the left bank on 26 September) meant that hundreds of lives were squandered, not to speak about the thousands of war invalids that returned to the USA after months of hospitalisation in Europe. Of course there are always extenuating circumstances and considerations that need to be factored in to any judgement; but the fact remains that the dominance of the German artillery on the Heights and the failure to allow for that dominance was a – if not the – crucial factor in holding up the whole offensive.

The first phase of the offensive on the left bank effectively was bogged down after three days of dogged fighting (officially it lasted from 26 September to 3 October). After the reorganization of the AEF divisions involved, the attack resumed on 4 October. Of course the Germans also fully exploited the lull in the fighting and consequently the attack of the AEF's First Army made little progress, owing in large part to the HE (high explosive) and gas shells fired from the Meuse Heights.

Four days later, on 8 October, the French XVII Corps, part of the American First Army, was ordered to advance and clear the heights. This combined American-French attack was to remove the Germans from the Meuse-Heights in a mere three days. Again, underestimation of the enemy's strength and artillery power resulted in limited success. It should be sufficient to note that the goals were only reached thirty-eight days later and that it required eight US/French divisions instead of the three that started the campaign.

### The consequences of ignoring the risk from the right bank.

1. From 23 September onwards, the Germans reinforced the right bank with fresh troops. On 8 October six divisions held the Meuse Heights; on 15 October this number had increased to eight. Several regiments and divisions were used to plug holes in the German defences on the left bank, thereby preventing an American breakthrough.

2. While the fighting in the area between the Meuse River and the Argonne Forest raged on, the German artillery was continually reinforced. Twelve new heavy battery positions (a battery includes four guns) were built and occupied; sixteen old ones were reoccupied. In addition, nine new long-range guns were brought into the action.

3. Maas Gruppe Ost (by this stage in the war, 'Corps' as a formal formation description in the German army was almost obsolete) was reinforced from the General Reserve; whilst reserve divisions from, in particular, St. Mihiel were moved closer to the Meuse Heights.

4. The Germans used their guns in enfilade positions before and beyond Montfaucon (centrally situated between the Meuse and the Argonne Forest) and essentially destroyed – certainly severely disrupted – American attacks before they had really started. As the American divisions advanced north the German gunners were even able to lay barrages behind them.

5. Railway lines, roads and waterways, the sinews of war, situated on the right bank were still intact, making it relatively easy for the Germans to resupply or to move reinforcements from A to B. On the contrary, the infrastructure on the left bank had been destroyed by German artillery, making it difficult for the Americans to resupply men and munitions or to move guns to the front, to name but a few consequences.

From 23 September 1918, General von Gallwitz, commander of the German Fifth Army, was certain that the Americans were going to attack east of the Meuse, ie on the *right* bank. However, it had not been possible to determine whether the attack would extend to the left bank. When the Americans launched the attack on the *left* bank instead, the German High Command was rather surprised but acted accordingly. Orders were issued to move fresh divisions from the right bank to the left. Consequently, as soon as 27 September, one day into the Meuse-Argonne Offensive, troops were moved to Dun-sur-Meuse, from where they crossed the river and moved into their designated sectors. This is one of the main reasons why the Germans were able to deploy fresh divisions so quickly (within two days) after the initial surprise of the American attack in the Meuse-Argonne.

**General von Gallwitz (1852-1937).**

General von der Marwitz, who succeeded von Gallwitz on 27 September, thought it wise to continue to reinforce the right bank positions. He thought it very possible that the Americans would extend the attack across the River Meuse.

**General von der Marwitz (1856-1929).**

'German HQ, 23 September 1918.

According to the news that we possess, the enemy is going to attack Fifth Army east of the Meuse and try to push toward Longuyon-Sedan, the most important artery of the Army of the West. Moreover, the intention of the enemy is to render it impossible for us to continue the exploitation of the Bassin de Briey, upon which our steel production depends in a large measure.

Thus it has come about that the hardest part of the task may fall upon the Fifth Army in the course of the fighting of the next few weeks; it is upon that task that the security of the Fatherland may rest.

It is on the invincible Verdun Front that the fate of a great part of the Western Front depends and, perhaps, the fate of our people.

The Fatherland must be able to count on every leader and every man knowing the grandeur of his mission and that he will do his duty till the end. If things come out thus, the enemy's assault, as in the past, will break against their firm will to hold.

Von der Marwitz.'

# List of Maps

1. Northern France, Belgium and Luxembourg.                          ix
2. Starting point of the walks and car tours.                         x
3. The Western Front between 1915 and 1918.                          xvi
4. German defensive positions in the Meuse-Argonne 1918.            xviii
5. German Spring Offensives of 1918.                                  2
6. Allied attacks on the Western Front,
   26 September-11 November 1918.                                     3
7. German defensive positions in the St. Mihiel Salient.             6
8. Plan of attack in the Meuse-Argonne, 26 September 1918.          12
9. The Second Phase of the Meuse-Argonne Offensive.                 16
10. The Third Phase of the Meuse-Argonne Offensive.                 18
11. 33rd Division's sector, 26 September-7 October 1918.            22
12. XVII Corps plan of attack.                                      28
13. 33rd Division's plan of attack.                                30
14. The 29th Division's sector 8-30 October 1918.                  38
15. 29th Division's plan of attack.                                50
16. 26th Division, 1-11 November.                                  62
17. 79th Division, 30 October-11 November.                         72
18. Operations of the 32nd Division, 8-11 November.                91
19. Operations of the 5th Division 5-8 November.                   97
20. Operations of the 5th Division 8-11 November.                 108
21. **Car Tour 1:** The 29th and 33rd Divisions' sector.          111
22. German trench map showing defences between
    Consenvoye and Brabant.                                       113
23. **Car Tour 2:** The 26th and 79th Divisions' sector.         138
24. **Car Tour 3:** The 5th and 32nd Divisions' sector.          160
25. **Car Tour 4:** The 5th Division-the Meuse Crossings.         183
26. The crossing of the Meuse, 3-5 November 1918.                184
27. Battle map of the Cléry, Doulcon and
    Dun area, November 1918.                                     190
28. **Walk 1:** The 26th and 79th Divisions – Ormont Hill.       205
29. **The Henry Gunther Tour.**                                  215
30. German defences on the right bank, October-November 1918.   217
31. Trench map of the Chaumont area, 1918                        218

Proud Austro-Hungarian (KuK) soldiers showing off their medals.

An Austro-Hungarian infantry shield. (*Coll Meuse-Argonne 1918, courtesy B. Metselaar*)

# CHAPTER 1

# The Americans in the Meuse

**From the start of the Hundred Days' Offensive to the Meuse-Argonne.**
The Spring Offensive of the German army on the Western Front started
on 21 March 1918, commencing with Operation Michael. The German
High Command hoped to win the war or at least force a favourable
draw before the Americans arrived in sufficient numbers to make the
Allied manpower advantage overwhelming. By the end of July, after
a series of major attacks along the northern and central part of the
Western Front, the German offensives had been defeated. The Germans
had managed to advance as far as the River Marne and, as in 1914,
were halted, this time with the aid of several American divisions, about
seventy kilometres from Paris. Once more they had failed to achieve a
decisive breakthrough. When it was clear that the Germans had ended
their run of offensives in July 1918, it was the sign for the Allied
*Supremo*, Ferdinand Foch, to order a counter offensive, later known
as the Second Battle of the Marne. The AEF, with over 250,000 men
fighting under French command, gained their first major battlefield
experience here. The men who fought at the Marne later successfully
put to use the lessons learnt there during the Meuse-Argonne Offensive
in September, October and November 1918. The American 3rd ('Rock
of the Marne') Division even coined its nickname during the fighting
in this area.

The Germans, having largely spent their offensive capabilities,
were forced to withdraw from the Marne and were pushed back to
the north. For this first Allied victory of 1918, Foch was granted the
rank of Marshal of France. After this success, Foch felt increasingly
confident and considered the time had arrived for a return to the
offensive. By now the AEF was present in large numbers and gave
new hope to the Allied commanders. The Americans were landing
in France at an average rate of 300,000 men per month by July.
However, Pershing was determined to use the AEF as an independent
command, one that fitted the American commitment to the war as an
associated power.

1

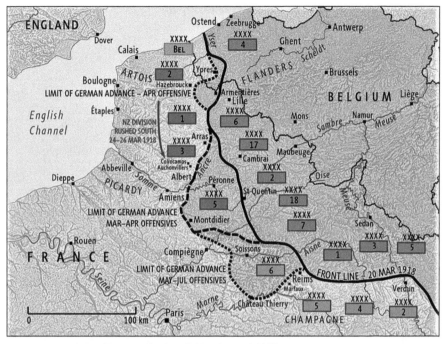

**Map of the German Spring Offensives of 1918.**

The American 27th, 30th, 37th and 91st Divisions had already reinforced the BEF, the British Expeditionary Force; the French were using several other American divisions to take over quiet sectors of the line in order to acquaint the fresh troops with trench life and to free experienced French divisions to fight elsewhere.

In the course of the Hundred Days' Offensive the Allies launched a series of offensives against the Germans on the Western Front from 8 August to 11 November 1918; they forced the Germans to retreat beyond the Hindenburg Line and ultimately the series of attacks led to the Germans being forced to sign the Armistice. The term 'The Hundred Days'

**Marshal Ferdinand Foch (1851-1929).**

Offensive' does not refer to a specific battle but rather the rapid series of Allied victories along much of the length of the Western Front, starting with the Battle of Amiens on 8 August, and which were co-ordinated by Foch.

During the Battle of Amiens the Allies advanced over eleven kilometres on the first day, one of the greatest advances of the war. The effects of this victory on the morale of both sides was very significant; it resulted in the surrender of a huge number of German troops. On one day alone they suffered 30,000 casualties. The German losses were so heavy that Erich Ludendorff described the first day of the battle as 'a black day of the German army', a view with which Hindenburg, Chief of the General Staff, agreed.

In the midst of the Battle of Amiens, the American First Army formally came into being on 10 August 1918; it was soon by far the biggest army-sized formation put into the field on the Western Front by any combatant power during the war. Its commander, General Pershing, was also the C-in-C of the AEF, who thus had a very weighty command function, almost an intolerable burden; with the formation of the Second American Army (12 October 1918), he gave up command of the First. In truth, he found it difficult not to meddle – or at least to try to.

**The Allied offensives of late September. St. Mihiel, bottom right.**

3

**The Allied offensives of late September.**

After several significant victories, a co-ordinated offensive by the French, British, Belgian and American armies, under the overall direction of Foch, started on 26 September 1918 in an all-out effort to force the German army out of France and Belgium and to bring the war to a conclusion, with the hope that this might be achieved before the end of 1918. Foch's planning for this dated back to late August and early September, with the various national commands being informed in early September of their contribution. In France, the American army was assigned the south-eastern part of the line, near Verdun, stretching from the Argonne Forest in the west to the River Meuse in the east, some thirty-five kilometres long, which became known as the Meuse-Argonne Sector. It also operated in other parts of the line and various AEF divisions still served with the British and the French. The French supported the AEF on its flanks. However, before Pershing could aim his guns on the Meuse-Argonne, the AEF first had to eliminate the St. Mihiel Salient, a bulge in the German line sticking out into French territory and which could be used by the Germans as a suitable jump-off position to attack the Americans in the rear.

**The St. Mihiel Offensive.**

The St. Mihiel Offensive started on 12 September 1918 and was the first operation undertaken in the First World War by an independent American Army; it was supported by 110,000 French troops. The plan to develop an American Army near St. Mihiel, when sufficient troops were available, and to reduce the salient there as a preliminary to more extensive operations in the same vicinity (Metz), was proposed by Pershing and was agreed to by the French High Command at a conference shortly after the arrival of the American Army Headquarters in France. The Americans constantly had this plan in mind and, beginning in January 1918, the front near St. Mihiel was used to give front line experience to American divisions and to acquaint them with the region in which they would later attack.

However, the succession of German attacks in the spring of 1918 made it necessary to postpone the original plan, as all available American troops were urgently needed to bolster the French and British armies, who were at risk of collapse in other sectors of the front, finally (and most notably from the American point of view) in the Marne region, not far from Paris. Although by July there were already more than 1,200,000 American soldiers in France, American combat formations were widely distributed along the entire front, either serving in the line with the French and British Armies or undergoing training – which had been generally inadequate at home in the United States, possibly the kindest description possible – in rear areas.

When at the start of August (close to the end of the Second Battle of the Marne of 15 July-6 August 1918) it became clear that the reduction of the German-held Aisne-Marne Salient was nearly completed, General Pershing pointed out to Foch that the improved situation made possible the concentration of American formations and insisted that the plan for the creation of an American Army be resumed. Although the French, but more outspokenly the British, urged that American units be left with their forces, Pershing stuck to his position. After much debate and palpable reluctance, an understanding was reached that most of the American formations would soon be concentrated into an independent American Army in the St. Mihiel area. For the time being, only the American 27th and the 30th Divisions stayed with the British.

On 13 August, at the newly established American First Army Headquarters in Neufchâteau, the Army staff set up shop and preparations were started for the reduction of the Salient. The assembling of formations started soon thereafter and, on 30 August, the American First Army took over command of the front line from Port-sur-Seille, nine kilometres east of the River Moselle, to Watronville, fourteen kilometres south-east of Verdun, a sector that also included the St. Mihiel Salient.

The Salient was shaped roughly like a triangle, with its points near St. Mihiel (to the south) Pont-à-Mousson, (east) and Verdun (north). At its base, it was forty-five kilometres wide, extended thirty kilometres into the Allied lines and had remained almost unchanged in shape since the end of 1914.

Within the German lines at the southern face of the Salient were the high and isolated hills of Loupmont and Montsec. These afforded the Germans excellent views of a large area of ground behind the French lines. Two German defensive zones, the Wilhelm and the Schroeter Zones, had been prepared in front of the Michel Zone and all had been strengthened by elaborate systems of trenches, barbed-wire entanglements, concrete shelters and machine-gun emplacements. The Michel Zone, however, was the most powerful of the three; since late 1917 this zone had been changed into a veritable fortress and close to one thousand pillboxes had been built on a sixty kilometres' wide front, a substantial number of which remain in existence today. The Michel Zone was to remain intact and in German hands until the Armistice.

The value of the Salient to the Germans was that it protected the city of Metz and the German border; protected the important Briey iron ore basin and large coal deposits; interrupted traffic on the main Paris-Nancy railroad; cut the Verdun-Toul railway; threatened the Allied territory in

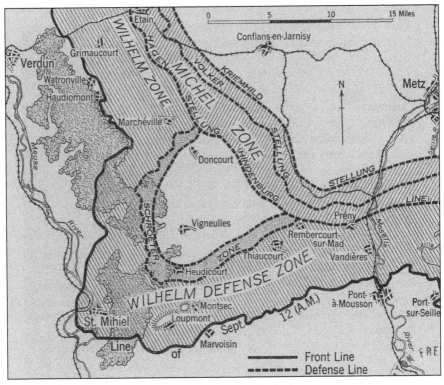

**German defensive positions in the St. Mihiel Salient.**

its vicinity, especially west of the Meuse; and forced the French to keep thousands of troops and large quantities of supplies in the area.

On the other hand, the Germans also recognised that it was vulnerable to a pincer attack, thus trapping many of the defenders; that the interior lines of communication were not good, largely due to the marshy ground; that if abandoned it would shorten the German line and thus the number of men required to defend it.

Foch appreciated that it was essential for the St. Mihiel Salient to be eliminated before any great offensive could be launched in the Meuse-Argonne.

The final American preparations for the attack against the Salient had been underway for just two weeks when, on 30 August, Marshal Foch unexpectedly suggested to General Pershing that the attack on St. Mihiel should be greatly downsized and that most of the American divisions should be used for another attack to be launched around 20 September between Verdun and the Argonne Forest. In the new plans, the American divisions would be assigned to operate under French command. Knowing that Pershing was almost fixated on deploying the American army as a whole, Foch pressed Pershing to undertake not one but two offensives. Additionally, such a course of action would free French divisions that could now be deployed elsewhere along the front.

An extremely annoyed, not to say angry, General Pershing felt that the St. Mihiel Offensive should be carried out as planned and definitively stated that the American divisions would fight *only* as part of an independent American army. On 2 September, after a series of conferences with Foch, it was agreed that the assault would be carried out, but that its objectives would both be strictly limited and severely time-limited. This meant that the American First Army could quickly undertake another major attack, the Meuse-Argonne Offensive, ten days after the capture of the planned initial objectives for the St. Mihiel 'drive' on 16 September. Although quite ambitious, to say the least, but eager to show the French and the British what the Americans were capable of, Pershing agreed.

More than 500,000 Americans (216,000 in line) and about 110,000 French were involved in the offensive. On the night of 11-12 September, First Army was in position, ready to reduce the St. Mihiel Salient.

On the German side, although no official orders had been issued, from the start of September supplies and weaponry were gradually moved from the front line position to the Schroeter Zone, a system of defences in the centre of the Salient, and further back. On Tuesday 10 September, Ludendorff wrote to Army Group Galwitz HQ:

'I request that you abandon the proposed attack [*in case of a small-scale American operation the Germans had been contemplating a counter-attack*] and begin to execute the measures for the occupation of the Michel Positions according to plan. The withdrawal of the troops from their present positions and the resultant abandonment of the position itself is, if possible, to be postponed as long as the tactical situation will permit, even after the evacuation of the St. Mihiel foreground, in order that time may be gained to improve the general situation.'

**The Americans attack.**
[For a full account of this action, see *The St. Mihiel Offensive* in this series.]

On Thursday 12 September, at 5.00 am, the rain-sodden infantry climbed out of their trenches into No Man's Land. Despite the lack of tanks – only a few had come up in time to assist the troops through the

7

wire entanglements – the attack advanced on schedule. According to the plan, the greatest advance was to be made by IV Corps and the left of I Corps; to gain the objectives of 12 September required an advance of ten kilometres. In its execution the 1st Division, on the left flank of the main attack, captured Nonsard and entered the woods to the north; the 42nd Division pushed on beyond the villages of Essey and Pannes, while the 89th seized Bouillonville. In I Corps' sector, the 2nd Division captured Thiaucourt, and the 5th drove through Vieville-en-Haye, with its eastern flank bent back to connect with the 90th Division, which was at the pivot of the main attack on the first day.

On the western face of the Salient the intensive fire of the French artillery continued until 8.00 am, when the infantry of V Corps launched its assault from the north. The Germans, not knowing what day the attack was going to take place, were surprised by the severity of the assault and were forced to give up ground on all fronts. As a result the official German order to retreat to the Michel Zone, the so-called Loki Movement, was given around midday. However, the speed of the American and French attacks was such that thousands of German soldiers and large quantities of equipment fell into American hands. At nightfall V Corps had advanced about four kilometres.

While the attacks on the two faces were progressing, reports indicated that the Germans were retiring from the tip of the Salient in front of the French troops, although French raids into the German lines near the town of St. Mihiel met with considerable opposition, mainly from machine-gun units.

**Troops of the 1st Division in a trench near Bouconville, St. Mihiel, 12 September 1918.**

Early in the evening of 12 September General Pershing, with the idea of cutting off the retreat of as many Germans as possible, directed that troops of IV and V Corps be rushed with all speed to link up in the vicinity of Vigneulles. Part of the 26th Division marched along a narrow forest road directly to the heart of the Salient; soon after 2.00 am Vigneulles was in American hands but the two divisions had not yet joined up.

At dawn on Friday 13 September, the 26th Division met patrols of the 1st Division just north-east of Vigneulles. This marked the closing of the Salient and the German soldiers who had not retired beyond that point were cut off and captured. Practically all objectives had been gained by the evening of 13 September, and the organization of the new position, roughly along the line between Vandières and Haudiomont, was begun. Because the attack had gone so well, the transfer of American units to the Meuse-Argonne region was started on the night of 13 September, three days before the completion of the St. Mihiel Offensive.

### The Meuse-Argonne Offensive.

Eliminating the St. Mihiel Salient had been, fortunately, a fairly easy task for the Americans. The downside of this 'easy' victory (8,600 casualties!) was that it made many of the Americans at higher command level unduly confident; they seriously underestimated the strength of German resistance in the Meuse-Argonne. The German troops who were waiting for them here knew that the Hindenburg Line, or better Zone, was the last barrier between the enemy and Germany, whereas at St. Mihiel the Germans had merely *withdrawn,* admittedly in some considerable disorder and at the cost of thousands of prisoners, to the Hindenburg Line/Michel Zone, a significant difference; the Germans were now fighting for their homes and to protect their kith and kin.

After the offensive at St. Mihiel was ended on 16 September, the attention of Pershing's staff was focused on the preparations for the offensive in the Meuse-Argonne, some forty kilometres to the north west of St. Mihiel. This was a monumental task for these staff officers, organising the switching of thousands and thousands of troops, men and their equipment, and hundreds of guns and aircraft from one front to another, either immediately, for the opening of the new attack, or within days of its start. Immediately after the battle, the veteran 4th Division was transported to the new line. All the other divisions that moved into the Meuse-Argonne sector for the opening of the offensive were fresh divisions from elsewhere. These latter divisions were transported close to their destination by train and marched off from disembarkation points to French barrack camps during the nights preceding the offensive. Soon afterwards they were moved into the forested area south of the old 1916 front line, where all sorts of hasty preparations were under way for the forthcoming attack. About 220,00 French soldiers had been moved out of the sector and over 600,000 Americans were moved into it. The troop movements were all done under cover of night. This was done to make the Germans believe that the Meuse-Argonne sector was still occupied by the French and that the main American thrust was going to take place in the St. Mihiel area against Metz. On the down side, this meant that the average American soldier had very little idea of where he was or what he was about to do, especially difficult for the more recent arrivals on the Western Front.

On the night of 25-26 September the First Army stood on its new front, ready for the battle that was to begin at dawn the next day. First Army was organized in four corps, three American and one French, each comprising four divisions, including one in reserve. The three American corps were tasked to attack between the Argonne Forest and the River Meuse; the fourth corps, the French XVII Corps, stationed on the right bank of the Meuse, was merely there to hold the front line. This corps was commanded by General Henri Édouard Claudel and was attached to First Army. It protected the right flank of the AEF.

**American soldiers enjoying motorised transport, with the added bonus of being well out of artillery range.**

Although the right bank was excluded from the attack, the artillery of III Corps, on the left bank of the Meuse, was especially charged with suppressing the enemy guns located on the dominating Meuse Heights. One might have doubts about how this could be achieved; a substantial number of the American gun batteries were equipped with the light (although excellent) French 75mm field gun, with an effective range of approximately nine kilometres. Furthermore, the opening barrage lasted for only six hours and no doubt most of the guns were targeted on the left bank. In addition, the American supply system was a shambles and there was simply not enough ammunition to prevent the German guns on the right bank from coming into action.

**General Henri Édouard Claudel (1871-1956).**

As a result the German guns, concealed in well-built and camouflaged positions, shot up, broke up and destroyed many of the American assaults. It has been estimated by one authority that, on average, seventy per cent of the casualties of the First World War were caused by artillery fire; this sort of percentage was no exception in the Meuse-Argonne

Although the 33rd Division, the formation to the immediate west of the Meuse, was to wheel to the right during the first phase of the fighting, the limit of their advance was to extend the American position north along the left bank of the River Meuse. Having successfully reached these positions on the first day of the offensive, the order to cross the river did not come before 8 October, a little over two weeks after the start of the offensive, which had been bogged down for some days after an initial sweeping move forward. With the AEF by now inching its way to the Hindenburg Zone, their advance had been such (the front line had moved north on average about eight to ten kilometres) that it was possible for the German gunners on the right bank not only to pour a deadly fire into the flank but also into the rear of the attacking Americans. In addition, this incessant, well-directed artillery fire seriously disrupted the still feeble American supply lines.

On the night before the attack on 26 September, the German defenders along the Meuse-Argonne front comprised five German divisions, at the most a theoretical 65,000 men, opposite some 193,000 Americans. They were commanded by General von der Marwitz, as part of the Fifth Army. On the right bank, General Franz Ludwig Freiherr von Soden was in command of Maas Gruppe Ost [Meuse Group East], a mixed German – Austro-Hungarian force. By this stage in the war it was quite common in the German army for corps commands to become 'group' commands – it gave added flexibility. British readers, in particular, may have heard of

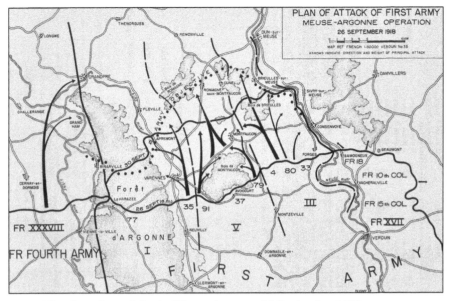

**The plan of attack in the Meuse-Argonne, 26 September 1918.**

von Soden – he commanded the division facing the British on 1 July 1916, defending the line from Gommecourt to the area of the Ancre. Several divisions were held in reserve.

As soon as the German high command realized the severity of the American assault, they began withdrawing reinforcements from nearby parts of the Western Front (St. Mihiel, Vosges). Within five days, they had rushed five more divisions into the Meuse-Argonne region. The Germans simply could not afford losing the Meuse-Argonne. If the lines in this region would be breeched it could mean the loss of Northern France. On the other hand, von Gallwitz was not at first persuaded that this attack was a full blooded offensive, thinking it a feint so as to encourage the Germans to pull troops from the more strategically significant area to the south east of Verdun and the scene of the American triumph at St. Mihiel.

### The First Phase, 26-30 September.

On the morning of 26 September, nine U.S. divisions, effectively 193,000 men on the ground, attacked the Germans along a line that was thirty-five kilometres in length. The first two lines of defence were lightly held by the Germans, who were by now following the well established principles of an elastic defence. As a result, the Americans made rapid progress; but within a few kilometres it seemed that with every

US soldiers in a trench; they all wear an overseas cap under their helmet against the cold. The centre soldier is holding a Chauchat machine gun.

German MG crew in 1918; note the helmet covers and trench knives.

13

hundred metres gained German resistance was stiffening. At nightfall on 28 September the AEF's objectives had been realized, most notably the German observation posts on Montfaucon; but over the next five days only slight progress was made. The slowing down of the advance, which ground to a halt in front of the German main positions, the Hindenburg Zone, was due to four principal factors.

First, there was the increasing resistance put up by the Germans, which had slowed down the advance to such a point that the Americans could advance no further. Secondly, the congestion of the roads and poor planning, a consequence of the haste with which the operation was put together, proved to be a major obstacle in trying to resupply the fighting men. It was almost impossible to bring supplies and guns (and shells) to the front but, more seriously, certainly for morale, the provision of medical care and the evacuation of the wounded were severely impeded. Thirdly, the inexperience and lack of sufficient and relevant training of the American soldiers, at all levels and in all arms, made itself evident and resulted in the inability of most American divisions to exploit their success. Fourthly, artillery played a vital role in the German defensive strategy. As the positions east of the River Meuse, the Meuse Heights, were not included in the American battle plans, the German artillery managed to destroy many American attacks before they even had a chance to materialize. German air superiority and a flawed American battle plan for their own aircraft added much to the success of their gunners. The downside for the Germans was that, in spite of having artillery and ammunition in abundance, there were insufficient infantry to launch counter-attacks and thus recapture important positions and lines – a vital element in their defensive strategy. The reason for this lack of manpower was, of course, that simultaneously the Germans were facing attacks by the French and the Belgians; whilst the British had penetrated the Hindenburg Line defences. This was a completely new experience for the German army on the Western Front. Added to this was the severe depletion of formations in the series of German offensives in the first six months or so of 1918; German divisions might have an establishment of 12-15,000 men, but the reality was that, by this stage in the war, many were only 8,000 strong, some having even fewer men, and of this figure there might be only 5,000 'bayonets', ie front line soldiers.

## The Second Phase, 1-31 October.

The attack resumed on 4 October. Having broken through the Hagen and Etzel Lines, the first two lines of the German defences, which had been comparatively lightly held, the doughboys were now up against the main German position, the Hindenburg Line. This line, in fact 'zone' is more appropriate and less misleading, was about two kilometres deep and was built on the wooded heights running east to west between the River Meuse and the Argonne Forest.

By now several American divisions had been relieved by fresh divisions. The supply situation had been, eventually, improved and ammunition and supply trains worked flat out so that by then they had enough guns, ammunition and other weaponry to be able to continue the advance. The drawback of the five days' pause in the fighting was that the Germans had also had time to bolster their positions.

Early on the morning of Friday, 4 October, the Americans moved across open terrain up to the Hindenburg Line. In most places the advance was hidden by a heavy morning mist. The men advanced behind an artillery barrage but as the fog lifted they were met with a deluge of ordnance of all calibres; the Germans had been quick to retaliate. As soon as the American troops on the centre and right of their attack appeared out of the woods or trenches, artillery from the Meuse Heights swept the front with an avalanche of shells, high explosive and shrapnel. To make matters worse, one out of three shells was filled with gas. Machine guns sprayed bullets in a coordinated and highly effective display of effective deployment. Along the entire front line the Germans put up a considerably fiercer resistance than, with St. Mihiel in the back of American minds, had been anticipated. Not surprisingly, again the key role of the German defences was played by the German gunners. It proved to be the start of the heaviest fighting of the war for the AEF, lasting almost a month. In the centre of the attack, looking north in the direction of Romagne and Cunel, the fighting was fierce. There were AEF divisions that had to be relieved after a week, spent, after an advance of a mere thousand metres.

To take an example, Cunel, just two kilometres as the crow flies from the start line of 4 October, was only taken on 14 October, after ten days of dogged fighting. On 30 October, sixteen days later, the lines had been pushed a mere three kilometres beyond that same village.

During this phase the first battles on the right bank were fought by the 26th, 29th and 33rd Divisions. These fights mainly took place in the area between Samogneux, Consenvoye and Chaumont. The terrain taken from the Germans and Austrians defending this sector did not eliminate the immediate threat of the German guns, it merely dented their outpost positions. The Americans captured several gun positions, observation posts and took about 4,000 prisoners. It caused the Germans to increase the number of divisions in the Meuse-Argonne and to retreat to the more favourable defences of the Giselher Line, part of the infamous Hindenburg Zone. The American attack on the right bank was a relatively

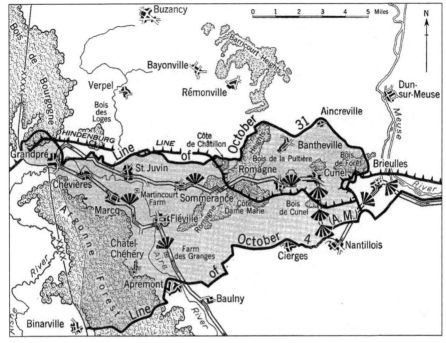

**The Second Phase of the Meuse-Argonne Offensive.**

small-scale operation; apparently the high command still did not grasp the gravity of the situation.

In spite of huge losses, the second phase of the Meuse-Argonne Offensive proved to be decisive. On 14 October, at Romagne, the backbone of the German defence system, the Hindenburg Line, was snapped and by the end of that same month the Germans were in full but largely organized retreat; on the other hand, the Americans were in no state to take advantage of that situation. However, on the right bank the Kriemhilde Line remained unbroken and as powerful as ever.

A key development in the conduct of the battle was the appointment of I Corps commander, Hunter Liggett, as the commander of First Army, formally

**The entrance of a Hindenburg Line shelter.**

16

assuming command on 16 October. The whole discussion over the command of the offensive and Pershing's perceived inadequacies (at least partially a consequence of 'wearing too many hats', to say the least) in this battle is one that has resulted in numerous books and articles and is beyond the scope of this book. However, it would seem that everyone agrees that Hunter Liggett was a competent, methodical and effective GOC (General Officer Commanding) of First Army. The Army needed him – for example, he commented that the Army up to this stage had the staggering figure of some 100,000 'stragglers' and the situation had to be taken in hand.

### The Third Phase: 1-11 November.

After the Hindenburg Line was breached on the west bank, the Germans were left with no alternative but to retreat. First, they wanted to cross the River Meuse in order to save as much equipment and as many soldiers as possible. If the armistice negotiations that were now on the way failed, the Germans could maintain hostilities from the right bank of the River Meuse, using the river as a natural barrier/defence line. Secondly, they hoped to slow down the American advance from positions on the right bank and, in doing so, buy time to allow an orderly retreat to some form of prepared positions to the rear. Thirdly, by now, the Germans were faced with severe and increasing social unrest at home, their army was facing unrelenting pressure and they could not afford to lose any more soldiers or guns; on balance it was preferable to have a functioning army, albeit a very weak one, in the light of domestic political turmoil.

At last the American high command decided to start a large scale attack on the right bank. Besides four American divisions (the 5th, 26th, 32nd and 79th), the French 15th Colonial Infantry Division was involved. This division had proved itself whilst fighting under American command at St. Mihiel.

At the opening of the third phase of the Offensive, some American divisions advanced as much on one day as during the entire second phase. The Americans aimed to keep the Germans under pressure, which was a successful strategy and every day the Americans made huge territorial gains. However, it was clear that the German army had almost come to the end of its fighting capability – it must not be forgotten that the line was crumbling all along the Western Front, from the North Sea in Belgium in the west to Verdun in the east, in the face of substantial blows by the Allies. Battle fatigue, malnutrition, the spread of the catastrophic Spanish influenza pandemic and the explosive social and political situation in Germany played havoc within the ranks. On top of this her allies had, or were, collapsing.

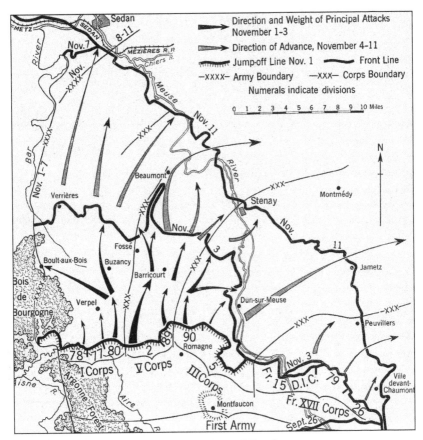

**The Third Phase of the Meuse-Argonne Offensive.**

**German prisoners marching into captivity.**

18

However, this by no means meant that the Germans were giving up the struggle overnight. The army was still putting up stiff resistance and every square metre of ground was heavily contested, in the Meuse-Argonne as much as elsewhere. They could still deploy masses of artillery and the ammunition to go with it; they constantly and effectively harassed the American advance, continually claiming lives until almost the very last minute before the Armistice was due to come into effect.

All along the Western Front the allied armies had forced the Germans into a fighting retreat. A further achievement of the American attacks in the Meuse-Argonne had been to pull in to their area substantial numbers of troops who would otherwise have been available to stiffen the opposition to the various major assaults by French and British armies elsewhere along the Western Front.

**American troops queuing for baths and delousing, a relatively rare treat. The opportunity to fumigate their clothes was often taken at this time.**

# CHAPTER 2

# The 33rd, 29th and 26th Divisions:
# 26 September – 31 October

**Summary: The 33rd 'Prairie' Division.**
The 33rd Division, commanded by Major General George Bell Jr., provided the right flank of III Corps. The 33rd, a National Guard division, was activated in July 1917 and was trained at Camp Logan, Houston, Texas. The Division (129th, 130th, 131st and 132nd Regiments) went overseas in May 1918. Upon arrival in France it was subjected to an intensive training program with the British and Australian forces. The first major engagement with the Germans was at Le Hamel, immediately south of the River Somme, on 4 July, in support of a limited but important attack by the Australian Corps. On 23 August, the Prairie Division was moved to the Toul sector, south of St. Mihiel. On 5 September, after a short period of rest and training, the division was moved into the Meuse-Argonne front to take over an infamous section of front line from the French known as Cote [Hill] 304 and the Mort Homme, Dead Man's Hill. This sector was utterly destroyed during the Battles of Verdun. The bitter fighting here lasted for the better part of 1916 and in August and September 1917 a second wave of destruction raged through the area.

A few days before the start of the Meuse-Argonne Offensive, the 33rd division was withdrawn from this sector and positioned between the 80th Division and the River Meuse. They were tasked with breaking through three German lines, the Wiesenschlenken, Hagen and Etzel lines, the last one located just beyond the village of Dannevoux. Their sector included Forges Wood and the villages of Forges, Drillancourt and the hamlet of Gercourt. Forges Wood was known to be heavily fortified and the first two German lines to be broken were in this area. To add to the difficulties, the Forges Creek had been shelled so heavily during the fights of 1916 and 1917 that a substantial area had turned into a morass. Another serious problem were the German

**Major General
G Bell Jr (1859-1926).**

20

guns positioned on Meuse Heights. It was anticipated that these guns would inflict considerable casualties on the attacking doughboys, having the advantage of being able to fire into any attack in enfilade. This assumption proved to be right; the movements of the 37th, 79th, 4th and 80th Divisions were all seriously hampered by enemy artillery fire; but for some reason the 33rd, notably the formation nearest to the guns, escaped this fate.

### Thursday 26 September.

The weather was extremely foggy. It obscured the Americans from German observation but it also caused scores of soldiers to lose their way in the unknown and hostile country. Just before dawn the soldiers of 66 Brigade, the 131st and 132nd Regiments, supported by the 124th Machine Gun Battalion, were on their way to the destroyed village of Forges and the banks of the River Meuse. The creek had been completely wiped away by shellfire and the whole area now resembled a swamp. Human remains, rusted barbed wire and broken equipment were scattered all around. During the night, however, the engineers had prepared numerous passages across this hellish terrain. They had also built several footbridges and marked the passages with white tape that provided essential help during this foggy morning.

Although somewhat aided by the flashes of the exploding shells of the rolling barrage, the going was so difficult in the dark and the fog that the men soon fell behind it. Alarmed by the barrage, the German gunners joined in the spirit of the occasion and it was not long before shells started to fall all around the Americans. It was fortunate that many of the shells exploded after they had been buried in the mud. The Meuse was reached at 10.10 am. Around noon the Americans seized Forges and captured about 1,000 prisoners; the attack had come as a complete surprise to the Germans. They clearly had not expected an attack in this sector over the destroyed terrain and difficult country; in fact, they deemed it impossible. Therefore the Forges Wood defences were poorly garrisoned and it did not help that the Germans troops defending the lines were Alsatians, natives of the Franco-German border region of Alsace-Lorraine, not far from the Meuse. Most Alsatians had family ties in both France and Germany and were bilingual. Fed up with the war, their morale was so low that many were easily persuaded to surrender.

Early in the afternoon the sun broke through the fog and the assault moved towards the Wiesenschlenken Line. Fortunately it was only lightly held and most of the garrison quickly surrendered. However, in some sectors the fighting was bitter. Often snipers and machine gunners needed

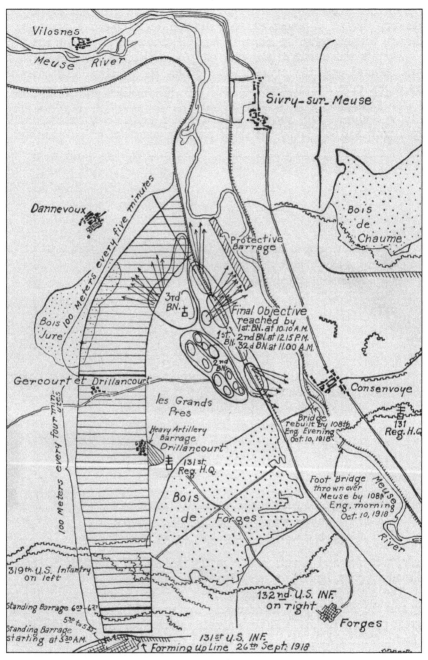

**33rd Division's sector, 26 September – 7 October 1918.**

**No Man's Land, with Forges Wood in the distance.**

further convincing to surrender and, according to the divisional history, the Americans 'obliged in the form of hand grenades and machine-gun fire'. The number of casualties on both sides remained low. The attack continued in the direction of the Hagen Line but most of the time there was not much resistance from the enemy; but there were exceptions. In some cases fanatical resistance was offered by German snipers, machine-gun and trench mortar crews. On the outskirts of Forges Wood the fighting was so fierce that two men, Captain George Henry Mallon and Sergeant William Berry Sandlin, were both awarded the Medal of Honor for their heroic actions that day.

Captain Mallon recalled:

'We were fighting in a heavy [sic – thick] wood against machine guns, and the men, of course, got separated. I had nine men with me, and we were having a fine time cleaning out machine-gun nests. All at once we came out into a clearing and imagine my surprise to see a whole battery of German artillery firing. All I could think to do was to charge, and we went at them with bayonets and pistols, and we were too close for them to shoot at us. I got off to the Germans with my fists. I suppose they thought there were more of us. It only took three to four minutes to clean them up, for most of them made a 'strategic retreat'. I expect if we had more time to think I would have started the other way as they [out] numbered [us] ten to one [sic], and if they had had our nerve there would be a different story to tell.'

**Captain Mallon, MoH (1877-1934).**

23

The exceptional gallantry and determination displayed by Captain Mallon resulted in the capture of one hundred prisoners, eleven machine guns, four 155 millimetre howitzers and one anti-aircraft gun.

The second Medal of Honor was awarded to Sergeant William Berry Sandlin. In an interview, his brother John Sandlin explained:

'The line had been ordered to stop the advance and the men lay down on the ground to avoid the machine-gun fire. But not Sergeant William Sandlin. Above and beyond the call of duty, he charged the machine-gun nest alone, armed with four grenades, a bayonet and his pack and rifle on his back. When he had advanced to within seventy-five yards of the nest, he threw his first grenade, which fell about fifteen steps short of the nest and exploded without effect. He then ran some thirty yards toward the nest and threw the second grenade, which hit the nest. After throwing the other two grenades, he charged the nest. Finding two men still unhurt, he put them out of action with his bayonet. While Sandlin was charging the nest, the enemy emptied two automatic revolvers at him.'

**Sergeant Sandlin, MoH (1890-1949).**

Sandlin single-handedly destroyed three German machine-gun nests and killed twenty-four of the enemy.

On the first day of the Meuse-Argonne Offensive the 33$^{rd}$ was one of the few American divisions to reach its final objective on time. On reaching the Meuse between Dannevoux (not captured yet by the 80$^{th}$ Division) and Sivry-sur-Meuse (still in German hands and situated on the opposite bank), parts of the 33$^{rd}$ Division wheeled right and started to take up positions along the river in full view of the Germans on the left bank. Not before long shells started to fall in the vicinity of the digging troops, fortunately without doing much harm due to the muddy terrain.

**Friday 27 September.**
Under cover of night the new American trenches along the Meuse were abandoned and a new line was dug 150 metres to the rear, behind the small rise provided by the Stenay-Verdun railway embankment. The Germans did not discover the withdrawal and thus continued to shell the original forward positions. At around midnight the neighbouring

American soldiers along the Forges-Brieulles road (D123). The line of trees mark the River Meuse, Consenvoye is on the left and Chaume Wood is on the hills in the distance.

The German view over the Meuse between Forges (left) and Consenvoye (right), looking towards the American position on the photo above.

80th Division had finally managed to take Dannevoux. This secured the 33rd Division's left flank. The next day, the 80th Division pushed on to the Meuse and attacked the woods north of Dannevoux. The latter attack took almost all day and their main target of that day, Brieulles, was not reached. In the meantime, the 131st and 132nd Regiments, 33rd Division, were frantically working on securing their trenches along the river; it was feared that the Germans were preparing for a counter-attack from the river side. If this materialized, it would seriously endanger the American III Corps' flank and rear.

### Saturday 28 September.
On the early morning of Saturday 28 September the Germans launched the expected counter-attack. However, it came from the direction of Brieulles, north of the front line and not from the Meuse. The attack was repulsed by the 320th Regiment, 80th Division, after which the 320th continued to Brieulles. Côte Laimont Wood and Brieulles Wood, both situated on a high rise in the terrain, were taken practically unopposed but the village itself could not be liberated. Built at the bottom of a four kilometres wide and barren valley, it proved impossible to reach. As soon as the soldiers of the 80th and 33rd Division showed themselves the Germans started a punishingly effective barrage.

### Monday 29 September.
The 80th Division was withdrawn from Brieulles Wood and the left bank opposite Sivry. They were relieved by the 129th and 130th Regiments of the 33rd Division, who were now tasked to guard and defend the whole sector. The American High Command decided that the series of wide valleys between Nantillois and Brieulles were so dangerous that the area would not be attacked for the time being. Indeed, Brieulles was not liberated until 1 November. The best news for the troops was that finally the rolling kitchens had reached the front line; this meant that they had their first hot meal in five days. Unfortunately there was no shelter from the torrential rain that had been deluging the battlefield since the second day of the offensive.

### Tuesday 30 September to Sunday 6 October.
While everywhere else along the Meuse-Argonne front the Americans were engaged in heavy fighting, the 33rd Division continued to occupy the relatively quiet Meuse front. During this time it lost twenty-seven killed and about 350 casualties, almost entirely as a consequence of a German gas attack. Forty men were evacuated with lung complications, the remainder with eye or body burns.

*Right*: A US gas mask; note the drill instruction card. (*Coll. Museum Meuse-Argonne 1918*)

*Below*: An American field kitchen at work.

## Monday 7 October.

With the failure of the Second Phase's goal to pierce the outer defences of the (left bank) Kriemhild Zone on 4 October, General Claudel's XVII Corps, which had remained in place on the right bank since the start of the Meuse-Argonne Offensive, was ordered to prepare a frontal attack on the Meuse Heights. The second phase of the offensive was supposed to deal several hammer blows to the Germans; instead the Americans had been stopped in their tracks by devastating artillery barrages from the guns on the right bank. It was (finally!) clear that something needed to be done.

On 7 October, the 33rd Division was put under the XVII Corps' command for practical reasons, with orders to hold its defensive position on the left bank and at the same time ready a part of its forces (132nd Regiment) to cross the river. The mission of XVII Corps was to seize and hold the approximately ten kilometres wide Meuse Heights sector between the Meuse and Thinte Creek. Its forces included the French 18th and 26th Divisions, reinforced by six Senegalese battalions. The 58th Brigade of the American 29th Division was positioned between the US 33rd and the French 18th Divisions. From left to right, looking north, the 33rd was to cross the Meuse and take Brabant and Consenvoye. When these villages were secured, they were to swing to the left (north) and advance in the direction of Sivry and

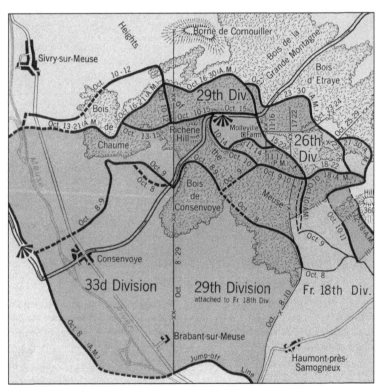

**XVII Corps plan of attack.**

28

Chaume Wood. The 29th Division started from the right bank village of Samogneux and were to advance north to attack Brabant-sur-Meuse, Malbrouck Hill and Consenvoye Wood. The French 18th Division, commanded by General Andelauer, was tasked to drive the Austro-Hungarian troops from Haumont-près-Samogneux and to advance on Ormont Farm.

The sector of the right bank that the US 33rd Division was to attack was defended by the 1st Austro-Hungarian [KuK – *Kaiserlich und Königlich*, Imperial and Royal] Division and the German 7th Reserve Division. These divisions were part of Maas Gruppe Ost. The 1st KuK, directly opposite the US 33rd Division, comprised, from left to right, the 5th, the 112th and the 61st Regiments KuK. The Austro-Hungarian troops were soon to be reinforced by the German 32nd Division and elements of the 228th Division (see Appendix 5 for the German order of battle).

**Tuesday 8 October.**
During the night of 7-8 October, two battalions of the 132nd Regiment began making preparations to cross the Meuse to attack the German positions on the right bank of the river. The 132nd crossed the river before dawn and advanced northward to Consenvoye. The first objective was to occupy Chaume Wood, on the ridge between Sivry and Consenvoye and part of the Etzel Line defences. The adjacent 29th and the French 18th divisions, on the right, were to capture the observation posts and defences on Malbrouck Hill and Haumont Wood respectively.

At 5.00 am, without artillery preparation, the combined American and French forces between Samogneux (west) and Beaumont (east) began their attack. Just before 6.00 am the 33rd crossed the Meuse on footbridges between Brabant and Consenvoye. Orders were given to occupy Brabant and to continue to Consenvoye. Meanwhile, as the day was dawning, construction of more sturdy passages over the river had begun under heavy enemy artillery fire, averaging ninety shells an hour. Many of these were gas shells and gas masks had to be worn all the time. Supported by several machine-gun companies, the 132nd advanced north of Brabant. At 11.00 am, learning that the 58th Brigade (115th and 116th Regiments) of the 29th Division had reached Malbrouck Hill and Brabant Wood on the 33rd Division's right flank, the 132nd Regiment advanced to the road (the present-day D19) running north east out of Consenvoye. In the meantime, Company D of the 124th Machine Gun Battalion, among other American troops, was sent to Consenvoye Wood with orders to remove the Austro-Hungarians from the edge of the wood and beyond. Immediately after they set out, however, the Americans were pinned down by heavy machine-gun fire.

29

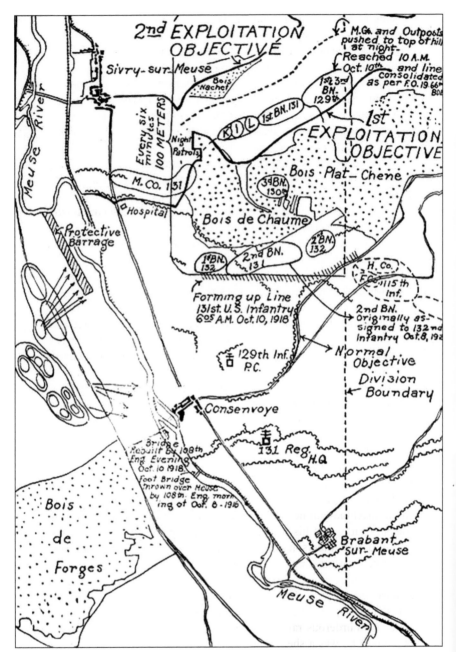

**33rd Division's plan of attack; Sivry (top left) was not reached until 6 November.**

Observing Austrian soldiers under cover some fifty metres away from his own position, Private Clayton Slack, 124th Machine Gun Battalion, on his own initiative, rushed them with his rifle and single-handedly captured ten prisoners and two heavy Maxim machine guns. Following his example, several of the enemy positions were rushed and this relieved some of the pressure on the 132nd Regiment, trying to reach the D19. In 1921 Slack was awarded the Medal of Honor.

**Private Slack (1896-1976).**

After the war Slack earned a living by touring the US showing war films and giving short, ten minute, speeches afterwards. One of the highlights of his stage presentation were the two Maxim machine guns he had captured from the Germans and which he had managed to send to the US when the war was over. In 1969 Slack told a most remarkable story to the *Daily Telegram*:

'While playing the Shubert Theatre in New York City, a man approached my dressing room after the film showing and introduced himself as Heinrich Kühler. I was flabbergasted. Kühler was a German [sic – in fact Austrian] sergeant I captured when I got the machine-gun nest. He was playing the snare drum in a German beer garden in Jersey City and saw the ad in the paper, and came to see my show in the theatre. He came to America after the war, married an American girl and became a citizen. I hired him for a while.'

Slack was not the only one showing initiative that day. First Sergeant Johannes Anderson's Company B, 132nd Regiment, was among the many units held up by the intense artillery and machine-gun fire. Anderson noticed that most of the machine-gun fire came from a single machine-gun nest just ahead of his company's position. Its fire was so deadly that his men could not advance; it would have meant instant death. Anderson quickly formed a plan. Leaving his company, he crept forward alone across No Man's Land. Besides his Colt M1911 pistol, he also carried a sawn-off shotgun. The ground was flat and open; Anderson's only protection from the murderous rain of bullets and exploding shells over his head was a shell hole here and there that afforded him a moment's rest. Crawling steadily forward, however, he worked his way around the enemy machine-gun nest and to the rear of it. Reaching a shell hole just beyond the machine-gun crew, Anderson dropped into it and awaited his opportunity. There were twenty-five men around the gun and they were pumping it for all they were worth. At last they had to stop to replenish their ammunition; this was the moment Anderson had been waiting for. After two blasts from the shotgun, killing two Austrians outright and wounding several others, twenty-three men surrendered. The Austrian-Hungarians were taken completely by surprise and his actions earned Anderson the Medal of Honor. However, there were many more nests that were not destroyed and this made the going extremely difficult.

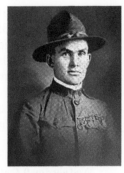

**First Sergeant Johannes Anderson (1887-1950).**

Despite continuous flanking fire from Consenvoye Wood on the immediate right, the objective, the road, was reached around noon. At the same time, because of the danger of a counter-attack, the 131st Regiment, 33rd Division, had been ordered to cross the river at Consenvoye. Under cover of a two hour standing and rolling barrage, the line inched its way towards the wood, only to be stopped by a withering counter barrage. Finally, at nightfall, the devastated Americans dug in on the southern edge of Chaume Wood; it had taken eight hours to battle their way across two kilometres of empty fields, most of the time in full view of German and KuK observers. By now communications were a shambles; of course no supplies reached the front at this point and many soldiers had lost their way. That day the twelve batteries of 52nd Field Artillery Brigade had fired 13,000 rounds in support of the attack.

The US 29th and the French 18th Divisions had also done reasonably well. Communications between the divisions were virtually non-existent, but the 1st Austro-Hungarian (KuK) Division was severely damaged and the 15th German Division had been pushed back all along the front line that now approximately ran from the southern edge of Chaume Wood through Consenvoye Wood and Ormont Farm in the east. The French 18th occupied the latter. Consenvoye and Brabant had been liberated too; troops and supplies

**Members of the 108th Engineers, 33rd Division, rebuilding a destroyed bridge, October 1918.**

now slowly made their way to the front across the two bridges that the 108th Engineers, 33rd Division, had been tirelessly working on all day.

The attack had come as a surprise to Gruppe Maas Ost; the Allies had penetrated four kilometres deep into the enemy lines and over 4,000 prisoners, mainly Austrian-Hungarians, were taken. The German High Command, surprised by the gravity of the attack, immediately ordered the 32nd Division to bolster the 1st KuK Division. They were marched to the front and arrived during the night and early morning of 9 October.

**Wednesday 9 October.**
In stubborn retreat before the advance of the Franco-American forces along its front, General Franz Ludwig Freiherr von Soden, commander of Gruppe Maas Ost, ordered its artillery to make the 'widest possible use of gas ammunition with slight use of HE [high explosive]' through the night of 8-9 October. From north to south, Consenvoye, Brabant, Samogneux and Forges, as well as the lost trenches and dugouts of the Brabant and Hagen Line, were kept under heavy fire to prevent further reinforcements coming over from the left bank. The Americans resumed the attack at 6.40 am. Supported by a 6,000 round artillery barrage, the 132nd advanced north from the southern edge of Chaume Wood.

When Private Berger Loman's Company H, 132nd Regiment, had reached a point within one hundred metres of Chaume Wood, to which it was advancing under terrific machine-gun fire, Loman voluntarily and unaided made his way forward after all others had taken shelter from the direct fire of an enemy machine gun. He crawled to a flank position of the gun and, after killing the entire crew, turned the machine gun on the retreating enemy. It is claimed that Loman killed or captured a total of 147 Germans during the war; he was awarded the Medal of Honor in 1919.

Meanwhile, the pressure proved too much for the remaining 1,500 soldiers of the Austrian 5th KuK Regiment; their defences were swamped by 3,500 Americans. Still, it was not before noon until Chaume Wood was entirely in American hands. The Austrians, supported by their notorious Skoda guns, had put up a considerable fight and consequently losses on both sides were substantial. Even today there are still many surviving gun pits and remains of deep dugouts in Chaume Wood, a silent but eloquent indication of the strength of the position.

**Private Loman (1886-1968).**

33

For the US 29th Division, the morning started somewhat differently; 'Germans! Germans! counter-attack!' That morning the Germans launched a concerted counter-attack against the 29th and the French 18th Divisions. The 102nd and the 177th Regiments of the freshly arrived 32nd Division assaulted the American and French troops, driving them back from the north of Consenvoye Wood. This seriously endangered the 33rd Division's right flank, which was now left exposed to the enemy. In spite of this, the 132nd Regiment of the 33rd Division continued the attack alongside the River Meuse and advanced north of Chaume Wood. At 2 pm, and against all odds, they reached the Giselher Line in the vicinity of the road from Sivry to Villeneuve Farm, beyond the Grande

An unknown Austrian prisoner; the effects of war are written on his face and in his eyes.

Montagne, that in a later attack would cost the US 79th Division so dearly. The German and KuK gunners who had been busy supporting the counter-attack were also ordered to support the outnumbered German troops defending Romagne and Cunel, geographically centrally positioned between the Argonne Forest and the Meuse River. Therefore the gun fire slackened in front of Chaume Woods, permitting the 132nd to advance. On the left bank, the Americans were well on the way to breaching the Hindenburg Zone in several places (although this did not actually materialize until 14 October) and the German gunners were working round the clock to prevent this from happening.

On the right bank there was more trouble for the Americans on the way. About the same time that the US 132nd Regiment reached the Giselher Line, the German 102nd Regiment wheeled left and hit the US 131st Regiment in the right flank between Consenvoye and Chaume Wood. Simultaneously, the 232nd Reserve Regiment and the 105th Storm Battalion of the 1st KuK struck the battalions of the US 132nd Regiment below Sivry. At the risk of being cut off and annihilated, they were forced to retreat two kilometres. The combined KuK and German forces recaptured Chaume Woods and the adjacent Plat-Chêne Wood. The Americans lost one officer and thirty-seven men killed and eleven officers and 315 men wounded.

A 33rd Division painted helmet. (*Coll Museum Meuse-Argonne 1918*)

Hundreds more had been exposed to a combination of HE and gas shells; over 200 severe cases were evacuated from the battlefield. Pounded from three sides by artillery shells, the Americans were in a poor shape and in no condition to continue the attack; but they managed to retain a line south from Chaume Wood.

### Thursday 10 October.

That night Brigadier General Wolf of 66 Brigade (129th and 130th Regiment, 33rd Division) ordered all the troops he could spare across the Meuse; almost the entire 33rd Division was thrown into the fray. During the night the German artillery kept the left and right bank of the Meuse continuously under fire with gas and HE shells. The 'fresh' reinforcements, who had been in the line since 26 September, were moved to their new positions on the right bank; no one slept a wink that night.

The orders for that day were to recapture Chaume and Plat Chêne Woods, exploiting the line towards the Sivry-Villeneuve Farm Road. The neighbouring US 29th and French 18th Divisions would recapture the ground lost the day before and continue their advance to Grande Montagne and Ormont Woods. Both woods lay more or less on the same alignment with the Sivry-Villeneuve Farm Road. At 6.00 am the combined allied force clambered out of their wet trenches and set off. At 10.50 am, the vanguard of the 33rd Regiment, supported by the US 29th Division on the right, gained their objective. However, an intense artillery barrage made it impossible to hold on to their positions. Gas masks were worn all the time at this stage. American reinforcements from the 129th and 130th Regiments had reached Chaume Woods by 2.00 pm, but meanwhile the Germans and Austro-Hungarians were preparing a counter-attack. Weakened by shell fire and a kilometre-wide gap between the 33rd and 29th Divisions, it was fortunate that the enemy attack did not materialize. In spite of a terrific artillery barrage and German planes strafing the Americans, they somehow managed to take positions on the north face of the Vaux de Mille Mais Ravine, a little south of the Sivry-Villeneuve Farm Road.

That night 33rd Division's HQ received a message from the 121st Regiment at 8.15 pm:

'... counter-attack imminent as enemy has been massing troops all day. Front thinly held. Support is absolutely necessary if we hold. Need support. Valley [Vaux de Mille Mais Ravine] is gassed. Casualties estimated at 50%, my right flank entirely open.'

To make the situation worse, Plat Chêne Wood, to the 33rd Division's immediate rear, was recaptured by the German 102nd Regiment.

**View from Consenvoye to Chaume Wood, January 2020.**

The rest of XVII Corps had fared a little better; the US 29th Division reached a line north of Molleville Farm and the French 18th Division was clinging on to the southern slope of Ormont Wood.

**Friday 11 to Sunday 13 October.**
Throughout the night of 10-11 October and the following day enemy artillery hampered the division as it sought to round up stragglers, reorganize units and set up a defensive line on the northern edge of Chaume Wood. The positions reached on the previous day were held, but just. Confusion and chaos reigned. The shelling, lack of food, sleep and dry clothes weighed heavy on the exhausted and rain sodden men. The situation remained unchanged until 13 October.

The hard-pressed German and Austro-Hungarian troops were hardly better off and no counter-attacks were made. The 1st KuK Division had suffered terribly; about 80 per cent of the 8,500 men that had initially made up the division had been killed, wounded or taken prisoner. Late in the afternoon of 12 October the sad remains were relieved by the German 228th Division. This division had been heavily engaged at Cunel and had been weakened over the previous days but was still a coherent fighting formation.

A typewriter found in 2018 at the location of a former HQ of the 33rd Division. (*Coll Paul 'Oz' Osman*)

## Monday 14 October to Sunday 20 October.

No attacks were undertaken during this period other than small-scale operations to straighten the lines in order to obtain more favourable positions. Both sides worked continually to improve their defences. On 21 October the 33rd Division was relieved by the French 15th Colonial Division.

## Summary: The 29th 'Blue and Gray' Division, 8-31 October.

The 29th Division, a National Guard Division, was commanded by Major General Charles G. Morton. Activated on 18 July 1917, the Division's infantry was made up of the 113th, 114th, 115th and 116th Regiments from New Jersey, Maryland, Delaware and Virginia. The division was composed of men from states that had units that fought for both the North and South during the American Civil War. Therefore it was nicknamed the 'Blue and Gray' Division, after the colours of both the Union and the Confederate uniforms during that war. The Division was trained at Camp McClellan, Alabama, and sailed for France in June 1918. It arrived in Brest Harbour on 8 June, although several of its composite units, like the 54th Field Artillery Brigade, landed in the UK, in Liverpool and London. After additional training with the French the Division was moved to a quiet sector in Alsace (in eastern France, near Belfort) to get accustomed to front line life. However, during their time in this 'quiet' part of the front line they were raided by the Germans at least four times. Realizing that they had a new division opposite their front, the Germans were searching for information about them and also hoped to intimidate the green troops.

**Major General Charles G. Morton (1861-1933).**

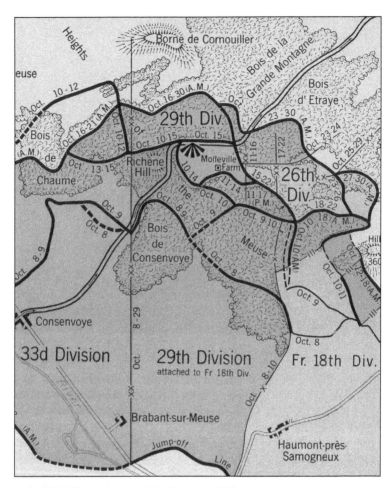

**The 29th Division's sector, 8-30 October 1918.**

On 23 September they were marched to the Meuse-Argonne area as one of the three divisions in First Army Reserve. On 1 October, after another forced night march through the driving rain, the division was billeted in Blercourt and surroundings, some fifteen kilometres south of the front. Two days later the 29th Division was relieved from this task and put under the command of the French XVII Corps, the easternmost corps of the American First Army. They were ordered to go into the line on the east of the Meuse River for an attack soon to be launched from this point. The 29th was to be placed between the US 33rd Division on the left and the French 18th Division on the right. They were only moved into the line on 7 October. However, because of the nature of the terrain and possibly because this was the first time that the 29th was to participate in a major battle, it was deemed not practicable to put the whole division in the line at one time. Therefore, only 58 Brigade (the 115th and 116th Regiments), commanded by Colonel Vernon A. Caldwell, was to be sent in.

**Monday 7 October.**
An anonymous soldier recalls:

> 'We assembled at about 7.00 pm in a heavy rain and hiked ten kilometres to a woods which were rather bare and showed considerable evidences of war. [This was in the barren, mud-churned wasteland of the Verdun battlefield.] The Germans were bombing the road, which delayed our march considerably, and as a consequence we didn't arrive at our destination until 1.00 am. Orders were not received to pitch tents, so we lay around in the wet until morning, resting the best we could.'

The initial front of 58 Brigade was nearly 2,000 metres wide; the planned depth of the advance was to be seven kilometres. The 115th took up a position 500 metres south of Brabant; the left flank of the 116th was some 350 metres north of Samogneux. At this point they were the only American formation on the right bank of the Meuse. However, the 33rd Division was ready to cross the river as footbridges had been constructed during the night between Brabant and Consenvoye.

**Tuesday 8 October.**
The goal of the assault was to break through the German first line (Brabant), the second line (Hagen) and to drive the Austro-Hungarians out of Malbrouck Wood and Consenvoye Wood, the third (Volker) line. The attack started without a preliminary bombardment so as not to arouse suspicion among the enemy's sentries.

Promptly at 5.00 am the 158th Field Artillery Brigade fired the first round and soon every gun in the sector joined in. The whistles of the First Battalion's company and platoon leaders set the various lines in motion; the standing barrage had been laid 300 metres in front of their jumping-off positions. On reaching this point the infantry moved forward behind a rolling barrage at a rate of one hundred metres every four minutes. Support troops followed at 500, reserve troops at 1,000 metres. Making their way across No Man's Land was not easy. During the two years following the Battle of Verdun in 1916 the Germans had organized the terrain into an interconnected series of defensive entrenchments. Deep dugouts, well-built communication trenches,

**View from Haumont to Malbrouck Wood, 29ᵗʰ Division's sector.**

**The excellent British Lewis Gun.** (*Coll Museum Meuse-Argonne 1918*)

observation and machine-gun posts, telephone lines, search lights and signalling stations were at the enemy's disposal.

The Austro-Hungarians defending the trenches opposite the US 58 Brigade were completely caught on the hop. Their artillery did not start a counter barrage until 5.30 am; but when it did start it was most vigorous. Fortunately, by then the barbed wire entanglements in front of the Brabant Line, the first objective, were already cut. Still, the going was so difficult – uphill, negotiating ravines, continuous artillery fire and gas – that it took the 29ᵗʰ until 6.20 to reach this line, which was lightly held. A few Austrian prisoners were sent to the rear and the advance continued. However, there are reports that in many instances the Austro-Hungarians did not appear until after the first American waves had passed over and the support waves were approaching. Then KuK soldiers emerged, armed with Lewis machine guns, and started to blaze away at anything that moved. (Large quantities of British Lewis guns had been captured from the British in the Spring Offensives and were pushed into German/KuK service, mainly with reserve or second rate units.) Heavy fighting broke out but it did not stop the advanced battalions from pushing on to the Hagen Line, which was reached at around 7.00 am.

## The 115th Regiment.

With the German and KuK artillery mainly focussed on the 33rd Division, busy crossing the Meuse and building bridges, the 115th Regiment found somewhat easier going in its part of the sector. It reached the first objective, a line between the present-day Consenvoye German Cemetery along the D964 and Malbrouck Hill, on schedule and continued to the second, the Consenvoye-Étraye Road, the present-day D19. Here, the ground was open and rolling and the southern edge of Consenvoye Wood could just be seen. This edge was strongly held but, because the 112th KuK were engaged in so many other places, resistance was quickly overcome. A likely favourable factor was that because of the topography the battalions of the 115th Regiment were less exposed to direct observation and therefore gunfire. Handwritten notes by Second Lieutenant John E. Theriault, Company C, in the margin of the 29th Division's History in the author's personal collection seem to confirm that often communications were poor.

'Co A & Co B of the 115th were the first line companies. The extreme left flank of the division is Company B. My platoon, myself in command, was the scout platoon or guard platoon. ["Immediately after the departure and during the march forward, each company in the first line will be preceded by a platoon deployed at very great intervals, which will be used as a forward guard for the second line companies."] As we advanced, the left flank was exposed as the 33rd Division was on the east bank of the Meuse River and did not arrive until some time later [at 9.00 am].'

The Second Battalion, now spearheading the assault, fought its way through the south-western tip of Consenvoye Wood and was quite successful in doing so. Company H, on the left flank, overcame numerous machine-gun nests and literally hacked their way to their main objective, the Consenvoye-Étraye Road.

When the advance of Company H was held up by machine-gun fire and a request was made for a Browning automatic rifle (BAR) team to

**The view from Samogneux to Malbrouck Wood.**

charge the nest, Baltimore born Private Henry Costin was the first to volunteer. Advancing with his platoon, under the terrific fire of enemy artillery, machine guns and trench mortars, he continued after all his comrades had become casualties and he himself was seriously wounded. He fired his rifle until he collapsed. His act resulted in the capture of about a hundred prisoners and several machine guns.

Only twenty years old, Costin succumbed from the effects of his wounds shortly after the accomplishment of his heroic deed; he was posthumously awarded the Medal of Honor. On 5 April 1919 The Washington Post reported that in a ceremony held in the Blue Room in the Belvedere Hotel in Baltimore, Hythron Johnston Costin, Private Costin's young widow, was presented with his Medal of Honor by General Beaumont Bonaparte Buck. After the repatriation of his body to the US, Costin was buried in Loudon Park National Cemetery, in Baltimore, Maryland.

The second man to perform deeds that day that resulted in the award of the Medal of Honor was Second Lieutenant Patrick Regan. While leading his platoon against a strong enemy machine-gun nest, which was holding up the advance of two companies, Regan divided his men into three groups, sending one group to either flank, and he himself, leading the third, attacking with a Browning automatic rifle team from the front. Two of the team were killed outright by machine-gun bullets while Regan and another man were seriously wounded, the latter unable to advance. Despite his wounds, Regan dashed with an empty pistol into the machine-gun nest, capturing thirty Austrian gunners and

**Private Costin, MoH (1898-1918).**

42

four machine guns. The elimination of the machine guns permitted the companies to advance, hitherto impossible. Despite his wounds, Regan continued to lead his platoon forward until ordered to the rear by his commanding officer. He received the Medal of Honor on 12 April 1919.

Thanks to local successes like the ones described above, the Consenvoye-Étraye Road was reached at about 4.30 pm. To establish liaison with the 116th Regiment, the right flank of the 115th was pulled back slightly.

Company E, on the right of the Second Battalion, also made good progress, although the fighting here was equally hard. Moving steadily forward, they took many prisoners and also found an abandoned ammunition dump and an engineer depot. Meanwhile, the Third Battalion, which had started the day in reserve, began its advance at 12.30 pm. According to the official 29th Division History, they pressed on to the line occupied by the Second Battalion, 'where it dug in and established liaison with the 33rd Division on the left'. This line was reached at about 4.30 pm.

Second Lieutenant Regan, MoH (1882-1943).

### The 116th Regiment.

Enemy resistance had begun to stiffen as the 116th Regiment attacked up hill and slowly approached the Austro-Hungarian's main position, the Volker Line. A part of that position was reached at 9.30 am by the third battalion of the 116th Regiment. The French on their right flank, however, were entangled in such heavy fighting in Haumont Wood that they had not yet reached this line. Contact with the 115th Regiment on the left also had been lost. The attack ground to a halt in the face of combined machine-gun, rifle, grenade and minenwerfer (trench mortar) fire when within 200 metres of the strongly fortified Malbrouck Hill. The Americans answered with a powerful rifle grenade and automatic rifle barrage, which beat down the opposition and enabled the Americans to take the enemy front line trench at bayonet point. As soon as the KuK line was breached, many of the enemy surrendered. However, this development had not gone unnoticed by the Austrian gunners and before long a terrible barrage began to fall upon the battalions of the 116th Regiment. While the doughboys clung on to their isolated position on the barren slope, the Austro-Hungarians did everything in their power to remove them from the edge of Malbrouck Hill. A bombardment opened up and the Americans were hard-pressed. In addition, the Third Battalion suffered terribly when a squadron of German planes swept the lines, first with bombs and then with machine guns.

*Left*: German troops stand to in a well constructed trench.

*Below*: American troops in a front line trench; the soldier in the foreground holds a hand grenade.

Timely American reinforcements were on their way. At 11.00 am the First and Second Battalion, 116th, reached Boussières Ravine, just south of Malbrouck Hill. At this time heavy machine-gun fire rendered a further advance extremely hazardous. With the Third Battalion pinned down in a few trenches at the southern tip of Malbrouck Hill, the situation was extremely critical. Subjected to heavy fire, without support on the flanks and deprived of supplies, one powerful counter-attack could have been enough to chase the entire 116th Regiment from their positions. This did not happen, yet again a clear indication of the desperate manpower situation facing the Germans.

A breakthrough was achieved by Captain Johnston, Company L, Third Battalion. On his own initiative he launched a sudden attack against the hill. Company K, under Lieutenant Stone, was immediately ordered to his support and the attack was driven home with the bayonet. Resistance was soon overcome thanks to the speed of their advance; Malbrouck Hill and part of Brabant Wood were now in American hands. In Brabant Wood eighteen heavy machine guns, dozens of Lewis guns, five guns, two anti-tank rifles and minenwerfers were captured, in addition to a food and ammunition dump. By about 1.00 pm the entire front and the flanks had been sufficiently cleared of Austro-Hungarians to permit the First Battalion to pass through the line held by the Third Battalion and to become the front line attackers.

For his actions Captain Ewart Johnston (as well as the promoted Captain Stone) was awarded the Distinguished Service Cross. (It is difficult to see why Johnston's was not the Medal of Honor, considering the train of events that he set in motion.) Besides single-handedly jump-starting the advance of the 116th Regiment, Johnston, with the aid of Company L, of course, is credited with the capture of 210 prisoners, including a battalion commander and his staff.

The fighting continued north of Brabant Wood into Consenvoye Wood. Again, the Americans were pinned down by machine and artillery fire. Sheltering behind trees, in abandoned trenches and shallow holes in the ground, Sergeant Earl Gregory became increasingly irritated by the situation. With the remark 'I will get them', Gregory seized a rifle and a trench-mortar shell, which he used as a hand grenade, left his detachment of the trench mortar platoon and, advancing ahead of the infantry, captured a machine gun and three Austrians. Advancing still farther from the machine-gun nest, he captured a 75 millimetre mountain howitzer and jumped into a dugout in the immediate vicinity. When he reappeared on the surface, he had captured nineteen more Austrians.

On 11 October, three days after the ferocious fighting in Consenvoye Wood, Gregory and his unit were attempting to take an enemy trench line when an artillery shell landed amongst his unit. Flying shrapnel wounded Gregory in the leg, causing him to be hospitalized for six months, first in France, before being shipped to Camp Lee, Virginia. On 7 March 1919, it was announced that he was to be awarded the Medal of Honor. Gregory was discharged from the army on 25 April 1919 and four days later he was presented the Medal of Honor by Major General Omar Bundy at a ceremony on the camp's parade field.

**Sergeant Gregory, MoH (1897-1972).**

By 3.40 pm Captain Alexander's First Battalion had reached a line on the northern slope of Molleville Woods, a sub-division of Consenvoye Wood, but had to fall back to the high ground overlooking Bourvaux Ravine in order to make firm contact with the French 18th Division. The French had been held up all day by notably accurate artillery fire and were in no state to continue fighting without resupply and reorganisation – in fact, this situation was true of the Americans as well. Still, the advance of the 29th/18th Divisions had been successful; they had penetrated four kilometres into enemy territory. Contact with the neighbouring 115th Regiment on the left, however, was effectively lost. That night, the remnants of the hard-hit 1st KuK Division were reinforced by the German 32nd Division.

**Wednesday 9 October.**

The night was spent without incident and the troops were kept busy consolidating the new line in preparation to resist counter-attacks. Shelling continued through the night and 'some gas' was reported. The bulk of the German guns were used to harass the Meuse crossings in the 33rd Division's sector.

The Germans had not been sitting idle during the hours of darkness either. At dawn (and hidden by a heavy fog) twenty German battalions, some 10,000 men from five different divisions, participated in a general counter-attack over a ten kilometres wide front, from Chaume to Caures Wood. General von der Marwitz had ordered Maas Gruppe Ost to 'retake the main line of resistance [Etzel Line], and at the very least, the Volker Stellung'. This was literally the line XVII Corps was clinging on to; the line was one of the backbones of the German defences on the Meuse Heights. At some places along the line, as on the 33rd Division front, things seemed perilous, but in other places in the 29th Division's sector the half-hearted attack was quickly repulsed. That morning, the German army lost another 1,000 men they could not afford to lose. During the remainder of the day the 58th Brigade advanced a little north and secured a large part of Consenvoye Wood. Contact between the 33$^{rd}$ on the left and the French 18$^{th}$ on the right was established. Once more, preparations were made to withstand further counter-attacks; the troops dug in and waited for things to come.

## Thursday 10 October.

During the night, part of 57 Brigade (the 113$^{th}$ Regiment and the 111$^{th}$ Machine Gun Battalion) was supposed to pass through 58 Brigade and to continue the advance; but the resistance met by the French 18$^{th}$ Division below Ormont Wood was such that General Claudel required the whole brigade in this sector. General Morton of the US 29$^{th}$ Division was not pleased; without any other reinforcements available he had to soldier on with what he had at his disposal; a renewed attack with fresh troops was out of the question.

Consequently, Morton ordered 58 Brigade to resume the attack in concert with the 33$^{rd}$ Division. The main objectives for this day were Richene Hill, Plat Chêne Wood and the clearing of Molleville Farm. Richene Hill housed an important observation position built on one of the highest hills (382 metres) of the Meuse Heights; it was in fact one of the most important targets of this whole campaign. The installations here were the eyes of the German artillery in this sector. If the Americans could seize this important tactical position it would be a slap in the face for the Germans and would seriously disrupt artillery operations.

**Molleville Ravine on a foggy morning in January 2020; Molleville Farm is just visible in the centre. Note the American trench in the foreground.**

**Members of the 308th Engineers, 33rd Division, repairing a footbridge near Brabant, 10 October 1918.**

Once more the attack was launched without artillery preparation. Some progress was made but the area was bristling with machine-gun nests. This held up the advance to such an extent that after the capture of Richene Hill by the 115th the fighting virtually came to a standstill. The 116th did not fare any better; after literally fighting for every square metre of ground, they managed to take Bossois Wood, a small strip of Molleville Wood. Again, the Molleville Farm clearing appeared too hard a nut to crack. By now German resistance was steadily increasing; the Americans were now facing the outposts of their principal line, the Etzel Zone and for the Germans it was an essential stand.

### Right flank: the US 57 Brigade, 29th Division and the French 18th Division.

That night the 113th Regiment crossed the Meuse but just as the last platoon reached the far side an artillery shell destroyed the pontoon bridge, preventing the supply trains from reaching the east side. An unknown private of Company M recalls:

'Many found the shell holes a convenient place in which to wash and clean up. Most of us obtained water for drinking purposes, although we well knew that it was the grave of hundreds. At 4.00 am on October 10th we were up and at it, rolling our packs and making ready for our departure.'

Half an hour later the 113th was silently marching over a series of hilly ravines from the Côte des Roches [La Quartière on modern maps] and through Haumont Wood to take up position. From left to right, the Second Battalion was on the south-eastern edge of Molleville Wood, with the 116th on its left flank. The Third Battalion took up position in an abandoned German trench system that ran from Molleville Wood to a little east of Ormont Farm and continued to Coassinvaux Ravine (or Death Valley, as it quickly became known). Soon thereafter the Austrians started to drop tear gas. The men started sneezing and breathing became increasingly difficult so that it became necessary to wear gas masks. At 9.00 am, after being lost for some time, the attacking companies took their positions in the jump-off trenches – effectively an irregular line of shell holes. At the time it was not entirely clear where the enemy were, how strong they were and whether Germans or Austrians occupied the sector.

At 10.40 am orders came to fix bayonets and sling packs. The barrage started at 10.45 am and fifteen minutes later the men went over the top. The half-baked artillery preparation was of little effect. It was a simple matter for the Austrians to jump into their deep dugouts and come up unscratched after the bombardment. An unknown private noted:

'The 1st and 4th Platoons, the attacking waves, were met almost immediately upon going over with a heavy machine-gun fire from a camouflaged trench, not over 150 yards ahead, which none of us knew about. A sweeping fire of shot and shell poured from Bois d'Ormont and Bois de la Reine upon our platoons, rushing one moment and crawling the next but ever onward. Suddenly a barrage rocket went up from the enemy's trenches and a rain of big shells from his artillery was the immediate answer.

The company, with considerable depleted ranks, kept pressing slowly forward. A few short dashes and the enemy's first position, 200 yards in front of our jump-off trench, was reached. It comprised a series of small posts, large enough to accommodate three or four men with a machine gun, lying just over the crest of a little knoll and camouflaged with branches and partially protected by tin [sheet metal] and wire. Ten terrified Huns who had left their

**29th Division's plan of attack, 8 October 1918.**

posts as the company reached their trench came leaping out with upheld hands, crying *Kamerad*! These were our first but by no means our last prisoners. [Private] Louis London could scarcely be restrained from shooting them down, but Lieutenant Webb, who lay near so seriously wounded that we accepted his death as inevitable, ordered him to spare them. They were undoubtedly the Germans [Hungarians] who had wounded the Lieutenant.'

Meanwhile, the French 18th Division's advance had not kept up with the 113th. This left the whole right flank exposed to machine-gun fire from emplacements and from trees in Bois d'Ormont. They also failed to connect up with the 116th on the right and the net result of a day's fighting was the gain of a couple of hundred metres.

**Elmer Frederick Stauch, Co E, 113th Regiment, 29th Division.**
Born in 1894 in Baltimore City, Maryland, Second Lieutenant Fred Stauch, an American with German roots, went overseas in June 1918. After the arrival in Brest, the green 29th Division trained with the French in a quiet sector in Alsace. Soon after arrival in the front line trenches, the 115th and 116th Regiments were raided by the Germans, who had set out to take prisoners for interrogation. On 23 September, the Blue and Gray Division was transferred to Verdun to participate in the Meuse-Argonne Offensive, more specifically in the right bank operations. During the night of 9-10 October, Stauch's Company E crossed the Meuse; the 113th was to operate on the right flank of the 29th Division and keep in contact with the French 18th Division.

The mess kit shown on the photographs was found in the summer of 2018 in Consenvoye Wood and clearly shows battlefield damage.

This is not surprising, as for most of the time that Stauch spent in the area the Americans were under heavy German shell or machine-gun fire. Stauch scratched his name and unit on the bottom of his mess kit, as well as a German Iron Cross.

The 29th was relieved on 30 October by the 79th Division and would not return to the battlefield before the Armistice. After the battle, Stauch was promoted to 1st Lieutenant in the Quarter Master's Corps, HQ. The officers of his new outfit sailed home on 30 June 1919. Stauch died in 1930, aged only 35.

## Friday 11 to Monday 14 October.

At 6.00 am, after thirty minutes of preparatory fire to 'soften up' the Germans, the attack was resumed. The two regiments (115th and 116th) were to advance side by side, each having one battalion, a machine-gun company, a 37mm gun platoon and a Stokes Mortar platoon attached, on the two kilometres wide front line, in total about 2,500 men. The objectives remained the same: Plat Chêne Wood and the northern end of the clearing at Molleville Farm, the present-day D19 Consenvoye-Étraye Road. If these goals were met, they were to push on to Hill 370, just north of the D19, extending into Grande Montagne Wood two kilometres further north. Initially, the advance went quite well; Molleville Wood was finally taken and the Americans were now able to attempt to cross the clearing at Molleville Farm. Several platoons of the 116th now advanced across the open ground until suddenly they were met with intense machine-gun fire from Grande Montagne Wood and Hill 370, just across the road. They fell back to the edge of the woods in disarray. It was clear that the Germans had sacrificed Molleville Wood in order to turn the ravine into a killing zone. Added to this was that the progress of the French 18th Division and the 113th Regiment of the 29th on the right flank had been slow. As a result, the Germans were still in possession of Bultroy Wood, east of Molleville Ravine, and were therefore able to fire in enfilade.

The assistance of the artillery was called for at 2.00 pm and before long a devastating barrage of heavy 155mm Schneider shells made sure that every German machine gunner in the area was keeping his head down. This enabled the Americans to take up the advance and to pick up momentum. Heavy fighting continued during the day; a strong German counter-attack was repulsed at the point where the 115th and 116th Regiment met. In spite of this, the 115th penetrated the Plat Chêne Wood for a couple of hundred metres and the 116th even made it into the Vaux de St. Martin Ravine, just before Grande Montagne Wood. Outnumbered by the Americans, the Germans called upon their artillery

**Trenches in Molleville Wood, January 2020.**

to clear the outpost zone of the Etzel Line. Soon an unprecedented artillery barrage of both gas and HE shells chased the Americans almost back to their starting points, across Molleville Valley to the northern edge of Molleville Wood. Once more Montagne Wood was beyond reach and the Americans had suffered a severe beating, enduring heavy casualties and in some cases companies had been entirely stripped of their officers.

By this point in the battle the German artillery had become more active than ever, part of a well-considered doctrine. The 29th Division's gas report of October 1959 explains: 'In the opening days of the campaign the 29th Division had reason to think that gas on this front might not be a serious difficulty after all. While it was German policy to lull new units facing them with desultory gas fire until they grew careless.'

The losses were terrible on both sides. The 1st KuK suffered a casualty rate of 80 per cent; during the night of 12-13 October they were relieved by the German 228th Division.

For the next three days the situation remained unchanged; the 115th occupied the southern edge of Plat Chêne Woods and the 116th the northern edge of Molleville Wood. The 113th Regiment, attached to the 18th French Division, were still struggling to connect its front line with the right flank of the 116th. This would not take place until 17 October. It is worth noting that during this period General Morton visited the front line. The story goes that during the visit Morton was caught in a German artillery barrage. However, he refused to take cover. Coolly, Morton ordered the rest of his staff to seek shelter in an abandoned German dugout. They probably did not need much encouragement to obey the general's orders.

Except for skirmishes between patrols and limited local actions, 13 and 14 October passed relatively quietly. As best as was possible, the regiments were reorganised, positions reinforced, outposts established; but the front line remained unchanged. Artillery bombardments continued during this whole period. Meanwhile, on 14 October on the left bank, the Americans (in this case the 32nd Division) had finally been able to achieve a breach in the Kriemhild Line after three weeks of dogged fighting.

### Right flank: the US 57 Brigade, 29th Division and the French 18th Division.

On the night of 11-12 October XVII Corps ordered the last of its reserves, the 114th Regiment, 29th Division, to move up from Côte des Roches, Brabant, to Ormont Farm and Coassinvaux Ravine. Passing through the French 18th, it was to attack the fortified heights of Ormont Wood. Only the French 66th Regiment would remain in the front line. At noon, after a series of attacks, the western edge of the wood had been taken with the assistance of the 113th Regiment from La Reine Wood. They paid a heavy toll; the 114th lost 118 men killed and 812 wounded, of which between 300 and 500 were gas casualties. Company D, First Battalion, was severely battered; it came out of the battle with thirty-six men, leaving behind 196. Only limited gains were made during those few days, although two German counter-attacks were defeated.

### Tuesday 15 October.

The 58 Brigade was ordered to renew the attack on Grande Montagne Woods in conjunction with the 33rd Division on the left and 57 Brigade, still operating under the French 18th Division, on the right. The capture of the section of the Giselher Line that ran along the heights of the Grande Montagne was the main objective. The rate of advance was to be a hundred metres in six minutes. Because of a shortage of ammunition (the exploitation of the breaking of the Kriemhild Line at Romagne, among others, had priority over the actions on the right bank) the artillery preparation was limited to only thirty minutes, or three rounds per gun per minute.

**A British 18 pdr shrapnel shell sectioned for demonstration purposes.** (*Coll Museum Meuse-Argonne 1918*)

**The 115th Regiment.**
The Third Battalion, commanded by Captain Woodcock, had gone
forward to the attack at 8.00 am. Keeping in touch with the 33rd Division
on the left and the 116th on the right, it met with intense machine-gun
and heavy artillery fire. The one goal they achieved was a slightly better
position to resume a future attack but for this day this was about the
maximum they could do. Nevertheless, this slight shift of the line also
put the 115th Regimental front line in contact with its neighbours.

**The 116th Regiment.**
Heavy fog shrouded Molleville Valley when the Third Battalion took the
lead. However, scarcely had they had cleared the woods and moved out
into the open than heavy machine-gun fire started from Bultroy Wood,
on the right side of the clearing. Nonetheless, they managed to reach
the northern edge of Molleville Valley and continued into the woods on
the opposite side of the road (the D19). At 9.00 am the southern edge
of Grande Montagne Wood was reached. Here, Major Opie, HQ Group
of the Third Battalion, established his command post but found himself
in an isolated position. While sending a request for reinforcements, the
improvised HQ was fired upon by several German machine guns, killing
one officer and wounding several, including Major Opie. Seriously
wounded, he remained in command and organized the defences until
by nightfall he was relieved by Captain Barksdale. After the war Major
Opie was awarded the Distinguished Service Cross and the French Croix
de Guerre. On the right of the 116th Regiment, Companies L and M
spent most of the day fighting in Bultroy Wood. By nightfall they had
occupied a small strip of the woods at a heavy cost in dead and wounded.
However, there was no contact with the 113th Regiment and the French.
Company C, First Battalion, 116th, was sent forward to fill the gap and
was promptly subjected to two German counter-attacks during the night.

By the end of the day the Third Battalion, 116th Regiment, had
only nine officers and 257 men left, out of the twenty-four officers and
790 men it had started out with.

**Right flank: the US 57 Brigade, 29th Division and the French
18th Division.**
Company F of the 113th, still under the command of the French, was ordered
to launch yet another attack on Molleville Wood, to cross the ravine and to
continue to Bultroy Wood. An anonymous private of Company F recounts:

'Three nests, containing altogether seven machine guns, were
encountered and an automatic crew was sent in to flank them on

the left. Private Sample, of Oklahoma, was caught fast in the wire and was killed by machine-gun fire. Private Gaspani pushed on, and wiped out a nest of three guns, piling up twelve Germans in the pit. Private Talmore, fighting coolly, had shot two of the enemy, and injured a third, when he himself was wounded and had to be evacuated. All the guns were soon silenced and destroyed, and the advance continued; more machine guns and snipers were encountered. Privates Belowitz and Marsavich were wounded, and Private Zenski, while kneeling behind a stump, firing at a machine gunner, was shot through the temple and instantly killed with his rifle in position to fire. Snipers, with machine guns, were located in trees and shot from their platforms, while others, fighting Indian fashion, dodging from tree to tree, were driven back, and we finally formed a line of resistance along the edge of a road at the top of the hill.'

Molleville Ravine was now partly in American hands; but the deluge of shell and machine-gun fire made it impossible to gain a foothold in Bultroy Wood. Although Bultroy Wood is only about 500 metres wide, no contact was made between Companies L and M of the 116th. Gas was now a real issue in their sector as 57 Brigade and the French 18th Division held a series of ravines. Because gas is heavier than air, ravines and other low places such as trenches, shell holes and dugouts, were to be avoided. The lack of water also became a serious problem as the wells and creeks were seriously contaminated with gas. The front line was nothing more than a series of consolidated shell holes that were under continuous artillery fire.

### Wednesday 16 to Saturday 19 October.

The Americans continued the attack after thirty minutes of artillery preparation. It was met by the usual machine-gun fire but, to everyone's surprise, the advance went quite well. What really made the difference was a notable decrease in the German artillery fire. Countless German machine-gun nests were cleared but the going was somewhat easier in comparison to the previous day. The fighting raged back and forth, but by the end of the day the Americans had moved the front line five hundred metres further north; the Plat Chêne Wood and also the southern part of Grande Montagne Wood were now firmly in American hands. However, the right flank still did not manage to overcome German resistance in Bultroy Wood and Ormont Wood, two kilometres to the south east. The advance could not continue as long as the right flank of XVII Corps was in danger of a flanking attack and flanking fire from the east. At this stage even an attack from the rear was possible.

Orders were given to dig in, reinforce positions and to prepare for a German counter-attack. By now, the French 18th Division had been so badly mauled that it was relieved by the American 26th Division. Part of the 113th Regiment's right flank facing Ormont Hill was taken over by the 104th Regiment, 26th Division.

Thursday 17, Friday 18 and Saturday 19 October passed without incident. On Friday, after days of fog and rain, the sun came out, which naturally had a positive effect on the men's morale. Also, for the first time in ten days, the infantry fighting had ceased, although, naturally, both sides continued shelling.

### Sunday 20 to Tuesday 22 October.

On 16 October the French 18th Division was relieved by the American 26th Division. This meant that 57 Brigade was released from French command, re-equipped as well as possible under the circumstances and returned to the 29th Division. Now, in spite of the fairly good results of the previous week, the biggest obstacles on XVII Corps' right flank were still in German possession. These were, from north to south, Étraye Wood, Bultroy Wood, Bélieu Wood, Chênes Wood and Ormont Wood. These woods are largely situated on hill tops and ridges and were heavily fortified. The German defences were organized in such a way that the positions covered each other with machine guns and artillery, providing mutual support. While the garrison on one of the hills sought refuge in deep dugouts and elaborate tunnel systems that were practically impervious to incoming fire, artillery and machine-gun units from another swept the area. This way, the hill tops could be easily rid of the enemy. When the shelling stopped, the garrison would come out with machine guns, trench mortars and hand grenades to eliminate the remainder of the attacking force.

As the advance further north bogged down because of German artillery fire coming from the rear and flanks, there was also a serious threat of an attack from the rear. Furthermore, the capture of Étraye Wood was the key to reinvigorate the attack to the north; and the only route to the capture of Grande Montagne and Réville Woods in the direction of Sivry-sur-Meuse was the elimination of this series of woods. On 20 October orders were issued to start preparations for a combined attack by the 29th and 26th Divisions. In addition to the usual machine-gun company,

**A painted helmet of the 29th Division. (*Coll Museum Meuse-Argonne 1918*)**

Stokes Mortar crew and 37mm gun platoons, a 75mm gun battery was assigned to each regiment in order to provide close artillery support. On the left flank, liaison was established between the French 15th Colonial Division and the American 29th.

**Wednesday 23 October.**
During the night the battalions who were to lead the assault were moved into the front line trenches. At 5.00 am, the First Battalion, 113th Regiment and a company of the 111th Machine Gun Battalion, were on their way to the front and moved into Coassinvaux Ravine, approximately 1,000 metres south of Molleville Farm. As ill luck would have it, the German artillery dropped about 400 shells onto their positions, of which an estimated 200 were gas. The shelling continued for about twenty minutes and part of the attached machine-gun company was severely gassed.

The American artillery barrage lasted for an hour, from 5.15 am to 6.15 am, and was joined by the French 15th Colonial Division's and XVII French Corps' batteries. The jumping-off line ran practically north and south through Molleville Farm and the attack was due east, with the 115th on the left, the 116th in the centre and the 113th on the right. The 26th Division was to eliminate all opposition from Houppy, Bélieu, Chênes and Ormont Wood. The leading battalions moved forward behind a protective artillery barrage but as soon as the Germans spotted any movement in front of their lines the Americans were strafed by intense shell and machine-gun fire.

**The devastation around Molleville Farm; a ruined narrow gauge railway line.**

In spite of this, the 115th had little difficulty when it moved into Grande Montagne Wood, north of Étraye Wood and took up a position in Vaux St. Martin Ravine. The 116th Regiment (centre) gained little ground in Étraye Wood but managed to take Hill 361, an important German observation area. The 113th Regiment removed all German opposition from Molleville Wood and took up a line 300 metres east of Molleville Ravine. The line was extended to make the connection with the 26th Division, which now occupied Houppy Wood and the southern part of Étraye Wood. However, a local but strong German counter-attack drove the 26th Division out of the woods and forced them to withdraw to La Reine Wood. The result of a day of heavy fighting was an advance of about 1,000 metres toward the east over a front of 800 metres.

**Thursday 24 to Saturday 26 October.**
With the help of a concentrated machine-gun barrage, an all-out effort was made to push the Germans out of Étraye Wood. Houppy and Bultroy Wood were finally cleared. Also about a third of Étraye Wood was now rid of the Germans, including Hill 361 and the so-called Pylone Observation Tower. Over sixty Maxim machine guns were captured. This new front line remained unchanged until 30 October. During the night of 24-25 October, the 113th Regiment was relieved by the 114th. An anonymous member of the former, in Company E, recalled:

'Relieved at 4.00 am. The company retired to the Battalion PC and was ordered to go to Molleville Farm and await the rest of the battalion, the final halt being made at the Molleville Farm ruins. A few minutes later, the ruins were bombarded again. We would have been wiped out had we continued to the farm itself. […] We marched through the Bois de Molleville in single file and came out by way of Brabant. Reaching Hill 338 another rest was taken and our rifles unloaded for the first time in weeks. After a ten minutes' rest, punctuated by Boche artillery fire, the men moved on to Brabant, in excellent spirits, singing and joking as they went. We stopped at the kitchen of some engineer unit to get our first cup of coffee in sixteen days, the men of this unknown outfit sharing their breakfast with us.'

Saturday brought the news that the 114th Regiment on the right flank of the 29th Division was to participate in an attack in concert with the 26th Division. Bélieu Wood, Ormont Wood and Moirey Wood were still in German hands. For weeks the stubborn defenders of the German

**A German observation tower on Hill 361, Étraye Wood.**

32nd Division and the 1st Landsturm Division had managed to repulse attacks from the American 26th, 29th and French 18th Divisions. Part of the fresh (at least to this battlefield) German 192nd Division had just arrived to reinforce the sector.

### Sunday 27 to Wednesday 30 October.

The artillery opened up at 10.00 am, followed by the infantry attack at 11.00 am. Close liaison between the 114th Regiment and the 26th Division was maintained and thanks to the artillery preparation the advance moved quickly and with comparatively light losses. The machine-gun companies did their utmost to keep the German gunners' heads down. During the afternoon, the Germans launched a counter-attack but this was beaten off and eventually the enemy was pushed back. A modest advance had been made and Bélieu and Moirey Woods were now in American possession. Ormont Hill, however, remained partly in German hands.

On 30 October the rested and re-equipped 79th Division relieved the 29th Division. During the night of 30-31 October the division was marched to Verdun. The 29th had been in the line for twenty-one consecutive days and was reduced to one third of its original infantry strength. It was marched off to a rest area, where it stayed until the armistice, during which time it received 5,000 replacements.

### The 26th 'Yankee' Division, 15-31 October.

The 26th Division (101st, 102nd, 103rd and 104th Regiments), a National Guard division, was commanded by Major General Clarence R. Edwards. A major formation of the Massachusetts Army National Guard, it was based in Boston and was activated at Camp Edwards, Massachusetts on 22 August 1917. Having done hardly any training, the Division sailed for France; the men of the 26th Division arrived at Saint-Nazaire on 21 September 1917. Interestingly, it was the second division of the AEF (after the 1st) to arrive in France and the first division newly organized in the United States. On arrival the Division immediately moved to Neufchâteau for training with the French; most of the men were very raw recruits. The 26th later trained extensively with the 1st, 2nd and 42nd Divisions, organized as I Corps in January 1918, and was moved to a quiet sector on the Chemin des Dames, where it stayed for several months to gain front line experience.

On 3 April 1918 the Division arrived by train in the St. Mihiel area and thus were familiar with the terrain over which that offensive was going to take place. The Germans became quite active once they discovered that there were Americans in the sector. Their attacks were primarily designed to intimidate the fresh, relatively untrained, American troops; but the Germans also wanted to take prisoners in order to find out what American intentions might be. Once in the front line, therefore, the 26th Division was seriously put to the test by the Germans. Thus during their very first week in the line, the 26th Division experienced a large raid but held its ground. Both sides suffered substantial losses. At the end of April the Germans launched an attack on Seicheprey; with the help of overwhelming artillery support, they captured the village. Before the Americans could make a counter-attack the Germans had retreated, having inflicted 634 American casualties, including eighty killed. Approximately 130 Americans were captured and taken back to the German lines, a devastating blow to morale.

On 28 June the 26th Division was moved to the Château Thierry sector. Pressure had been exerted all along the central to northern part of the Allied front since the beginning of the German Spring Offensive in March 1918, and this spread to the Aisne and the Marne in May. During the fierce fighting in the Château Thierry area, the

**Major General CR Edwards (1859-1931).**

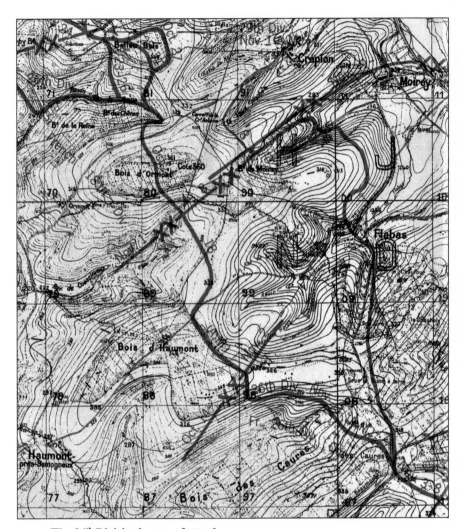

**The 26ᵗʰ Division's area of attack.**

26ᵗʰ lost over 4,000 casualties. With the line stabilised, by 31 August the 26ᵗʰ was back in the St. Mihiel sector. In the opening stage (12 September) of the offensive there it had the important task of making an unprecedented advance of fifteen kilometres in a south-easterly direction to meet up with the 1ˢᵗ Division to cut off the tip of the Salient. The 26ᵗʰ remained in the area after the St. Mihiel Offensive ended on 16 September. On 8 October it was transferred to the Citadel of Verdun, where it became part of First

Army Reserve. This period of relative rest and training did not last long. On 13-14 October the 29th moved into reserve positions in the area of the XVII French Corps, where it relieved the French 18th Division.

## Wednesday 16 October.

The first day in line was not a glorious one. Part of Haumont Wood was still in German hands and before the French 18th Division was entirely relieved the 104th Regiment of the Yankee Division was told to complete the capture of the woods. The French units that were still in line supported the 104th. The other regiments, from north to south the 101st, 102nd and 103rd, were to take up positions along the Chemin d'Ormont and Coassinvaux Ravine (known as Death Valley). After a forced march in the night of 15-16 October, unfamiliar with the lie of the land and under horrible weather and ground conditions (pouring rain, deep mire), the attack of Companies A, D and E and one platoon each of Company G and H started.

The attack was begun at 5.40 am, without artillery preparation. In spite of the assistance of sixteen French Renault FT17 tanks the assault achieved nothing. Any visitor to the battlefield today will readily observe that the terrain, with its ravines and steep hills is totally unsuitable for tank warfare. The tanks quickly bogged down in the mire and were abandoned by their crews. Three companies of the 104th Regiment went in but achieved almost nothing. Without artillery assistance the Americans could make no progress against the German machine-gun defence. The heavy rains, deep mud and the gutted terrain also severely limited the movement of the troops. A second attack was made at 4.00 pm. With the aid of a rifle grenade and machine-gun barrage, the north eastern edge of Haumont Wood was taken and secured.

## Thursday 17 to Tuesday 22 October.

During this period there was a lull in the fighting that was used to relieve the French. However, both the German, American and French artillery remained very active and many men on both sides continued to be killed or wounded by gas or shrapnel shells. The French 18th Division had been entirely relieved on the 18th and the 'Sammies' now occupied a line from Molleville Ravine and Chênes Wood (51 Brigade, 101st and 102nd Regiments) in the north to the Côte de Poivre (Pepper Hill), near Vacherauville (52nd Brigade, 103rd and 104th Regiment) in the south. From here the line was continued by the French 26th Division, the hinge around which the attack pivoted. It is worth noting that on 21 October

28348

*Above*: Troops of the 103rd Field Artillery, 26th Division, in Death Valley. Note the AA machine gun. October 1918.

*Below*: The same place in January 2020.

the Germans launched an unsuccessful attack to test the 26th Division's strength. On 22 October orders were received for an assault in a north-easterly direction that was to be joined by the US 29th Division.

## Wednesday 23 October.

The 26th Division was to gain possession of the heights of Houppy, Bélieu, Chênes and Ormont Wood. At 5.30 am the artillery began a preparatory barrage on the enemy line and at 6.15 the rolling barrage started. This was not as intense as desired (shortage of ammunition) but better than nothing. By about 8.30 am the 101st Regiment had reached the southern edge of Houppy Wood. After regrouping the fighting continued and before noon the woods were in American possession.

In spite of the appalling weather conditions the assault made good progress and Bélieu Wood was also captured by elements of the 101st Regiment. However, they were later pushed back by a powerful German counter-attack and the shelling was such that they barely managed to cling on to the northern edge of La Reine Wood, Chênes Wood and Molleville Ravine. Incoming fire from the commanding heights on the left flank of 51 Brigade made almost any movement impossible and had to be dealt with first. Although a series of futile and costly attacks were made against one of these positions, Ormont Wood, crowned by the dominating Hill 360, the Germans remained in possession of the hill. Haumont Wood, however, was now largely in American possession.

Away from the front, on the same day the official 'Yankee Division' insignia was submitted for approval; its wearing was made compulsory after 29 November, a couple of weeks after the Armistice. At least it would be ready for the victory parade, whenever that might be, back in the States.

## Thursday 24 October.

It was learnt from prisoners and deserters that the German 1st Landsturm Division had just been reinforced by fresh troops of the 192nd Division, a third class formation. Late in the afternoon the attack was renewed. Supported by artillery, machine-gun fire and a smoke screen, the 2nd Battalion of the 101st Regiment once more advanced on Bélieu Wood, while the 102nd Regiment attacked a line in which the principal objective was Ormont Wood. Once more a violent battle ensued. Ranging from machine-gun nests hidden in trees, to the skilful concealment of snipers, to bombardment by minenwerfers guided by aerial observation, the Germans fought for every inch of ground. The fighting continued for hours until darkness brought it to an end. The divisional history talks about 'the first success'. However, only the lower slope of Hill 360 (also known as Ormont Hill) was secured; a mere 200 metres. Bélieu Wood, a little north of Ormont Hill, had been penetrated for about 500 metres; but as soon as darkness fell the German artillery blasted them from their positions, forcing them back into Chênes Wood. The net result of the day was that Houppy, Bultroy and Chênes Woods were finally cleared. The new line was secured by a line of outposts, essentially fortified shell holes each with a machine gun and observers out in No Man's Land.

**A zinc bucket, riddled by shrapnel, found in Bélieu Wood, November 2020.**

The Division's commander, General Edwards, was relieved from duty on 25 October and sent back to the US, officially to assist in the training of newly recruited troops. He was very popular amongst his men, who had trained and fought under his command from the beginning, and for many the news came as a blow. The reasons for his 'dismissal' are likely numerous, but he and Pershing did not get on at all in the pre war US army, with its small officer corps. Nor did he get on at all well with General Liggett, the new commander First Army. On top of this, his only child, by then married, died on 13 October, so Liggett and Pershing had a compassionate excuse for getting rid of him. In any case, Pershing was notorious for removing general officers, with a significant number being sacked in the days leading up to and the

**Brigadier General FE Bamford (1865-1932).**

first days after the launch of the Offensive. Another wave of dismissals followed after 12 October and the perceived – justified or not – relative lack of success in achieving the Division's objectives made Edwards a prime target and he was succeeded by Brigadier General Frank E. Bamford.

### Friday 25 October.
The 26th Divisional history 'New England in France 1917-1919' describes the day's action, once more a tale of initial success and then, effectively, failure:

> 'Night brought a new enemy reaction. Against the heavily tried battalion of the 101st no less than four furious counter-attacks were directed in quick succession. Three were resisted successfully, but the fourth pushed our troops back again beyond the western edge of the Bélieu Wood, only to have them reform and return to the attack at 2.30 am. This time they succeeded in establishing a

line well in advance of their original parallel of departure, while the 3rd Battalion, 101st Regiment, moved up and extended the new line westerly. Two companies of the brigade reserve (1st Battalion, 101st Regiment) were sent in to support the 2nd, which had suffered considerably. Once more the 51st Brigade went forward in an attempt to consolidate its first gains. At 11.30 am on 25 October, the 2nd and 3rd Battalions, 102nd Regiment, after a violent artillery preparation, moved out to the capture of Hill 360 [Ormont Hill], which adjoined the Bélieu Wood ridge on the south-east. But hardly had the infantry started, their intentions and objective having been made quite plain to the enemy from the direction and character of the artillery fire, than the enemy clamped down a really awful storm of gas and high explosive under which the assaulting waves simply melted away. The meagre hold which had been secured on the lower slopes of the formidable Hill 360 had to be abandoned, and the shattered battalions reeled back to their lines, spent and exhausted, though a few separated sections clung to their gains throughout the night.'

**Saturday 26 October.**
Following artillery preparation, the attack was renewed at 11.00 am. The Americans were literally stopped in their tracks by the heavy resistance

**Members of the 101st Regiment, 26th Division, in a trench near Haumont, 27 October 1918. One of them is taking the opportunity to have a shave.**

and artillery fire. Noon of the 26th found the lines no further advanced than they were on the afternoon of 23 October. The German defence, most skilfully executed by machine-gun and artillery fire, admirably directed by planes, had proved once more impregnable. In addition, sickness (the 26th was heavily affected by the Spanish Flu) and the casualties of battle severely weakened the Yankee Division's strength. Battalions, normally 1,100 men strong, were now reduced to company strength (270 men) and there was a terrible shortage of officers.

### Sunday 27 October to Friday 1 November.

Despite the loss of strength and therefore the loss of pressure on the German defenders, the attack on Ormont and Bélieu Woods continued at first daylight on the 27th. The nests that had been cleared on previous days were reoccupied and resupplied over night. During the heavy fighting in Bélieu Wood, countless machine-gun emplacements had to be eliminated for the second or third time. Often covered by other well-camouflaged nests, it was an extremely hazardous job.

Private First Class Michael J. Perkins, Company D, 101st Regiment of the 26th Division, single-handedly crawled to a small concrete shelter from which the Germans tossed hand grenades at his platoon. Awaiting his opportunity, when the door of the pillbox was again opened to throw another bomb, Perkins threw a hand grenade inside. The explosion burst the door open and, drawing his trench knife, he rushed into the bunker. In the hand-to-hand fighting that followed he killed and wounded several Germans, upon which the rest of the crew surrendered. Rolling up the defences, he captured twenty-five prisoners. This put seven machine guns out of action. Although seriously wounded by the fighting in the pillbox, he was not evacuated from the battlefield until the next day; and then disaster struck. While Perkins was transported to a first aid post an artillery shell killed him. Perkins, only 19 years old, was posthumously awarded the Medal of Honor on 7 March 1919.

Bélieu Wood, as well as Ormont Wood, were now partially in American hands. Five days of savage fighting had resulted in the capture of 500 metres of terrain. While extremely limited in terms of territorial gain, nonetheless it offered favourable jumping-off positions for a future attack in a drive to remove the German defenders from the heights altogether. However, it was by now painfully clear that fresh troops were needed to continue the fighting.

**Private Perkins, MoH (1899-1918).**

On 1 November, the 26th Division's positions were taken over by the rested and re-equipped 79th Division, the heroes of Montfaucon. The gutted 26th was moved a little to the south to take over the quiet sector held, ironically, by the French 26th Division. During the last phase of the war it would launch modest attacks against the Germans in the direction of Flabas and Moirey. They attempted to take Azannes, but this little village was not reached before the war was over. The story of the Yankee Division continues in chapter 3.

**A water-logged and frozen shell crater on Ormont Hill, February 2021.**

# CHAPTER 3

# The 79th, 26th and 32nd Divisions
# 3 – 11 November

**Summary: The 79th 'Liberty' Division.**
The 79th Division (313th, 314th, 315th and 316th Regiments), a National Division formed from conscripts, was commanded by Major General Joseph H. Kuhn. The Division was activated in August 1917 at Camp Meade, Maryland, and was composed primarily of draftees from Maryland and Pennsylvania. In July 1918, shortly before the Division was due to embark overseas, almost sixty per cent of its trained troops were taken for cadres and replacements elsewhere; in return it received 15,000 more or less untrained troops. This made the 79th one of the most inexperienced divisions on the front. Despite this, it was they who were selected for the task of capturing one of the most formidable series of defences culminating in the hill and village of Montfaucon. For the Americans, the hill was a key position that served as a gateway to the Hindenburg Line. When this line, or rather zone, of defences were broken it could mean the end of the German occupation of northern France.

The 79th Division failed to take Montfaucon on 26 September, the first day of the Meuse-Argonne Offensive; but the hill was taken on the second day, a remarkable achievement for such

**General Claudel, commander of XVII Corps, and Major General Kuhn of the 79th Division, 31 October 1918.**

70

an inexperienced division. During the following days they continued the advance to Nantillois but, exhausted by the fighting, the large number of 'shirkers', the rain and the lack of supplies, they were relieved by the 3rd and 80th Divisions. The Division was in such a bad state that it took the better part of October to become an effective fighting formation again. During this period it received over 6,000 replacements. In the First World War, the effective strength in the field of an average American division was 16,000 rifles: vastly bigger than the size of a division in other combatant armies – indeed probably three times bigger than many of the German divisions at this stage of the war. For more information on the 79th in this first phase of the offensive, see *Montfaucon* in this series.

**Saturday 26 October to 2 November.**
On 26 October the 79th was designated as reserve of the French XVII Corps, First Army. Orders were issued to relieve the 29th and part of the 26th Divisions in the front line. The 158th Brigade (315th and 316th Regiments) were ordered to relieve the 29th Division. From left to right, the 316th took over the sector Molleville Farm-Richêne Hill on 28-29 October and the 315th Étraye and Wavrille Woods during the night of 29-30 October.

Second Lieutenant Arthur H. Joel, 314th Regiment, recorded his impressions when he and his company marched toward the front.

'At the site of old Samogneux, marked only by a sign board and a few scattered piles of broken masonry, the officers met their units and the single file of men began its relief march through the dark, gassy Death Valley. From this point the different units wended their way along the wooded trails to the area of shell holes, dugouts and trenches occupied by the 26th Division. F Company crossed a hilly, open field, and the file of shadowy figures stumbled its way along the path bordering the narrow-gauge track leading directly into their new position. Reports, as well as the inspection made by the reconnoitring party, indicated that this part of the trail was by far the most dangerous. Whole sections of tracking had been torn completely asunder by powerful explosive shells, the jagged ends of the rails and metal ties curving upward over the deep shell craters beneath. Numerous corpses of Germans and Americans lay scattered along the track, some darkened with age, and most of them mangled or dismembered.'

On 30 October 157 Brigade (313th and 314th Regiments), already in the sector, was ordered to take over the 26th Division's sector, Bélieu, Chênes

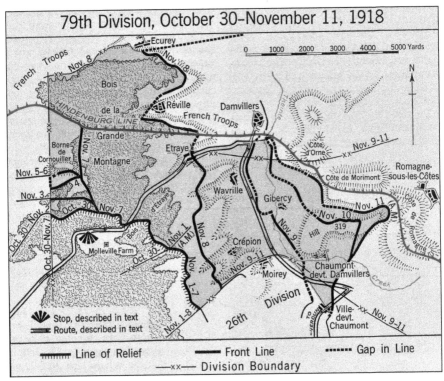

**79th Division, October 30–November 11, 1918**

79th Division's sector, 30 October-11 November.

and Ormont Woods. These woods were still partially in German hands. Second Lieutenant Arthur H. Joel recalled taking over the line:

> 'The seventy odd men that he still commanded were broken in nerve and spirit by repeated gas and shell attacks and constant exposures and privations. The relief was quickly completed, F men taking over the outposts, trenches and dugouts of Co. B. With curt instructions regarding the position and a few words of advice, the relieved men quickly departed. In the outposts of the dark, wooded hill [Ormont], in some places within fifty to one hundred yards of the enemy, the individual or small groups were left alone with their thoughts.'

The 79th Division's right flank was covered by the 26th Division, the latter relieving the French 26th Division in the quiet Flabas sector. The French 15th Colonial Division covered the left flank. Of course, the soldiers in the front line were frequently subjected to shelling.

On 1 November the third phase of the Meuse-Argonne Offensive started on the left bank. After the breaking of the Hindenburg Line on 14 October, the Germans had been conducting a fighting retreat towards the Freya Stellung. The First Army, meanwhile, now under Hunter Liggett for just over a fortnight, had used much of the time to reorganise, refit and prepare for this next phase. The main line of this largely unfinished defensive zone was built on the Barricourt Heights, a wooded ridge with many hills. One day later, the Americans, who were

*Above left*: **The 'Cross of Lorraine' insignia of the 79ᵗʰ Division only came into use after the Armistice.** (*Coll Museum Meuse-Argonne 1918*)

*Above right*: **Lieutenant General H Liggett (1857-1935).**

by now fighting at full throttle, smashed through the lines, forcing the Germans to retreat once more. This time, there was no other defensive line to retreat to but the River Meuse.

To prevent the build up of German troops on the right bank, it was decided that III Corps, the 5ᵗʰ and 90ᵗʰ Divisions, would cross the Meuse. The 5ᵗʰ Division was ordered to cross the river between Dun-sur-Meuse and Brieulles-sur-Meuse. The 90ᵗʰ Division was ordered to head for the crossings at Stenay, to the north. To put more pressure on the already crumbling German Army, XVII Corps on the right bank was ordered to advance in a north-easterly direction. For more information see chapter 4.

### Sunday 3 November: 158 Brigade.

The main objective of the renewed attack was the line Vilosnes-Haraumont-Écurey-Peuvillers, roughly along the present-day D110 road. From left to right, the French 15ᵗʰ Colonial Division was to advance to Sivry and Long Wood. It was expected that they would link up with the US 5ᵗʰ Division on the line Vilosnes-Brandeville only a few days later. On the right flank of the French was the 79ᵗʰ Division. They were to advance north, alongside the French, and their first targets were finally to remove the Germans from the commanding Hill 378 (Borne de Cornouiller, on present-day maps Le Haut Chêne) and Hill 370 in Grande Montagne Wood.

The large ravines between Sivry and Vilosnes, Grande Montagne Wood and the heights between Étraye and Wavrille were part of the fifth German defence line, the Giselher Line. In the 79ᵗʰ Division's sector, through the trees and across a ravine, they could see the barren and rounded top of Hill 378, perfectly clear of trees or brush. On the summit

**View from the German positions on Hill 378 towards, from left to right, Grande Montagne, Vaux de Mille Mais, Chaume Wood and Sivry.**

the Germans had built a powerful stronghold from which all previous American attacks had been broken up. From hidden observation posts they could see any movement made and machine-gun nests covered every approach to the hill. It was in fact a key position of the Giselher Line and the main centre of German observation for the Meuse Valley, with uninterrupted views to the west and north west. With the elimination of Hill 378, the whole of the Giselher Line could be rolled up. Before striking across the Woëvre Plain to the east, therefore, it was first necessary to remove the menace of Hill 378.

**157 Brigade.**
The front of 157 Brigade, which comprised the 314th Regiment, one battalion of the 313th Regiment and one company of the 111th Machine Gun Battalion, was about two kilometres in length. The main targets were, from north to south, Wavrille, Bélieu and Ormont Woods. The period from 2 to 7 November was one of patrolling only but there were still many casualties as a consequence of persistent German shelling.

**Monday 4 November: 158 Brigade.**
At 6.00 am, after a short artillery barrage – still no priority in ammunition supply was given to actions on the right bank, and then under the protective cover of a rolling barrage, the patrols of the 315th and 316th Regiments advanced. Both regiments were met with a hail of machine-gun fire before they had gone a hundred metres. By 10.00 am, removing the nests one by one, the line had advanced 1,200 metres. There were many casualties; the Germans frequently gassed the valleys leading up to Hill 378. Lieutenant Harold B. Alston of the 312th Machine Gun Battalion wrote of what happened that day:

**Lieutenant Ira Lady, 312th Machine Gun Battalion (1891-1918).**

**Headstone of Lieutenant Peterson in Meuse-Argonne Cemetery, Romagne, plot E.26.11**

'Nothing better indicates the strength of the enemy defences in this sector than the fact that during the first four or five hours we advanced only about 150 metres. The woods were thick with machine guns and it was practically impossible for us to go ahead. Lieutenant Lady [of the Headquarters Company] was hit in the knee so I made a tourniquet above the wound and propped him against the side of a shell hole. [Second Lieutenant Ira Lady died on 22 November 1918 in hospital, two weeks after his leg was amputated.] This shell hole was covered by an enemy machine gun, which made it impossible to evacuate him immediately. I detailed a man to stay with him, while I crawled out and proceeded to cut in the road on the flank of the gun that was holding up our attack.

Here I met Lieutenant Peterson. He yelled at me to duck and as I did so he aimed a rifle at a Boche. But a bullet hit him and he lunged forward, dead. I signalled to three infantrymen and we started crawling into the woods to get the machine-gun nest. We crawled forward a few yards, a low mist prevented our being seen, and finally I could see the enemy gun. Having a grenade I tossed it over and it luckily landed just a few feet in front of the gunner, tearing his head completely off. This was our signal to rush [the nest] and we did so. On the rush, two of my men were killed about twenty-five yards from the gun. I rushed on with the other man and we got to them before they could fire. My one remaining man was wounded. I emerged from the woods with fourteen prisoners and sent them to the rear.'

Unable to advance any further, a foothold was gained on Hill 378 and into the woods on Hill 370. The next day the fighting continued but no further advance on Hill 378 could be made. The attack on Hill 370, however, was very successful; machine-gun post after machine-gun post was destroyed and by the end of the day the hill was cleared of the enemy. Aerial reconnaissance also made it clear that troops and materiel were withdrawn to the rear. In the meantime, the French 15th Colonial Division successfully liberated Chaume Woods, near Sivry; it was clear that the Giselher Line was about to crumble.

**Tuesday 5 November: 158 Brigade.**
By now the US 5th Division had made several successful crossings across the Meuse. This made it very hard for the Germans to maintain the Giselher Line; the US 5th Division attacked in the rear and the French 15th and American 79th in the front. The biggest success of the day was the capture of Hill 378 by the 316th Regiment with the 315th in support. After heavy fighting and with the American artillery sweeping the crest, the Germans finally retreated. However, the Americans could not occupy the summit; it was under constant German artillery fire. The conquest of the hill came with a heavy toll; according to the 79th Division history, the effective strength of the 316th, normally 4,400 men, had been reduced to 600.

1st Sgt Joseph F. Killroy, Co K, 315th Regiment, noted:

'The battle of Hill 378 was the worst shambles I have ever seen. The first two hours of the battle the Boches counter-attacked us three times. The battle was simply indescribable. So much happened in such a short space that no ten men could give a full, graphic report of the complete affair. The Germans came out with hand grenades, in mob formation and threw at us what is known as the potato masher grenade. Well, each time they came out our boys stood up and slaughtered them with rifle and automatic rifle fire. But we were not doing all the dirty work, for when we stood up to fire at the Boches the German machine guns rained death and agony among us.'

**Wednesday 6 November: 158 Brigade.**
The 316th was relieved during the night. The artillery of the rolling barrage was scheduled at 8.00 am. The attack of 6 November, however, did not materialize. Although the Germans were now beaten back and in serious trouble, the American/French attack that was to exploit the breakthrough at Sivry, Hill 378 and Grande Montagne Wood went nowhere. The terrible concentration of gas, shrapnel and high explosives made it impossible to advance even a single metre. Thirty-seven Americans were killed, a few hundred wounded.

**Thursday 7 November.**
**158 Brigade:**

On the night of 6-7 November the control of the left bank passed from XVII (French Corps) to the French II Colonial Corps. General Claudel, however, remaining in command. From Dun to Brieulles, the Germans were retreating east. Orders were issued to keep in contact with the enemy, to leave him no time to rest. The French advanced on Sivry, Vilosnes and Haraumont; the 79th on Grande Montagne Woods and Réville.

Patrols that were sent out to see whether Grande Montagne Woods had been evacuated by the enemy soon found out when they were met

*Right*: **Interior of a German shelter, Grande Montagne Wood, November 2020.**

*Below*: **A tank barrier between Sivry and Réville, 31 January 1919.**

by a hail of machine-gun bullets. By 2.00 pm the Cul de la Vaux Ravine had been reached but the advance halted because of 'friendly' artillery fire. One hour later the ravine was crossed and the 316th dug in. Heavy machine-gun fire made it impossible to continue the advance.

**Friday 8 November: the 79th swings to the east.**
The 79th Division History sets the scene:

> 'Word from II Corps that the 15th French [Colonial] Division, on the left of the 158th Brigade, had swung through Haraumont Ridge and to the north-east, driving out the enemy in the Bois des Vaux at 17h [5 pm], November 7, solved one problem of the front line positions, this time at the extreme northern end of the sector. It meant that the 158th Brigade had no enemy to the north of it and could turn to the east after establishing liaison with the French further north.'

Therefore, the 79th Division was ordered to 'exercise its pressure' in the direction of Wavrille, Étraye, Réville and Écurey. The left flank boundary of the 79th Division was to be the Haraumont-Écurey Road, the present-day D110. The night of 7-8 November was used to move the troops to their new positions. Progress was slow and it was not until noon that the leading battalions started the advance. Patrols sent out before the attack soon reported that the area in front of the division was deserted by the Germans. Apart from occasional shelling and without much opposition, the line Écurey, Réville, Étraye, Wavrille Wood, Bélieu Wood and Ormont Wood was reached, the latter wood still not entirely cleared by the 26th Division on the 79th Division's right flank. After a month of heavy fighting, the Meuse Heights in this sector were almost cleared of Germans and their artillery. However, the Giselher and Kriemhild lines running from Étraye to Chaumont and Romagne-sous-les-Côtes remained to be dealt with.

**Saturday 9 November.**
During the night the French II Colonial Corps ordered the complete capture of the Meuse Heights. Therefore the tired 3rd Battalion of the 104th Regiment, 26th Division, was relieved by the 314th Regiment, 79th Division, to take care of the stubborn resistance at Ormont Hill. The attack was to be launched in the general direction of Romagne-sous-les-Côtes. The left flank boundary was the line Etraye-Côte d'Horgne (often misspelled in American books as Côte d'Orne), the right flank of Ormont Wood, Moirey (exclusive) and Azannes.

All through the night heavy explosions were heard; the Germans were destroying their ammunition depots. Night patrols that slipped down in the unknown valleys ahead reported that there was no sign of the enemy on the west bank of the Thinte Creek. At 6.00 am the 314th Regiment attacked; little opposition was encountered and by 10.15 am Crépion and Wavrille were occupied, including the so heavily contested Ormont Hill/Hill 360. When the advance continued onto the Woëvre Plains, resistance stiffened; the German guns once more made it impossible to continue the advance. As Second Lieutenant Arthur H. Joel noted:

'The pursuit progressed several miles before any unit encountered the slightest resistance. One began to wonder if the Germans had finally decided to spend the winter across the Rhine. The most noticeable feature of the deserted landscape was the series of dugout towns built in the slopes of narrow valleys. From a distance, these hillsides looked like the burrows of countless ground hogs. Upon close examination one found them to be underground camps, well equipped with kitchens, sleeping chambers, stables and store houses. Off to the left, rising above the sea of rapidly clearing fog, stood the rounded summits of a series of large hills. Surely, one concluded, the enemy had not abandoned even these excellent points of resistance in their quick retreat. To the advancing troops these numerous knolls were indicative of a combat with another wall of German defences. Crépion was completely deserted and Moirey just beyond was in a similar state. About this time there was a noticeable increase in the number of bursting shells. Since the enemy had left his position the previous afternoon, only an occasional shell came over and these few had not fallen too close for comfort. But when a series of 'big boys' hit true on the road out of Moirey, and several others struck the town itself, suspicion was fastened on the big, oval Hill 328, just across the swamp beyond the town.'

Second Lieutenant Joel was right; Hill 328, or Buisson Chaumont Wood on today's maps, was part of the Giselher defences and was fortified with bunkers, trenches and deep dugouts. When the shelling stopped briefly, the Thinte Creek was reached and crossed and the troops started to dig in. Joel continues:

'The advance led through swamps and muck beds and across a narrow stream. 'F' Company held the right flank, and, as the result of the position, was suddenly exposed to flank fire from

*Above*: The ruins of Haumont, in the distance, seen from Death Valley, 27 October 1918.

*Left*: A German trench mortar pit on the edge of Ormont Hill, looking towards Death Valley and Haumont, November 2020.

Chaumont over on the right of the hill. To hear the angry cracks of bullets coming from a flank and watch the leads bite up the dust along your line of exposed men is a demoralizing situation to say the least. A covered position soon corrected this and Fritz's lead sung harmlessly overhead.'

To the left, contact was established with the French 15th Colonial Division, but on the right there was a 1,500 metres' wide gap between the 79th and 26th Divisions.

**Sunday 10 November.**
The 158 Brigade was to continue its attack to the Côte de Marimont, a wooded ridge east of Romagne-sous-les-Côtes. The 157 Brigade in the south was ordered to capture Hill 328 (Buisson Chaumont Wood), Hill 319 and the Côte de Romagne.

Second Lieutenant Joel, 314th Regiment:

'At daylight, on November 10, the battalion fell back to the railroad, while our artillery pounded the top of the hill. It then attacked behind the advancing barrage, passing through a counter barrage, whose shells were throwing great spurts of mud and water as they exploded in the swamp in front of the hill. The waves of attack cleared the top of Hill 328, and started toward 319 but stopped short when the intense machine-gun barrage from the ridge of 319 made every wise doughboy look for a hole or rampart of some sort to escape the shower of bullets. For nine hours the Yanks were forced to stay below the barrage line, not a few being caught in depressions hardly big enough to stretch out in or to allow sitting up without exposure to the deadly hail of lead. Combat patrols from the left flank of the battalion suffered heavily as the result of several unsuccessful attempts to wipe out some of the machine gun nests. From seven in the morning until four in the afternoon it was necessary to lie low in a shell hole, road bed or other depression, and listen to the angry cracks of bullets flying from a few inches to several feet overhead, depending on the depth of the depressions. But with only a few inches to spare, a man could still lie low and avoid stopping a bullet.'

At 4.20 pm, following a thirty minute artillery barrage, the attack on Hill 319 was resumed. At dusk the last German pockets of resistance on Hill 328 and Hill 319 were cleared. A line was organized along the northern and southern slope facing north-east. Meanwhile, the 316th held

Machine gun crews of the 314th in position in shellholes on Hill 328. Note the Browning .30 calibre machine guns; the 79th was one of the first divisions to be equipped with this excellent weapon. However, only approximately 1,100 of them were shipped to Europe before the war ended.

A front line position near Rémoiville, November 1918.

**Headstone of Hugh McMonagle; he was killed on 10 November 1918 on Hill 328. Romagne American Cemetery, E.27.35.**

a line a little east of Gibercy, on the left flank of the 314th. This line continued north to the French troops who occupied Damvillers. Patrols were in contact with the 26th Division near Ville-devant-Chaumont.

### Monday 11 November.

The attack continued at 9.30 am. The positions of the division's regiments and their objectives, from north to south, were: the 316th, from Gibercy to Côte de Horgne; the 315th, from Gibercy to the Côte de Morimont; and the 314th, from Hill 319 to the Côte de Romagne and finally, the First Battalion of the 313th, from the line Chaumont-devant-Damvillers/Ville-devant-Chaumont to Thil Wood and Azannes.

At 11.00 am hostilities ceased. The American advance stopped not far from the last, great German defence line, the Hindenburg Line. Apart from sometimes intense shelling and machine-gun fire, the Germans had abandoned the area west of that line. Second Lieutenant Joel's diary, 314th Regiment, describes the last morning of the war.

'Morning found Hill 319 and the surrounding knolls and valleys covered with a sea of dense fog. It was impossible either to note the lay of the land or to observe the positions of the enemy. However, a German map of the area, captured the day previously, gave the company commander a good idea of the defences and topography ahead. An early summons to the major's dugout resulted in the receipt of orders to advance toward Côte de Romagne, the last hill and strongest natural defence in the area. It lay across the wooded ravine directly in front. F Company was to form the first waves on the right flank, with E Company on the left and G and H supporting. A machine-gun battalion was to support the advance with a strong overhead barrage.

'Pop! Pop! Pop! Pop! Pop! Zing! Zing! Crack! Crack! Crack!' The intense enemy machine-gun barrage caught the advancing men just after clearing the woods and starting up the slope of Côte de Romagne. The first bursts were over the troops' heads, for as the Germans told us after the armistice, they knew of the truce and were testing the seriousness of our intentions. But when a skirmish line had been formed behind a slight rise of ground and the men kept up a steady fire of rifles, automatics and rifle grenades, the Rhinelanders became angry, and began cutting up the dirt with more effective aim. There was still a dense fog so that the best any one could do was to fire into the haze in the direction of the general line he judged the enemy to hold.

A runner from Lieutenant Cabla on the right reported that patrols had come in contact with the enemy on that flank but had seen no signs of friendly troops. Another report from the left flank stated that we had lost contact with E Company, due to the failure of a sergeant to carry out specific orders to maintain contact at any cost. Exposed flanks were highly uncomfortable even in a fog and would be extremely dangerous if the fog cleared and the enemy became aware of our unsupported position.

Finally, at 11.10 am, an exhausted runner, Latchet, crawled through the fog to the side of the company commander and gave his message: 'War's over - Cease firing - major's orders'. About the same moment Private Purcel was shot in the wrist. Very few seconds slipped by between the command 'cease firing' and the turning of safety locks on the guns. At first there was a dead calm – no shells or bullets, but just the quiet of a peaceful countryside. But the calm quickly ended with the shouts and voices of excited and happy men. With the aid of a Pennsylvania Dutchman, acting as interpreter, arrangements were made with the Germans to ensure the end of strife. There was an exchange of cigarettes and wine, some snappy saluting by the clean-cut, neatly-uniformed Germans who held this position, and a rather hopeless attempt at conversation. No one seemed sorry that the war had ended.'

The last American who was killed in the 79th Division's sector was Henry Gunther, Co A, First Battalion, 313th Regiment. In the morning of 11 November, First Battalion was sent out to capture the important German logistical centre at Damvillers. One minute before the

**View of Hill 328 (left), Chaumont-devant-Damvillers (foreground left) and Hill 319 (right).**

armistice came into effect, Gunther was hit by a burst of machine-gun fire. He was later officially acknowledged to be the last American killed in the First World War. [For a full account of his story and the last two days of the 79th Division before the armistice, see The Henry Gunther Tour.]

### The 26th Division, 1-11 November.

On the night of 31 October – 1 November, 51 Brigade, the 101st and 102nd Regiments, of the Yankee Division were relieved by the 79th Division. The subsequent relief by the 26th of the French 26th Division on the line north and north-east was also ordered. The new boundaries, from north to south, ran from the western edge of Moirey Wood to the western edge of Beaumont. The French 10th Colonial Division (not part of XVII Corps) covered the right flank, but did not participate in any attack.

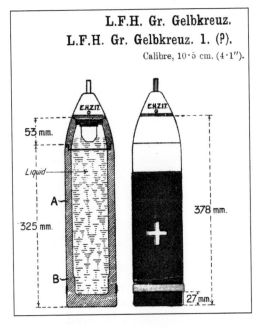

**L.F.H. Gr. Gelbkreuz.**
**L.F.H. Gr. Gelbkreuz. 1. (P).**
Calibre, 10·5 cm. (4·1″).

**Diagram of a German 105mm mustard (Gelbkreuz – yellow cross) gas shell.**

Meanwhile, the Germans were in full retreat on the left bank and the 5th Division, who successfully crossed the Meuse at the beginning of November, were also keeping the pressure on the enemy.

The 26th Division, guarding and protecting the 'hinge' of XVII Corps, received orders directing an advance to be made upon notification. Owing to the success of First Army's attack on the left bank, XVII Corps was ordered to prepare its divisions to 'push forward vigorously and exploit fully any retirement of the enemy on its front'.

During the period 4 to 7 November, there was no change in the front lines of the 26th Division.

**Friday 8 November.**

Early in the morning the 26th Division front line and battery positions were subjected to heavy shelling. An estimated 3,000 yellow cross shells (mustard gas) and at least 6,000 HE shells were the first clue of the German retreat. Around noon several outposts reported that the enemy was showing little or no activity in their sector. After the return of strong reconnaissance patrols it was clear that the Germans were showing signs of withdrawing. At 3.00 am, a general advance was ordered, with the high ground dominating the Moirey-Azannes Road (the present-day D905/D65) as the objective.

Strong patrols were sent out. Flabas was taken but found abandoned; the unnamed wooded ridge north of the village was also taken. Moirey, however, remained in German hands.

**Saturday 9 November.**

To support the 79th Division's attack on the 26th Division's left flank, the Yankee Division was ordered to change the direction of the attack from east to south-east. The attack resumed at 5.00 am, and was supported by eight battalions from all four regiments with four battalions left in reserve. Unfortunately, the Germans had retreated just a few kilometres east, only to establish a new defence line on the heights to the east of the Damvillers-Azannes Road, the D905/D65. Moirey was found abandoned and was quickly occupied by the Yankees, but Ville-devant-Chaumont was stubbornly defended by the Germans, in support of the retreating troops from Caures, Compte and Chaumont Woods. Still, by the end of the day, these woods were cleared of Germans occupation but any attempted advance onto the Woëvre Plains ended in disaster. Along the whole sector, both the 79th and 26th Divisions were again held up and forced to dig in because of terrifyingly accurate shell and machine-gun fire. Other sources, like the 26th Division gas report written by the US Army Chemical Corps Historical Office, dating from 1960, place a different light on the poor results of the division:

'Spirits were low, results were meagre and that [the previous] night was spent in reorganizing the line. A division historian said that '... the men were exhausted after fighting for weeks under continual rain, with scanty food and little or no shelter. They had been gassed and shelled heavily.' The troops were also having problems as a consequence of the relief [ie sacking] of several regimental commanders. "In at least one case," said the division's historian, "a new commander had the greatest difficulty in getting any response from his men. Straggling was very bad and I was able to muster only 240 men in the firing line from the entire regiment [the 101st] during the operations".'

By now the defences of the Meuse Heights were largely overcome but it was clear that the Germans had no intention of giving up any more terrain; in anticipation of the failure of the armistice negotiations they had merely straightened out the lines and taken up more favourable positions.

**Sunday 10 November.**
The attack that started at 6.00 am was met by unexpectedly heavy resistance; at some places the advance was checked after only 200 metres. Nevertheless, Bois de Ville Wood (the present-day Fôret Communale de Ville-devant-Chaumont) and by nightfall Ville-devant-Chaumont were taken, a nice bonus.

Members of Co D, 101<sup>st</sup> Regiment, 26<sup>th</sup> Division, taking a breather. Note the soldier drying out his socks, bottom right.

Men of 102<sup>nd</sup> Ambulance Co, 26<sup>th</sup> Division, collecting their 'chow' at their field kitchen, 1 November 1918.

**Monday 11 November.**

During the night the 101st Regiment was withdrawn from the battlefield. The regiment was reported 'shattered', its numerical strength weak and the men reluctant to obey orders; it was no longer an effective fighting formation. In the 101's defence, this situation was not unique, as many American regiments suffered from battle fatigue. The attack scheduled for early in the morning was at first called off but was later reinstated. Following an artillery preparation, the attack started at 9.30. The most notable gains that were made before the cessation of the fighting was that the Third Battalion of the 103rd Regiment reached Bonne Espérance Ridge, a few hundred metres south of Azannes. In line since 16 October, according to the ABMC history the 26th Division had lost an estimated 820 men killed and 3,850 wounded.

## The 32nd 'Red Arrow' Division.

The 32nd Division was formed from National Guard units from Wisconsin and Michigan and was commanded by Brigadier General William G. Haan. The 32nd Division was activated in July 1917 at Camp MacArthur, Waco, Texas. Wisconsin furnished approximately 15,000 men, and another 8,000 troops came from Michigan. The division was made up of 63 Brigade (125th and 126th Regiments) and 64 Brigade (127th and 128th Regiments). On 24 February 1918, the 32nd Division arrived in France. Upon arrival it became known that the Division was to serve as a replacement division – ie units would be detached to other formations as required, a rather devastating blow to morale. When in April it was finally assigned to front line duty, 9,000 largely untrained replacements were received. In that same month they were moved into a quiet sector in Alsace to familiarize the troops with trench life. Later, the 32nd participated in the fighting at Château Thierry, Fismes and Juvigny. On 10 September they were ordered to the Meuse, where 5,000 replacement troops were received. During the night of 25-26 September, the night before the opening of the Meuse-Argonne Offensive, they moved into new positions in Hesse Woods, just south of the front line.

When the Meuse-Argonne Offensive opened the 32nd Division was the reserve division of V Corps. On 30 September it relieved the 37th Division at Cierges and participated in the second phase of the attack, the breaking of the Hindenburg Zone. On 14 October the 32nd captured Romagne and Côte Dame Marie, both part of the inner Hindenburg Line defences. The first division (see *Meuse-Argonne 1918: Breaking the*

**Major General Haan (1863-1923).**

**The 32ⁿᵈ Division's patch.** (*Coll Museum Meuse-Argonne 1918*)

*Line* in this series) to pierce the Hindenburg Line, a line shot through with a red arrow was adopted as a shoulder patch in due course. On 20 October the division was relieved by the 89th Division. Following its relief it served in reserve with V Corps until 27 October and then of III Corps thereafter.

### Monday 4 to Friday 8 November.

On 4 November, the 32nd Division history explains, the 5th Division, which was fighting on the right flank of III Corps' front, forced a crossing of the river at Dun-sur-Meuse and formed a bridgehead. Up to that time the axis of attack had been generally north. Now it turned to the north-east on the right flank in an endeavour to connect with the French XVII Corps, which had been driving up the right bank of the river but considerably to the rear of III Corps' front. The 5th Division, however, attacked on too wide a front to make contact with the right flank. In addition, XVII Corps was still held up by a robust German defence and did not advance north as quickly as expected. Therefore, on the night of 5 November, First Army ordered the 32nd Division to send the 128th regiment to report to Major General Hanson E. Ely of the 5th Division for use in support of its right flank. The 128th Regiment, 32nd Division, crossed the Meuse at Brieulles on the night of 5 November. On 6 November, the regiment took up a position on the right flank of the 5th Division but failed to make contact with it. One of the many problems of the AEF was the lack of good maps. Reconnaissance patrols finally established liaison with the 5th Division, but the French 15th Colonial Division on their own right flank could not be located. During the next day, the 7th, they participated in the fighting in and around Brandeville, which was finally captured on 8 November. On that same day, the French 15th Colonial Division chased the Germans from the wooded ridge between the villages of Bréhéville and Écurey.

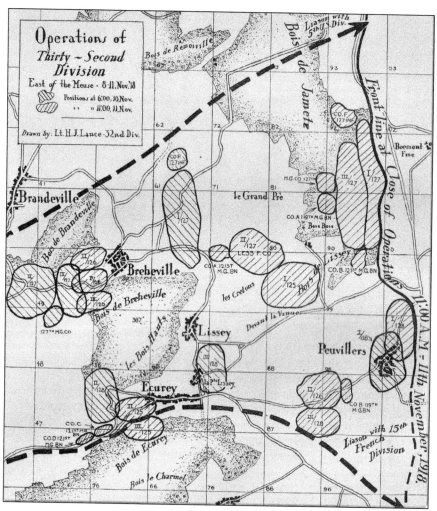

**Operations of the 32nd Division, 8-11 November 1918.**

## Saturday 9 November.

Orders were received for the remainder of the Division to cross the Meuse at Brieulles and go into line with the 128th, which was holding the position between the 5th and the French 15th Colonial divisions. The troops crossed the pontoon bridge during the night and took up the forward positions in their new sector between Brandeville (exclusive) and Écurey (inclusive). The crossing was an all night operation and was not completed until dawn – it had seemingly taken forever to move up to the front line and to occupy their new positions.

**Soldiers of the 32ⁿᵈ Division at Écurey, 11 November 1918.**

### Sunday 10 November.

That night new orders were issued. Because the Germans were in retreat all along the left bank, the 127th (north) and the 128th (south) Regiments were ordered to go into battle in 'pursuit formation'. This means that there was not a continuous front line but strong patrols probed forward, keeping in close contact with the German rear guards. The main target for the day was the Jametz-Damvillers Road, now the D905. The advance started at 6.00 am without any artillery preparation; the division's gunners were still struggling to get their guns and ammunition across the Meuse.

### 127th Regiment.

During the first two kilometres of the advance little opposition was met. However, when the 127th was about to enter Jametz Wood the mist cleared. Warned by the rattle of the American machine guns, a barrage opened up. Fortunately, the German guns were still trained on where the old front line ought to have been and no casualties were suffered. Overcoming the rearguards, the advance was steady until 4.30 pm, when it was stopped about 200 metres west of the Thinte Creek by machine-gun fire from the east bank. Heavy German shelling made any further advance impossible and orders were issued to dig in. Meanwhile, the 125th Regiment was moved into Lissey Wood to fill the gap between the 127th and 128th Regiments.

### 128th Regiment.

A heavy fog hid the advance and rapid progress was made in the general direction of Peuvillers. When the fog lifted, the 128th found themselves in the middle of a strong German position that they had no intention of giving up. The fighting started at once but it quickly became clear that any attempt to dislodge the Germans from their positions would fail without artillery support. The German artillery, of course, was very accurate and this ruled out any chance of success. The regiment withdrew in good order and by 2.00 pm they were back in line with the other regiments. No further advance was made.

A painted helmet of the 32nd Division. *(Coll Museum Meuse-Argonne 1918)*

### Monday 11 November.

By nightfall it became clear that the information that the Germans were retreating was not correct; they had merely withdrawn to a more favourable defence line, the Kriemhild Line. This well-prepared defensive zone was still largely intact. Reports coming back from neighbouring divisions indicated that they had likewise been able to make but little progress and that the Germans were not retreating at all. Orders were given to resume the attack along the whole front at 7.00 am. By now,

**German bullets found at Thinte Creek, January 2020.**

sufficient artillery batteries had come up to the front line to support the attack. The German positions were continually kept under fire during the night, increasing in volume just before the infantry set off. Meanwhile, the Germans were waiting for them, warned by the increase in shell fire. The German artillery started their own barrage and not before long it was raining shells both in front of and behind the tired troops of the 32nd. At 6.55 am, just five minutes before the attack was about to start, panting runners from HQ reached the lines and told the commanding officers that the war was over. Meanwhile, the artillery blazed on, trying to do as much damage to the Germans as possible before 11.00 am. During the last few days of the war the 32nd Division lost 192 dead and 510 wounded.

**The German-built road bridge crossing the Peuvillers-Damvillers railway line, May 2021.**

# CHAPTER 4

# The 5ᵗʰ Division
# 3–11 November

**Summary: The 5ᵗʰ 'Red Diamond' Division.**
The 5ᵗʰ Division, composed of 9 Brigade (60ᵗʰ and 61ˢᵗ Regiments) and 10 Brigade (6ᵗʰ and 11ᵗʰ Regiments) was a regular army division commanded by Major General Hanson E. Ely. The 5ᵗʰ Division was organized as a part of the programme of the War Department for the rapid expansion of the regular army and its establishment on a war footing for immediate service in France. Therefore, units that were already in existence at the declaration of war were selected to form a new division. The 60ᵗʰ and 61ˢᵗ Regiments were originally organized in Gettysburg, Pennsylvania during the Civil War, whereas the 6ᵗʰ and 11ᵗʰ Regiments' histories date back to the 1790s. The division was activated in December 1917 in Camp Logan, near Houston, Texas and sailed for Europe on 20 April. The larger part of the division landed in Liverpool, where they were rested before the Channel crossing was made to Le Havre. Some units came directly from New York to Brest, St. Nazaire or Bordeaux, French ports on the Atlantic coast.

The Division trained with the French in the Vosges in June 1918 and that was where it suffered its first casualties. From 4 to 8 September the division was moved into the St. Mihiel sector, where on 12 September the formation was part of a major attack that reduced the salient at St. Mihiel. It was relieved on 16 September.

The Meuse-Argonne Offensive started on 26 September. On 5 October the 5ᵗʰ Division moved into Hesse Wood, south of Vauquois, as the reserve of III Corps. During the night of 11-12 October it relieved the 80ᵗʰ Division near Cunel. Two days later it advanced north and east towards Bantheville, Pultière Wood and Rappes Wood, where it was involved in heavy fighting. During the night of 21-22 October, the 5ᵗʰ was relieved by the 90ᵗʰ Division, reorganized and received about 3,000 (largely untrained) replacements.

On 27 October they held the line from Rappes Wood to a little north of Brieulles, the latter town still in German hands.

**Major General Ely (1867-1958).**

To force the remaining Germans from the Hindenburg Line and the Freya Stellung, the 5<sup>th</sup> Division was ordered to make an attack in a north-eastern direction. Although the Germans on the left bank were in full retreat, Aincreville (30 October), Brieulles and Cléry-le-Grand (1 November), Cléry-le-Petit (2 November) and Doulcon (3 November) were only liberated after intense fighting with enemy rearguards. As was only to be expected, every bridge across the Meuse had been destroyed by the retreating enemy.

On 2 November, in spite of fog and rain, reconnaissance planes reported that the roads east of the Meuse were crowded with trains of trucks, wagons and heavy artillery moving north east. As a result, every American division in line was ordered to keep up the pressure on the enemy. To prevent the fleeing Germans on the left bank from taking up positions on the right bank of the Meuse, the 5<sup>th</sup> Division, fighting on the right flank of the III Corps front, was ordered to cross the Meuse between Dun-sur-Meuse and Vilosnes to form a bridgehead and to open the roads eastward and northward toward Montmédy and Longuyon.

Crossing the river between Dun and Vilosnes presented considerable difficulties. To reach the right bank, the 5<sup>th</sup> Division had to cross a 500 metres wide flood plain, then the Meuse River and finally the Canal de l'Est, which runs parallel with the river. The whole area is dominated by the Meuse Heights and was well within reach of the German machine guns and artillery. The 9<sup>th</sup> Brigade, 5<sup>th</sup> Division, operated between Sassey and Cléry-le-Petit inclusive. The 10<sup>th</sup> Brigade occupied the sector from Cléry-le-Petit exclusive to a point (L'Herminette) approximately one kilometre south of Brieulles. The leading role during this phase of the war was given to the 7<sup>th</sup> Engineer Regiment, responsible for building the bridges across the Meuse.

**Saturday 2 and Sunday 3 November.**

The attacks of the First Army on the left bank had been highly successful; by noon it had penetrated the last German defence lines and artillery positions. At 12.30 pm orders were issued to start the pursuit at once and that preparations would be made to extend the pursuit on the right bank; the German defences opposite the US 79<sup>th</sup> and the French 15<sup>th</sup> Colonial Division were slowly giving way. If the 5<sup>th</sup> Division could launch a successful attack between Brieulles and Dun, the Germans would be forced to abandon the Meuse Heights between Samogneux and Stenay altogether. All during the day, columns of smoke were seen on the right bank; the enemy was attempting to destroy anything that could be of use to the Americans.

*9 Brigade (60<sup>th</sup> and 61<sup>st</sup> Regiments).*

On 2 and 3 November, 9 Brigade was engaged in the sector between Doulcon and Mont Wood that became known as the 'Punch Bowl'.

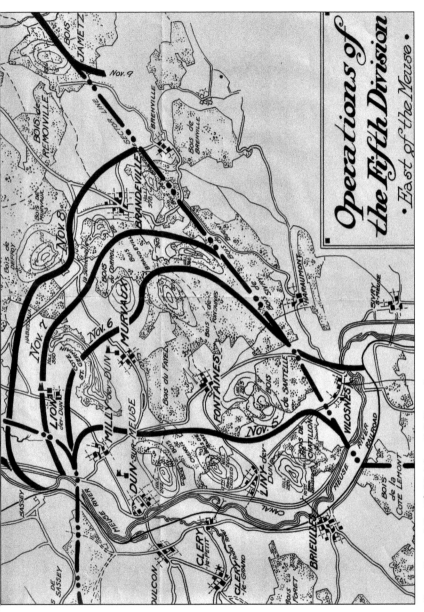

**Operations of the 5th Division, 5-8 November.**

This part of their history will be treated in a subsequent book in this series.

### 10 Brigade (6ᵗʰ and 11ᵗʰ Regiments).

On 2 November the 7ᵗʰ Engineers had practised several hours with a new type of pontoon bridge designed by the Engineer Corps. Later that day the material was hurried up to Brieulles to start the crossing at once. Of course it took forever to get the equipment to the right place and consequently time was lost. The first attempt at crossing the Meuse was made by Company D of the 7ᵗʰ Engineers at the southern point of the Meuse's curve in toward the large village. On 3 November, at 1.00 am, they succeeded in getting a patrol of twenty men across the river just north east of Brieulles. They acted as a covering detachment for Company F, which was busy constructing a pontoon footbridge at this point. It was to be followed by Company E as soon as the bridge was ready. Alas, at dawn, when the engineers were preparing to bring up construction material to bridge the adjacent canal and despite the cover of rain and fog, the Germans discovered what was going on and reacted accordingly. While Company E was waiting to cross the footbridge, there was a storm of machine-gun bullets from the east and the vicinity

**A pontoon footbridge at Moyenvaux Gully, near Liny, 5 November 1918.**

98

**The quay used by the 7th Engineers is still visible in 2020.**

of the bridge was bathing in lead. Meanwhile, the desultory artillery fire on Brieulles increased into a heavy bombardment. Pinned down behind the canal bank, there was no way that the crossing was to take place here during the day. It had become painfully clear that the Germans had not yet evacuated this part of the right bank. In the pouring rain, engineers were sent out to find out if there were perhaps more sheltered places to cross the river.

Fortunately there was or at least one, which was sufficient. At nightfall the 7th Engineers shifted their bridging material some 600 metres north along the canal to the point near the shattered remains of a 'blown' iron footbridge opposite a deep gully called Fossé Moyenvaux, near Liny, a natural drain between two hills, on the far side. Out of view of the Germans, under cover of a pitch black and rainy night, work on the two footbridges started. An already existing thirty metre wide platform with ramps made from dirt that was butted against the canal bank was reinforced while other men were building the actual pontoon bridge. The work lasted all night and the first attempt to cross the canal was made early on the morning of the next day.

**Monday 4 November.**
*9 Brigade.*
With the Germans withdrawn from the Punch Bowl at Doulcon, at 4.00 pm two battalions, with artillery support, were ordered to cross

*Above and below*: Then and now: the site of the 61st Regiment's (5th Division) crossings at Cléry-le-Petit, March 2020.

the Meuse at the Écluse de Warinvaux, northeast of Cléry. This spot was selected because at this point the river and canal are no longer separated but united into one stream. Under heavy German artillery fire, Companies B and C of the 7th Engineers tried to construct two light pontoon bridges. It soon became clear that these attempts would be in vain as accurate German shelling sank the pontoons as fast as they could be put in the water.

The engineers moved a kilometre to the south to a point where a cliff close to the river made them invisible from direct observation. The Germans were unaware of the change of position and the engineers continued to work on the bridges uninterrupted.

### 10 Brigade.

Shortly after midnight the bridges opposite Fossé Moyenvaux was completed. At 2.00 am two companies tried to rush across one of them but were driven back by enemy fire. Other attempts were made but failed miserably. The bridge remained under German fire all day and once again the Americans were forced to spend another day hugging the canal bank. At dusk, after an all-out bombardment of the German positions on the opposite bank, Companies E and G crossed the bridge and surprised the Germans in the quarry and gully on the far side. After a short but intense fight, a bridgehead was organized and quickly extended to its flanks. Two large chalk stone quarries on both sides of

**The overgrown quarry where the Third Battalion of the 6th Regiment crossed the Canal de l'Est, photographed in 2020.**

the bridgehead provided adequate shelter from incoming shells and were used to stockpile ammunition and other supplies. During the day one footbridge was destroyed by enemy fire but, before long, 900 men of the 2nd Battalion had made it to the other side.

In the afternoon the 6th Regiment, 3rd Battalion moved from Côte Laimont Woods into Brieulles to cross the river. While the attention of the German gunners was focussed on the 2nd Battalion, 10 Brigade, the 3rd Battalion, some 1,100 men, crossed the river and the canal by ferrying the troops over in French pontoons found in Brieulles and by using telegraph poles that were lashed together to make rafts. By 8.00 pm the entire battalion was in a quarry on the east side of the canal. Still undetected, the men moved about 300 metres south before they began marching up the slope of Hill 252 (marked 244 on modern maps). These operations took place during the better part of the night. Plans were drawn to extend the bridgehead by taking the adjacent Châtillon Wood in the morning.

**Tuesday 5 November.**
*9 Brigade.*
With two finished bridges across the river and canal south east of Cléry-le-Petit, the first troops to cross were a working party of the 7th Engineers. Company M of the 61st Regiment was also sent over to provide protection. By dawn two more bridges had been laid across the canal. When the companies of both the 60th and 61st Regiments were massing in the swampy area between the river and the canal, the German artillery opened up. Both bridges were damaged but fortunately most of the doughboys managed to make the crossing unscathed. Once on the right bank heavy fighting broke out; but the Americans were able to enlarge their bridgehead. The advance continued due east, towards Hill 260, where the Americans attacked the machine-gun nests on the western slope, after which they continued into Bussy Wood. Contact was made here with troops of 10 Brigade.

Meanwhile, the 61st Regiment moved north and by 10.30 am Hill 290, Côte de Jumont, was in American hands. After reorganizing the scattered platoons, the advance was continued on Dun, which was taken at around 1.00 pm. With the Germans retreating all along the 5th Division's front, it was decided to exploit the situation to the maximum; three hours later Milly-sur-Bradon, two kilometres north-east of Dun, was liberated, after which the 61st was ordered to join up with 10 Brigade west of Murvaux.

*10 Brigade.*
With most of the 3rd Battalion ferried across the river and canal, the attack on Châtillon Wood started at dawn. By 8.00 am (and without much

**A German shelter in Châtillon Wood, January 2020.**

opposition) the wood was cleared of Germans and a defence line organized along its eastern edge, today's D964. Patrols were sent to Vilosnes to make contact with the French but they had not yet reached the village. Meanwhile, the 1st Battalion, 6th Regiment, captured Hill 228 at the far end of Fossé Moyenvaux and linked up with the 3rd Battalion. Passing through the 6th Regiment, the 11th Regiment attacked Liny-devant-Dun and pushed home the attack to the southern edge of Hill 260, a little north of the town, thereby substantially enlarging the bridgehead on the right bank.

The attack had been so successful that by 8.30 the order was given to move north to Hill 290 (Côte de Jumont) and Dun and link up with 9 Brigade. The platoons of the 3rd Battalion, 11th Regiment, raced up the slopes of Hill 260 and surged into Bussy Wood, where just before midnight it took up positions along the eastern edge. Meanwhile, the 1st Battalion, originally in reserve, was sent to the front line in order to keep up the momentum. They moved north along the Meuse and protected the right flank of 9 Brigade. Hill 290 and Chênois Wood were taken and because of the successful attack on Dun by 9 Brigade, the 11th Regiment was ordered to advance east in the direction of Murvaux. At nightfall the Milly-Murvaux Road, the D102, was reached. The success of both brigades had made it possible to make further repairs on the bridges at Cléry-le-Petit. At 6.00 pm the 5th Division issued orders, based on orders from III Corps, for an attack at 8.00 am, with the objective the line Lion-devant-Dun, Côte St. Germain, Brandeville and the hills in between.

**Wednesday 6 November.**

At Dun, the crossing of the artillery units had begun. This was a dangerous job as artillery units ware favourite targets for German aviators. On the previous day, near Liny, one German pilot killed all the horses of an

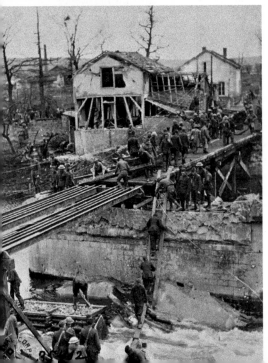

*Above*: **American troops cross the Meuse at Dun, 6 November 1918.**

*Left*: **Engineers constructing a heavy timber bridge at Dun, 8 November 1918. It was of vital importance to get guns and ammunition across to the right bank of the Meuse.**

American 75mm gun battery. The second vehicle to cross the bridge at Dun was an ambulance from the 30th Ambulance Company; they were starting to set up dressing and collecting stations at Dun and Milly. Hot food was also transported across the Meuse.

### 9 Brigade.

The 1st Battalion of the 60th Regiment crossed the Meuse and continued the attack north east. Around 9.00 it captured Murvaux. A little later it reached the Côte St. Germain, where it linked up with elements of the 61st Regiment that were already in control of the ridge. From here an attack on Lion was launched but heavy artillery fire made it impossible to reach the village. The opposition was such that the 61st withdrew to the north western slope of Côte St. Germain, where it remained for the night. During the night patrols were sent out to maintain contact with the German rearguards.

### 10 Brigade.

The 11th Regiment, starting from Hill 260, north east of Liny, renewed the attack around 8.30 am and large territorial gains were made. An hour past midnight, Brandeville Wood was reached. The village and the dominating Hill 388 remained in German hands.

At 8.40 am, the 6th Regiment, which had been taken up positions along the D964 between Liny and Vilosnes, started the advance on Sartel Wood. Around noon, the woods, including Hill 284, were taken without much opposition. Strong patrols were sent to Vilosnes, where the Germans were successfully preventing the French 15th Colonial Division from crossing the river. A surprise attack, launched from two sides, finally resulted in the evacuation of Vilosnes by the enemy. The village was quickly occupied by the French, who immediately started to rebuild the bridge there in order to expand the bridgehead.

With the Germans retreating to the east, the advance of the 5th Division between Mouzay and Vilosnes had been quite substantial. Probing for weak spots in the German rear guards and using every opportunity to push the front line back east, they had not yet linked up with the French. It was desirable to close this gap between them and the Colonial Division. To solve this problem the 128th Regiment of the 32nd Division crossed the river at Brieulles and followed the 6th Regiment. At nightfall, soldiers from both the 5th and 32nd Divisions had taken up positions along the easternmost boundary of Sartel Wood, just a kilometre short of Fontaines-St-Clair.

**Thursday 7 November.**

The 5th Division's movements were hampered by the lack of supplies of all sorts, ranging from ammunition to medical aid. Due to the lack of roads and the difficult terrain, the artillery was too far behind the infantry to be of any serious support. The German artillery, however, played a far bigger role, increasing with every kilometre the Americans moved east. Time was also needed to reorganize and to establish contact between regiments and divisions. The lack of good mapping also frustrated the advance. In spite of this, some regiments made good progress.

*9 Brigade.*

At 6.00 am, the 60th and 61st Regiments advanced on Lion, now abandoned by the Germans, and continued from Côte St. Germain into Habessaux Wood. Intense shellfire made it impossible to enter the woods; positions

**The 60th Regiment on the march from Lion to Louppy, November 1918.**

106

along the northern flank of Chaumusson Ridge and Corroi Wood were occupied.

### 10 Brigade.

The 11th Regiment occupied Chaumusson Ridge and Corroi Wood. Although this part of the battlefield was evacuated by the Germans during the previous night, it took them all day to secure this difficult terrain.

The 6th Regiment, on the far right, made no advance; their place in the front line was taken over by the 128th Regiment, 32nd Division, who finally managed to locate the French positions, thus closing the gap between the US 5th and the French 15th Colonial divisions. The 128th also organized a defensive position along the high ground south west of Brandeville. The Germans were still in control of the heights between Brandeville (inclusive) and Lissey.

Because of the successful advance of the 5th Division, the Colonial Division was able to make good progress; the two kilometres' gap between Vilosnes and Sivry was closed and an advance in a broadly easterly direction of a spectacular six kilometres had been made. To the left, the 90th Division was patrolling on the right bank and preparing for a push towards Stenay. From Verdun to Lion-devant-Dun, the right bank was in American/French hands and all along this line the Germans were pushed away from the river.

### Friday 8 November.
### 9 Brigade.

In 9 Brigade's zone there was not much change in the line and consequently the day was spent in consolidating the positions held.

### 10 Brigade.

The 128th Regiment, 32nd Division, on the right of the 5th Division, advanced northeast toward Brandeville. They entered the town at almost the same time as the 11th Regiment, 5th Division, when the heights between Brandeville and Lissey were also captured and cleared of Germans. Fontaines Wood was cleared by elements of the 6th Regiment. Most of the day was spent consolidating the new positions. During the night probing patrols were sent out to investigate Habessaux and Deffoy Woods.

The 15th Colonial Division advanced beyond Bréhéville. During the night orders came through that the French division was to be relieved by the 128th Regiment, 32nd Division. The regiment was to be reinforced by bringing up the rest of the 32nd Division.

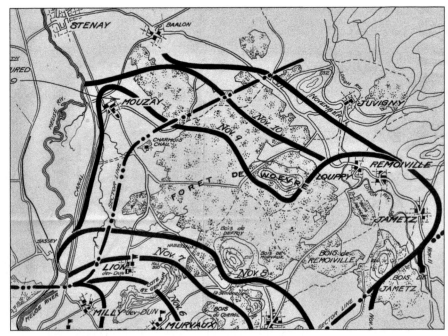

**Operations of the 5th Division, 8-11 November 1918.**

### Saturday 9 and Sunday 10 November.

By 2.00 pm reports were received that the Germans had withdrawn to the north east. Remoiville, Louppy, Jametz, Charmois, Juvigny and Mouzay were quickly cleaned out by patrols of the 5th Division. On the 10th the advance was largely ended. The speed of its attack had carried the division front eighteen kilometres east of the Meuse, the farthest point east reached by the AEF at the time of the armistice. The men were tired from the long marches and the hard fighting and needed time to rest and to reorganise. Consequently, no further advance was made on this day.

### Monday 11 November.

During the night, orders were issued that directed a renewal of the pursuit on the following morning in the direction of the River Chiers, Montmédy and Longuyon; but the armistice went into effect before the attack could take place.

Not yet aware of the armistice, the 11th Regiment prepared for an attack at Loison Valley. When the fog lifted, the Germans discovered the preparations. Immediately a white flag was waved and a man came forward from the German lines. He was an officer, spoke good English and explained to Colonel Peck: 'My God, sir, what are you doing? Don't you know the armistice goes into effect at 11 o'clock?' It is said that Peck replied: 'No, is that so! Then that spoils all my schemes!'

**The 89th and 90th Divisions.**
Both divisions crossed the Meuse on 10 and 11 November, but fall outside the scope of breaking the line on the Meuse Heights; their exploits will be treated in a subsequent book in this series.

*Above*: **Soldiers resting on the bank of l'Andon Creek near Cléry, 5 November 1918.**

*Below*: **The 60th Regiment arriving at Louppy.**

# Car Tour 1

# The sector of the 33rd and 29th Divisions

*Duration: A full day's tour*
*Distance: Thirty-five kilometres*
*Map: IGN 3112 ET, Verdun*

This circular tour starts and ends in Consenvoye at the bridges across the Meuse and is designed to cover the general area of the attack as fought by the 29th and 33rd Divisions. Starting on 8 October 1918, the 29th and 33rd were the first American divisions to fight on the right bank of the River Meuse in the Verdun sector.

Consenvoye is a large village with a petrol station, campsite and a restaurant, where you can get a cup of coffee or a cold beer as well as lunch, a *plat du jour* in French. Lunch only is served between 12.00 and 2.00 pm. With the exception of the restaurant, there are no public rest rooms along this route. Most of the points of interest are easy accessible by car; however, walking boots are recommended and a pair of binoculars would come in very useful as there are some spectacular views along the way. Make sure you bring some provisions, water etc. for a picnic.

**NOTE:** Stands 15a, 15b, 17 and 18 can best be located with the aid of a GPS device.

### GPS coordinates for Car Tour 1

| | | |
|---|---|---|
| (1) | Meuse crossing Consenvoye footbridge | (N49°16.692′ E005°17.466′) |
| (2) | Meuse crossing Consenvoye bridges | (N49°17.031′ E005°16.893′) |
| (3) | 'Then & Now' bridge | (N49°19.630′ E005°12.293′) |
| (4) | Consenvoye German Cemetery | (N49°16.777′ E005°17.783′) |
| (5) | Père Barnabé Monument | (N49°15.272′ E005°20.336′) |
| (6) | Samogneux church ruins | (N49°15.390′ E005°20.261′) |
| (7) | Père Barnabé Monument 2019 | (N49°15.382′ E005°20.247′) |

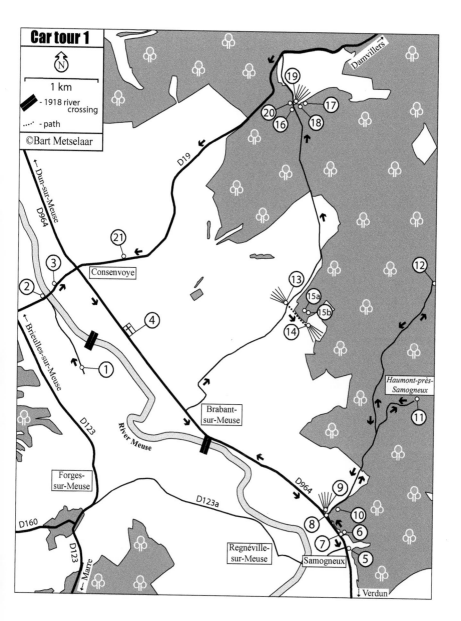

(8) Austro-Hungarian Monument    (N49°15.496′ E005°20.124′)

(9) Panorama 29th Division    (N49°15.577′ E005°20.242′)

(10) Grave of Captain Pierre    (N49°15.531′ E005°20.287′)
Juanahandy

| | | |
|---|---|---|
| (11) | Haumont-près-Samogneux, destroyed village | (N49°16.340′ E005°21.080′) |
| (12) | Death Valley bunkers | (N49°17.203′ E005°21.321′) |
| (13) | Panorama, 33rd Division area | (N49°17.004′ E005°19.649′) |
| (14) | Panorama, 29th Division area | (N49°16.876′ E005°19.831′) |
| (15) | Malbrouck Hill parking | (N49°16.916′ E005°19.762′) |
| (15a) | Observation post 1 | (N49°16.967′ E005°19.851′) |
| (15b) | Observation post 2 | (N49°16.976′ E005°19.902′) |
| (16) | German shelter/engine room | (N49°18.360′ E005°19.706′) |
| (17) | Gun pits and trenches | (N49°18.404′ E005°19.762′) |
| (18) | German shelter | (N49°18.417′ E005°19.717′) |
| (19) | Molleville Ravine | (N49°18.428′ E005°19.665′) |
| (20) | German generating station | (N49°18.435′ E005°19.662′) |
| (21) | 33rd Division HQ bunkers | (N49°17.312′ E005°17.785′) |

If you come from the direction of Stenay or Verdun, follow the D964 to Consenvoye. There is only one major crossroads in Consenvoye; take the D19 to Montfaucon. Immediately after you have crossed the *third* bridge, take a left turn onto a farm track. Continue for about 500 metres until you are at a T-junction (N49°16.526′ E005°17.292′). The Meuse River is about a hundred metres from where you stand. From here, you have a good

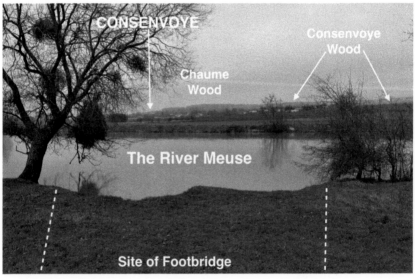

**The site of the Consenvoye footbridge of 8 October 1918.**

112

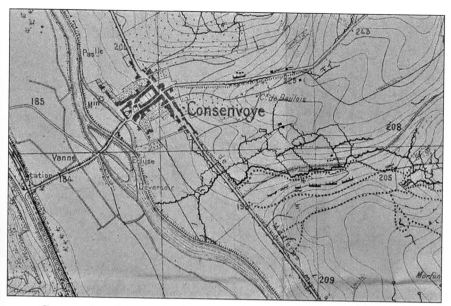

**German trench map showing the defences between Consenvoye and Brabant.**

view of the former site of the **Consenvoye footbridge (1)** (N49°16.692′ E005°17.466′). If there are no cattle in the fields you can walk along the track to the edge of the river. Remember to close the gates. The exact spot can be found by using the GPS coordinates above (1).

During the night of 7-8 October 1918, the 108th Engineers, 33rd Division, constructed a simple but effective pontoon bridge across the Meuse. At 5.00 am it was crossed by elements of the 132nd Regiment, 32nd Division, who were ordered to take Consenvoye and move north towards Consenvoye and Chaume Woods. Once the fog lifted and the rain started, the Germans continued to gas the area to such an extent that the engineers were forced to do this heavy work whilst wearing their gas masks all the time.

Return to your car, turn around and drive back to the main road, the D19. Just before you reach the D19, park your car and cross the D19 on foot to the other side of the bridge. From here it is possible to take a good look at the **Consenvoye bridges (2)** (N49°17.031′ E005°16.893′). The original bridges were destroyed by the Germans; in order to get supplies and artillery across the river the 108th Engineers used the old stone abutments to rebuild the bridges from timber. Besides the awful weather and the continuous shelling, it was a major challenge for the engineers, as they had to build no less than three bridges to get to the other side of the Meuse.

113

**The Consenvoye bridges were rebuilt by the 308<sup>th</sup> Engineers in order to get guns and supplies across the river.**

Once back in your car, turn right and cross the first bridge. Once at the **second bridge (3)** (N49°19.630′ E005°12.293′), take a look at the then and now photographs in the book. You can park on the left just before the bridge, or make a brief stop when there is no traffic, in which case do not forget to turn on your hazard lights. The original photograph was taken on 12 October 1918, just four days after the first crossing was made. Unfortunately the bell tower is now obscured by the line of trees behind the left railing.

Continue along the D19 until you are at the major crossroads. Turn right onto the D964 in the direction of Verdun. After about a kilometre you will see **Consenvoye German Cemetery (4)** (N49°16.777′ E005°17.783′) on the left. You can park opposite the entrance, on the right side of the D964.

This cemetery is the last resting place of 11,146 German soldiers, one nurse, one Russian soldier and sixty-two Austro-Hungarians. It is by far the largest and, arguably, most visited German cemetery of this region. The French, in accordance with an agreement with the treaty arrangements, started this concentration cemetery in 1920. Hundreds of small cemeteries and isolated graves that were scattered around the countryside, generally near by, were concentrated here. Graves that were discovered subsequently in the area, for example during road works or development projects, are buried here.

*Above and below*: Consenvoye, then and now.

27075

Work by the French ended in 1928. Interestingly, a second phase of reburials started after the French capitulation in 1940. During 1943, about 6,000 German graves were added by the German Graves Service. These graves came mainly from isolated and neglected sites in the Meuse Valley and from the Argonne Forest. The entrance, made from sand stone from the Vosges, was also started during this period but could not be finished before the liberation of the Meuse region by Patton's Third Army in September 1944. A major landscaping project took place in 1966; in 1978, as in many of the German cemeteries in France and Belgium, cast iron metal crosses replaced the original wooden crosses. These are placed on a heavy (thirty five kilograms) concrete base.

A bronze plaque at the entrance of the cemetery recalls the memorable occasion, on 22 September 1984, when the German Chancellor, Helmut Kohl, and the French President, François Mitterand, laid a wreath of reconciliation for the first time since the First World War. Together they declared: 'We have become wiser and become friends'. On 26 May 2016, the French President, François Hollande, and the German Chancellor, Angela Merkel, remembered the centenary of the Battle of Verdun here, celebrating their countries' reconciliation since the end of the world wars.

Another plaque at the entrance remembers the sixty-two Austro-Hungarians that are buried here. Most were killed on the right bank, either when they were defending their positions against the attacking

**Consenvoye German Cemetery contains 11,146 graves.**

**A LA MÉMOIRE
DES 62 SOLDATS DE L'ARMÉE
AUSTRO-HONGROISE ET UNITÉS DE LANDWEHR
QUI REPOSENT EN CE LIEU
1914 ~ 2014**

Croix Noire Autrichienne / Österreichisches Schwarzes Kreuz
Service des sépultures de guerre / Kriegsgräberfürsorge
Consulat Général d'Autriche / Österreichisches Generalkonsulat Strasbourg

**IM GEDENKEN
AN DIE 62 HIER RUHENDEN SOLDATEN
DER ÖSTERREICHISCH-UNGARISCHEN ARMEE
UND DER LANDWEHREN
1914 ~ 2014**

forces of the American 33<sup>rd</sup> and 29<sup>th</sup> Divisions between 8 and 12 October, or died from the Spanish Flu. Strangely enough, Consenvoye German Cemetery is one of the few German cemeteries that has headstones with dates between 26 September and 11 November 1918 (ie the Meuse-Argonne Offensive). As over 25,000 Germans died during this period in the offensive, one can only wonder where these bodies are buried. The same goes for the Austro-Hungarian dead; so far as is known, none were repatriated to Austria or Hungary.

Return to your car and continue along the D964 for about 5.5 kilometres until you reach Samogneux. The safest way to visit the next three points of interest is to turn right onto the D123a. You can park your car in the parking space in front of the Mairie (the Town Hall), opposite the church. If by any chance you should find the doors of Saint Rémi Church open it is worth going inside and view the painting by Lucien Lantier, 'Two Mothers'. It depicts a French and American mother grieving over their sons killed in battle. On the left side of the choir there is a modest bronze plaque donated by Mrs. Harlan Cleveland in honour of her son, Reverend Stanley Matthews Cleveland, 307<sup>th</sup> Regiment, 77<sup>th</sup> Division. Seriously wounded in the woods of Samogneux, he finally succumbed to his wounds on 25 September 1926 in Cincinnati, Hamilton County, Ohio, USA. His son, Harlan Cleveland, would later become the USA's permanent ambassador to NATO under Presidents Johnson and Nixon.

Walk to the D964; on the other side of this busy thoroughfare stands the **Père Barnabé Monument (5)** (N49°15.272′ E005°20.336′).

The statue depicts a character, Father Barnabas, created by Verdun-born journalist and writer Henri Frémont (1866-1944). From 1916 until the end of the war, Frémont published a weekly series about the adventures of Père Barnabé, a Meuse refugee from Samogneux. At the end of the war a book was published and the introduction was written by André Maginot, later Minister of Defence and inspirer of the eponymous Maginot Line, France's concrete defence line against Germany built in the 1930s. The concrete statue was first exhibited in Paris, later in Verdun and finally inaugurated in Samogneux on 6 July 1929. The memorial was financed by Mrs. Horace Gray (1860-1949), a wealthy American women who volunteered to work in military hospitals during the war. Mrs. Gray also happened to be the aunt of Reverend Stanley Matthews Cleveland, see above. Shocked by the death of her nephew and the destruction of the Meuse-Argonne, she and author Henri Frémont set up the Franco-American Organization for the reconstruction of Samogneux.

**The bronze memorial plaque of Stanley Matthews Cleveland, 77th Division.**

Facing the statue, turn left and proceed along the D964 for about fifty metres. At a certain point, a track branches off from the main road; walk up to the monument that is visible behind the fence and walk through the gate. You are now at the ruins of **Samogneux church (6)** (N49°15.390′ E005°20.261′), the only physical remains of the pre-war village. Today there are a few old walls and headstones but it also features the poignant Samogneux War Memorial, dating from 1933. The headstone on the left of the monument commemorates machine gunner Charles Daniel, a native of Samogneux. He was declared missing on 22 February 1916.

Originally, Samogneux was destined to join the nine villages that 'died for France' that are located in the Zone Rouge, the Red Zone, where no rebuilding is allowed. Amongst other reasons, this was done because the cost of rehabilitating the land was greater than its pre-war value. However, the energy put into the Franco-American Organization for the reconstruction of Samogneux by Mrs Gray and Henri Frémont influenced the decision of the French Government to change the classification of Samogneux from the monumental status of 'Died for France' to that of a destroyed village and in 1921 the reconstruction of the village started. One of the sources of financing the project was the

**Above:** The 1920s Père Barnabé monument, symbol of war refugees from the Meuse.

**Right:** The Samogneux War Memorial.

royalties from the translation into English of the Father Barnabas book. The last major building project in Samogneux was the bridge across the Meuse River. It was finally finished in 1935, only to be destroyed by the retreating French Army on 12 June 1940. A temporary bridge was laid in 1960. Finally, in 2010, the new permanent bridge was inaugurated, ninety-six years after German shells destroyed the original bridge.

**The Austro-Hungarian monument at Samogneux.**

Walk down from the church ruins towards the main road and turn right. After about fifty metres you come to the new **Père Barnabé Monument (7)** (N49°15.382′ E005°20.247′) at the foot of the old church. This new statue was built in 2019 to replace the old one; however the original statue has also recently been restored, resulting in the odd situation of having two nearly identical Barnabés one hundred metres apart along the same road.

Return to your car and head back to the D964 and turn left. Once outside Samogneux village limits take the first road (signposted Haumont-près-Samogneux) on your right into what looks like a truck stop. Park here. In the centre of the small strip of land between the D964 and the parallel road that you are on stands the **Austro-Hungarian Monument (8)** (N49°15.496′ E005°20.124′). This long overdue memorial was erected in 2014 at the start of the centenary commemorations. It remembers the thousands of Austro-Hungarian soldiers that fought and died or were wounded on the Western Front during the last months of the war; and also units like the Mörser Battalion Krakau, that were deployed under German command between 1914 and 1917. Only a few feet away from the monument stands a demarcation stone, the Borne Vauthier. In the 1920s, ninety-eight of these were placed in France, with varying degrees of accuracy, to mark the furthest point of the German advance.

**The new (2019) Père Barnabé monument.**

Next, turn around and cross the parallel road (not the D964) and go to the edge of the field. This **panorama (9)** (N49°15.577′ E005°20.242′) gives you some idea of the terrain that the troops of the 29th Division had to deal with before reaching the trenches of the 1st KuK Division.

*Above*: **An Austro-Hungarian knuckle duster, Graz, 1916.**

*Left*: **The Borne Vauthier marks the furthest point of the German advance.**

*Below*: **The area from where the 29th Division started their attack on the Meuse Heights on 8 October 1918, looking north-east.**

Two lines of lightly defended outposts ran across these slopes, namely the Brabant and Hagen lines. Of course, broad belts of barbed wire criss-crossed the fields and the air was heavy with gas and shrapnel during the attack. Apart from exploding shells and the staccato sound of machine guns, the continuous rain turned the area into a swamp. From this point, the 115th Regiment, 29th Division, set off to liberate Brabant (on your left, not visible); the 116th went up hill in the direction of Malbrouck Hill (not visible – it is behind the hill you are looking at).

Return to your car and turn right onto the narrow road that is signposted 'Haumont-près-Samogneux, village détruit'. After about a hundred metres, you will see a sign on the right side of the road that shows the way to the grave of **Captain Pierre Juanahandy (10)** (N49°15.531′ E005°20.287′) but **NOTE**: you have to be in good physical condition as the grave can only be reached after a steep climb. Juanahandy, a veteran of Morocco and Tunisia, recipient of the Croix de Guerre and the Legion d'Honneur, was a captain of the French 55th Regiment that participated in the French offensive to push the Germans back from the ground that they had won during the Battle of Verdun of 1916. Juanahandy, 41 years old, was killed approximately at this spot on 21 August 1917.

Once back in your car continue along the road until you come to a fork in the road; take the right fork. After about a kilometre, you enter **Haumont-près-Samogneux, (11)** (N49°16.340′ E005°21.080′) one of the nine destroyed villages and national war memorials. There is a car park next to the walls that are built around the chapel. In 1914 the village had 131 inhabitants and stayed in French hands until the opening days of the Battle of Verdun. As soon as the attack began on 21 February

**The almost invisible grave of Captain Pierre Juanahandy.**

1916, the German artillery concentrated their fire on Haumont, which they suspected to be one of the centres of resistance on their way to Verdun. Their firepower was so great that the forward lines of defence in Haumont Wood gave way; in heavy snowfall the Germans moved towards Haumont. At 4.00 pm the Germans launched the attack and overran the defenders of the French 362nd Regiment. On 22 February, after heavy fighting, the village fell into the hands of the Germans, who occupied it until amost the end of the war. On 8 October 1918 it was retaken by the French 18th Division as part of the attack to liberate the right bank and to cover the right flank of the American 29th Division.

The village is amongst the best presented of the Verdun battlefield *'villages détruits'*, each one of which still has a mayor. Beside explanatory information boards and a recommended route through the village, life-size photographs of some of the occupants placed on top of heaps of rubble that once were their homes, along with information about these people, make a visit to the remains of the village very moving. A chapel has been erected in its centre and there are also several German concrete shelters and observation posts that have escaped destruction. A short stroll among the ruins in this quiet spot to contemplate the suffering of men and beast during this black page in history is strongly recommended.

**A German bunker at Haumont, one of the nine destroyed villages around Verdun.**

Drive back until you once more arrive at the fork in the road; take a right turn and follow the track for about two kilometres until you see a large open space, which is in fact a large T-junction. Nowadays, this terrain is used to load and to park lumber trucks. Park your car somewhere on the right so that you do not block the road; you are now in the infamous **Death Valley (12)**. It runs parallel with the lumber road that goes to the right. There are four bunkers and the easiest way to find them is to use GPS coordinates. These are: bunker 1: (N49°17.203′ E005°21.321′), bunker 2: (N49°17.200′ E005°21.353′), bunker 3: (N49°17.196′ E005°21.380′) and bunker 4: (N49°17.190′ E005°21.399′). The four bunkers are built along a track that runs parallel with the lumber road, Death Valley, or Coassinvaux Ravine in French; the first bunker is located about fifty metres from the parking space.

**HAUMONT
PRÈS SAMOGNEUX
Village Détruit**

125

*Above*: The entrance of bunker 1.

*Left*: Shell damage at the entrance of bunker 1.

**A German water trough in Death Valley (not included in the tour).**

Second Lieutenant Arthur H. Joel of the 314th Regiment, 79th Division, noted in his diary:

'The long, narrow valley extended from the ruins of Samogneux, past the village of Haumont, to the wooded hill called Bois de Chênes: Death Valley, some of the dough boys labelled it, and such did its appearance and the near-future developments prove it to be. The summits of the ridges were covered with masses and bands of rusted barbed wire, while their slopes were so thoroughly pitted with shell craters that the earth at this point appeared to have been stricken with some pock disease. The masses of splintered tree trunks, all that remained of former groves and woods, also seemed to have been affected by some dreadful scourge.

On the reconnoitering trip, the afternoon of the day of the relief, one could hardly help but be impressed with the story of death and destruction as told by the great variety of battle debris scattered along the path and road leading from the canal near Samogneux to the battalion dug-out at the head of the valley. Mangled bodies of dead horses, the remains of blown-up kitchens and wagons, sheet iron slabs used in building dug-outs, shells and shell splinters, hand bombs, rusted rifles, loaves of bread, cans of meat, slabs of bacon, and many other odds and ends of supplies, ammunition

127

and equipment completed the weird picture of destruction – the result of several years of intermittent shelling and gassing by Hun artillery. There were no dead bodies visible along the path, but the small, scattered groups of rough wooden crosses told of quick burials, It did not require sensitive nostrils to smell the fumes of mustard gas at any time, but more especially when the hot sun increased evaporation of the deadly fumes. Such signs and conditions told a variety of tales of scattered ration details, gas attacks, box barrages, blown-up kitchens and ambulances, numerous casualties and other portentous battle events.'

Return to your car and drive back to the main road, the D964. Once there, turn right and go to Brabant-sur-Meuse. Turn right at the first crossroads that leads into Brabant proper and continue straight on to the church. Turn left at the T-junction and follow the road for about two kilometres

Panorama of the terrain covered by the 33rd Division on 8 October, looking north.

Panorama of the terrain covered by the 29th Division on 8 October, looking south and in the direction of stop (9).

until you are at the wooden electricity pole opposite Malbrouck Wood, see the map at the start of this tour. Park your car on the track that leads to the wood. Walk back to the pole and compare the view with the **panoramic photograph of the 33<sup>rd</sup> Division's sector (13)** (N49°17.004′ E005°19.649′ – see page 25). The attack started on 8 October 1918. From where you stand they advanced to the woods before you. The shelling was so intense and the losses so severe that on 21 October the 33<sup>rd</sup> Division was spent and was relieved by the French 15<sup>th</sup> Colonial Division. The area beyond Chaume Wood (Sivry, Vilosnes, Haraumont) could not be liberated until 5 November.

Continue along the track (Malbrouck Wood is on your left) until you come to a T-junction; stop here and compare the view with the **panoramic photograph of the 29<sup>th</sup> Division's sector (14)** (N49°16.876′ E005°19.831′). The 29<sup>th</sup> Division attacked Malbrouck Hill early in the morning of 8 October 1918.

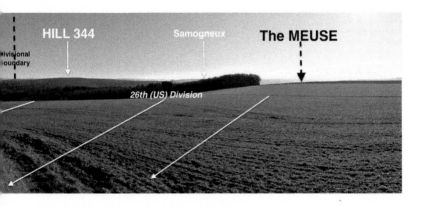

Turn your car and return to the main road until you are roughly half way back to it. The wood on your right is **Malbrouck Wood (15)** (N49°16.916′ E005°19.762′); park here. The best way to locate the two observation posts is to use the GPS coordinates: **observation post 1 (15a)** (N49°16.967′ E005°19.851′), **observation post 2 (15b)** (N49°16.976′ E005°19.902′). Another option is to use Car Tour map 1 but, frankly, the bunkers are very hard to find without GPS. The use of heavy machinery for logging has erased many of the traces of war; most of the trenches have all but disappeared. Still, when you look from the woods to the surrounding area you do not need much imagination to see that Malbrouck Hill once was a formidable natural bulwark. This sector was defended by the 1st KuK (i.e. Austro-Hungarian) Division.

Drive back to the road and turn right. Carry on for about two kilometres (the road changes into a track, which is in a bad state in some places) until you see a large clearing in the forest; this is Molleville Ravine. Park your car on the right side of the road (N49°19.630′ E005°12.293′). Walk back for about fifty metres until you see a large semi-round concrete entrance on your right. The original entrance is at the back wall of the bunker but it is just as easy to enter through the gap at the road side. The bunker was used as a **shelter/engine room (16)** (N49°18.360′ E005°19.706′) and is accessible at your own risk. Once inside you will see a concrete plinth where a generator stood. The metal Heinrich sheets that once supported

**An Austro-Hungarian observation post in Malbrouck Wood.**

130

**A German shelter in Consenvoye Wood.**

the roof have been removed after the war by metal scavengers but the imprint of the sheets are visible in the concrete. At the far end is the original entrance; behind it is another small room with a collapsed roof.

Leave the bunker and walk to the other side of the track and enter the forest. The easiest way to find the next two stands are by using GPS coordinates, or a careful study of the map at the start of this tour. Proceed for about fifty metres; if there is not too much underbrush, you should see several large mounds of earth on your left hand side. These are the remains of **German gun pits (17)** (N49°18.404′ E005°19.762′) and were probably built for large calibre guns, such as the 21 cm Mörser.

If you walk back towards the edge of the woods in the direction of your car, there are many trenches and other earthworks visible. The 29th Division was held up for weeks along this edge, as Molleville Ravine/clearing was under constant shell and machine-gun fire. On your way back to your car you will see the remains of a **German underground shelter (18)** (N49°18.417′ E005°19.717′). Around the entrance lie dozens of dried out cement bags; if you look carefully, you can still see the imprint of the canvas bags in the cement. It is time well spent exploring this part of the woods – but, to emphasise the point, watch out for unexploded ordnance and leave any you might find well alone.

Return to your car and take a look at **Molleville Ravine (19)** (N49°18.428′ E005°19.665′). The 26th, 29th and the 79th Divisions tried

A German gun pit in Molleville Wood.

A German shelter in Molleville Wood. Note the bags of concrete in the foreground.

time and again to cross this valley. It took almost four weeks until the ravine and the surrounding woods were firmly in American hands; the might of the German machine guns and artillery made it impossible to occupy the ravine permanently.

The 79th Division suffered particularly in this ravine; the wooded Hill 379 across the road proved a real death trap. Every time the Americans launched an attack they were forced to advance across the open grounds of Molleville Ravine. As soon as they were spotted by the Germans all hell broke loose. The hill itself was stubbornly defended by the German 228th Division; dozens of hidden machine-gun positions had to be overcome before the men of the 79th could finally continue the attack from Hill 379, a key position of the German Giselher defences, to the Borne de Cornouiller. 'Cornwilly Hill', as the Americans quickly dubbed it, was finally taken on 7 November, after five days of intense fighting. An anonymous soldier wrote in his diary:

'The 29th of October was a beautiful autumn day [this rarely occurred; most of the time it rained], but this showed to the regiment [the 316th] only a scene of desolation and carnage. The great trees of the woods were shattered and torn and the ground was gashed everywhere by shellfire. The open land across the road, sloping into the ravine of Molleville Farm, was pockmarked with enemy fire and the farm at the bottom was crumbled to a heap of stone. On the far side of the ravine, both to the east and north, the Germans held the woods and had the P.C. [of the 316th] and the road leading northward [where you are standing now] to the crossroad under perfect observation. The death dealing road was lined with broken water carts, dead horses, ammunition boxes, empty marmite cans and every description of equipment left by men killed while carrying supplies up to the lines.'

The situation only changed after the surrounding woods, Bultroy, Étraye and Grande Montagne, were wrested from the determined enemy; once these positions were taken at the end of October/start of November the attack in a northern direction could continue. A large part of the German guns that disrupted the American attacks on the left bank of the River Meuse were positioned in this area.

On the other side of the track from where you have parked your car is the entrance to a **German generating station (20)** (N49°18.435′ E005°19.662′). The original entrance is blocked but if you go to the right and walk around the huge structure you will see that there is another entrance at the back. Once inside you will notice that the roof has

**View across a foggy Molleville Ravine, looking east towards Molleville Farm; it was in similar weather when the men of the 29th Division first saw it.**

gone. According to local French historians, this large bunker was used to protect a large group of generators that delivered the power for the operation of several large search lights that were used for spotting French night bomber planes. From mid 1916 on, night raids were common and each month countless sorties were made by both French and German pilots. The Germans used the infamous 88mm, among other guns, as an effective countermeasure against the heavily laden enemy night bombers. The average top speed of a First World War plane did not exceed 200 km/h and bombers were a much slower target and thus easier to hit.

A careful study of the remains of the roof/ceiling reveals that two layers of tree trunks were used to support the roof and to double as form work for the concrete. The tree trunks have long gone, but one can still see the imprints of the wood in the concrete. Also visible is the tar paper that was used for water proofing the roof. To the left and right of the chamber, in the roof are large circular holes, five on each side. These were used to evacuate the toxic fumes of the generators but also to let in ample fresh air to keep the engines running. Close to the bunker there used to be a large engineer camp with kitchens, canteens, shops and dozens of barracks and shacks; these have long gone and the materials reused by locals.

Drive along the track until you come to the main road, the D19. Turn left here and drive back to Consenvoye. About a kilometre before you

**Entrance to the German generating station, Consenvoye Wood.**

**The ruins of the generating station in Consenvoye Wood, January 2020.**

**This German bunker served as an HQ for the 33rd Division on 8 October 1918.**

enter the village, you will see a white sign on the right of the road that reads 'Champ de Bataille 14-18 Argonne'. At the side of the road, flush with the road surface, are two German bunkers that were once part of the Hagen Line defences. In summer they are hard to spot as they are usually obscured by crops in the field. On 8 October these bunkers served as the **headquarters of the 33rd Division (21)** (N49°17.312′ E005°17.785′). Both shelters are now not accessible; the entrances are sealed off with earth. Carry on for a kilometre and you are back at the starting point of this tour.

# Car Tour 2

# The sector of the 26<sup>th</sup> and 79<sup>th</sup> Divisions

*Duration: A full day's tour*
*Distance: Forty-seven kilometres*
*Maps: IGN 3111 SB Stenay and 3212 SB Étain*

This non-circular tour starts at Sivry-sur-Meuse and ends in Gremilly. This car tour takes you along several points of interest in the 26<sup>th</sup> and 79<sup>th</sup> Division's sector. However, several points of interest, like Consenvoye Wood and Molleville Farm which are in the 79<sup>th</sup> Division's sector have already been visited in Car Tour 1. Ideally, if you start early, you can combine this car tour with the Henry Gunther Tour.

There is a petrol station, bakery and a supermarket in Damvillers but unfortunately there are no public toilets along the way. Walking shoes are not required, except if you decide to include the Henry Gunther Tour at Stand (9). A pair of binoculars are very useful as on various stops there are stunning views across the battlefield.

## GPS coordinates for Car Tour 2

| | | |
|---|---|---|
| (1) | German Monument | (N49°19.241' E005°16.305') |
| (2) | St. Pantéalon Chapel | (N49°19.398' E005°17.892') |
| (3) | 316<sup>th</sup> Infantry Regiment Monument | (N49°19.725' E005°18.576') |
| (4) | Gisheler Line shelters | (N49°20.444' E005°22.782') |
| (5) | Damvillers German Cemetery | (N49°20.948' E005°24.742') |
| (6) | Barbären Brunnen | (N49°19.272' E005°24.446') |
| (7) | German well | (N49°19.254' E005°24.529') |
| (8) | German gun battery | (N49°18.924' E005°24.030') |
| (9) | Henry Gunther Monument | (N49°18.928' E005°25.749') |
| (10) | Ville-devant-Chaumont German Cemetery | (N49°17.529' E005°25.470') |
| (11) | Feldbahnhof Frosch | (N49°17.890' E005°26.605') |
| (12) | Azannes-et-Soumazannes German Cemetery | (N49°17.576' E005°27.841') |
| (13) | Becker Monument | (N49°17.147' E005°28.559') |

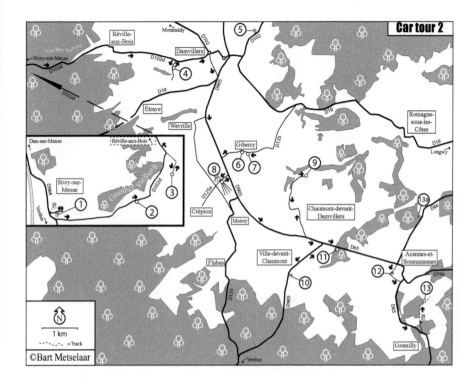

Sivry-sur-Meuse is situated along the busy D964 between Stenay and Verdun. When you come from the direction of Stenay, take a left turn immediately after you have passed the church. From Verdun, take a right turn just before the church onto the Rue de la Chaudoye. After about 150 metres you see Sivry communal cemetery appearing on your right hand; now carry on along the cemetery wall for another fifty metres until you arrive at the back wall. You can park your car on the side of the road. During the war, the sports field on the right side of the road was the site of a German cemetery. In the middle of the back wall you will find a **German Monument (1)** (N49°19.241′ E005°16.305′) dedicated to the 47th Field Artillery Regiment. On 24-25 August 1914 Sivry was largely abandoned by its inhabitants; men aged between 18 and 55 who had remained were arrested and sent to Camp Grafenwöhr, a work camp in Bavaria. In February 1916 the village was largely destroyed by shell fire during the Battle of Verdun and only the walls of Saint Rémi Church were spared.

The German cemetery was started in 1914 and was used throughout the war and originally held some 800 graves. After the war the majority of the German graves in Sivry were moved by the French authorities to concentration cemeteries in Brieulles and Consenvoye; but for some reason the burials along the back wall of the communal cemetery remained. Interestingly, the monument that is now in Sivry was originally built in Syrie Wood, east of Étain, where during the war a large German rest camp was established. In the winter of 1927/1928, on the instigation of the German authorities, the monument was moved from the former *Syrie Lager* to Sivry. Consequently the monument does not show on German photographs taken during the war. However, it does show on the photograph reproduced here, taken just after the restoration of the church towers in 1928. During the Second World War the Germans moved the remaining graves to Consenvoye but left the monument untouched. In a bad state after exposure to the elements for ninety years, the monument was beautifully restored to its former glory by Denis Mellinger in 2012.

Return to the D964 and turn left. After about two hundred metres, where the main road makes a 90° bend to the right a somewhat faded white sign, *Monument Américain*, indicates a left turn at a point. Do not continue in the direction of Verdun. Follow the minor road, *the Rue Pierre Pinton,* for about four hundred metres. At a crossroads, continue straight on and drive uphill. After a kilometre, you reach **St. Pantéalon Chapel (2)** (N49°19.398′ E005°17.892′). The chapel is beautifully situated on the approach to the US 316th Monument. Partially destroyed by shellfire in September/November 1918, the ruins of the chapel were used for shelter by an unknown French lieutenant of the 2nd Colonial Infantry Division who was seriously wounded on 4 November 1918. The lieutenant survived the war and upon his instigation the chapel was

*Above left*: **The Koniglich Sächsisches Erzatz Feld Artillerie Regiment 47 Monument in Sivry.**

*Above right*: **The cemetery in 1928; note the memorial in the wall below the church steeple.**

restored. The only thing that is now known about him is that he died on 4 November 1936, exactly eighteen years after he found refuge in the chapel.

Once outside the chapel, look toward the wooded hills on the other side of the valley. It is easy to appreciate from here why the 33$^{rd}$ Division could not advance any further after 20 October. The valley remained in No Man's Land and was under constant German observation and shellfire until 7 November, on which date the French finally took Sivry and the American 79$^{th}$ Division, after several costly attempts, finally captured Hill 378, or Cornwilly Hill. Facing the entrance of the chapel, the 316$^{th}$ Regiment Memorial can be seen on the left in the distance.

Return to your car and carry on for a few hundred metres until you come to a fork in the road; take the left turn. The going can be a bit rough but a car with sufficient bottom clearance will not experience any problems. Almost at the top of the hill, there is a sign pointing to the right that reads: 'To La Grande Montagne and the monument of the 316$^{th}$ Infantry AEF'. You should already see the pine trees (although these may have been felled, alas, by the time this book is published) that line the lengthy approach path leading up to the **316$^{th}$ Infantry Regiment, 79$^{th}$ Division Monument (3).** (N49°19.725′ E005°18.576′). Between 3-7 November this hill was freed of Germans by the 79$^{th}$ Division during the Third Phase of the Meuse-Argonne Offensive.

**The Chapel of St. Panthaléon; note the line of trees in the distance between it and the car marking the 316$^{th}$ Memorial in the background.**

The 316<sup>th</sup> Regiment, 79<sup>th</sup> Division Memorial in Sivry.

Once at the monument, there is a clear, indeed magnificent, view over the Meuse Valley; Montfaucon (both the memorial column and the very handy red and white television mast to its east) are clearly visible in the distance. Before the Americans wrested this hill from the Germans it was an important artillery observation position. In fact it was part of a whole range of artillery positions that were built on the Meuse Heights, of which the *Grande Montagne* formed just a small part. From these heights, especially as the American line pressed northwards, the Americans would have been increasingly hit in enfilade. Intense and terribly accurate gun fire, directed by observation posts situated such as this, made it extremely hard for the men of the 79<sup>th</sup> Division (and of course many other divisions) to reach their objectives. Most of the gun batteries were in action during the better part of the American attack and were responsible for a significant proportion of the American casualties.

The right bank of the River Meuse did not come under any significant attack until 8 October 1918 (it has to be said much to the surprise of the Germans) and the guns positioned there were mainly responsible for harrying the whole American offensive and for a high proportion of casualties. It is notable that the hill – and therefore all the advantages that it offered – remained in German hands until the last week of the war.

When you go to the hedgerow at the back of the monument, looking south, you can see, from right to left, Chaume Wood, Plat Chêne Wood and Grande Montagne Wood. On the heights the Germans built the Etzel and Volker lines, a continuation of the defences that also protected Montfaucon. This is where on 20 October the American offensive on the right bank petered out in the face of the endless and accurate shelling. The attack could not be continued to the north, so until the 5th Division crossed the Meuse (3-5 November) between Dun and Brieulles to knock on the backdoor of the Kriemhild Line defences, no further advance could be made. That is why the 79th Division only continued the attack after the 5th Division crossed the Meuse on 3 November. The Germans, threatened from the front and the rear, retreated to the east, the only route of escape. During the advance of the 79th the hill was under permanent artillery fire to deny the Americans the access to this formidable observation post. However, during the proceeding days the shellfire gradually weakened because the German gun batteries were withdrawn well behind the Kriemhild Line; the hill finally fell into American hands on 7 November.

The monument, erected in 1928, commemorates the casualties of the 316th Regiment of the 79th Division during the course of its operations in 1918; seventy-eight officers and 3,128 soldiers. With Captain Carl E Glock, a former member of the 316th Regiment, from Pittsburgh as the driving force behind the project, Marcel Delangle was hired to be the architect of this privately funded monument.

At the time of its construction the monument was a source of controversy. According to an American law *'no memorials should be erected to any unit of the American Army in France of lesser size than a division'*. General Pershing became the American Government's 'Supreme Coordinator' for American Battle Monuments abroad; he urged the French Government to destroy the monument. Fortunately, the French Prime Minister, André Tardieu, refused this request, coming up with a fistful of admirable bureaucratic reasons, the ace card being that it was erected on private property. Indeed, he was only surpassed in wiliness by the Regimental Association. He offered to amend the memorial by adding a bilingual memorial plaque, to be inscribed, 'In memory of the high achievements of the American troops that fought in this region during the World War'. This was reluctantly accepted by Pershing, but in the end the plaque was never added to the memorial. The row rumbled on for over nine years, involved three US Presidents, embassies, quite sophisticated spying techniques, including phone tapping, the Mayor of Verdun was a major pro memorial supporter (and who found a way around the problem) and French prime ministers. The controversy was on national US newspaper front pages several times and also brought in the American Gold Star Mothers in full voice, arguing in favour of the memorial.

Over time the controversy died away, the memorial remained and for that the modern battlefield visitor must be truly thankful. It has remained a fine and, pleasingly, recently restored (2016) regimental memorial.

Drive back along the track until you come to a tarmac road; turn right in the direction of Réville-aux-Bois. This route takes you more or less along the line where the Giselher Line defences were built. This line was the last line of defences before the Kriemhild Line, the German main line. When you enter Réville, take the right fork. At the next junction, take a right turn onto the D102d, the *Rue de Chaufour*, towards Damvillers. After you have passed two large barns/hangars on the right side of the D102d, take the first farm road on the right. After about fifty metres, you see a large German bunker in the field on your right.

This is one of five shelters that were built in 1917/1918 as part of the **Giselher Line defences (4)** (N49°20.444′ E005°22.782′). The garrison that manned the shelters defended the plains that lead to Damvillers; many railway lines of all gauges criss-crossed the valley floor and every village in this area was used in some way or another, varying from billeting, advanced dressing stations to supply dumps for the German war effort. At your own risk, and when there are no crops in the field, this is the only bunker that is accessible; the other four are flooded, even in summer. The shelter has two entrances with a flight of stairs that led into a central hallway. On the left side of the hallway there

German medics and their officer (right) taking their dogs for a walk in Réville, 1917.

**A typical 1917/1918 Kriemhilde Line shelter at Réville.**

are several niches for ammunition storage. On the right side, there are two entrances that led to the actual shelters. The roofs are made from corrugated iron, and each compartment used to be equipped with stoves and bunk beds.

Return to the main road and continue to Damvillers. When you come to the roundabout take the second exit, onto the D102. Follow the D102 until you come to a second roundabout. Here, take the third exit and continue straight until you leave the village. At the T-junction follow the road to the left; after two kilometres, **Damvillers German Cemetery (5)** (N49°20.948′ E005°24.742′) is on the left side of the road.

In preparation for the attack on Verdun (21 February-15 December 1916), German engineers erected numerous wooden barracks for

**The German Kriemhild Line defences between Réville and Damvillers.**

medical stations, an approximate equivalent to the British casualty clearing station; they were mainly dedicated to slightly injured soldiers. It has been estimated that between January and September 1916 about 8,400 wounded were treated here and it was around that time that the cemetery was started. Soldiers who were killed and brought back from the front, men, killed by accidents or died of disease are also buried here. These graves can be found on the boundaries of the cemetery. However, the main area of the cemetery has casualties almost entirely from 1917, many dating from August/September 1917, when the French launched a major counter-attack (the so-called Second Battle of Verdun) to retrieve ground that was lost to the Germans in 1916.

In the centre of the cemetery stands an original German monument that commemorates the fallen. It was erected in 1916 by the 48th Reserve Field Hospital Regiment. In total, 1,113 soldiers are buried here, including four Austro-Hungarian soldiers and two Belgian forced labourers. The memorial's plaque reads: In commemoration of the brave warriors that lie at rest here.

Now drive back to Damvillers and continue to the major crossroad; take a left turn off the D19 on to the D905 and carry on for about three kilometres. Take a left turn on to the D125 and proceed to Gibercy, a hamlet comprising not much more than a church and a few farms. On 9 November 1918 Gibercy was liberated by the 79th Division. On entering the village, follow the road around the church. The **Barbären Brunnen (6)** (N49°19.272′ E005°24.446′) is on the right hand side. The well was built by a German artillery unit. Because of the proximity of the River Thinte and numerous wells, besides billeting troops, Gibercy served as a so-called *Badeanstalt*, a bathing facility. Several washing

145

*Left*: The 48<sup>th</sup> Reserve Field Hospital Regiment Monument in Damvillers German Cemetery.

*Below*: The Barbären Brunnen in Gibercy, 2020.

*Der Barbaren-Brunnen in Gibercy.*

**The well during the German occupation.**

basins and wells were constructed by different German units during the occupation of the village.

Carry on for another hundred metres along the D125. Opposite the last house of the village, you can see the derelict and heavy overgrown remains of a second **German well (7)** (N49°19.254′ E005°24.529′). You can park on the side of the road.

**German bathing facilities in Gibercy.**

147

**A derelict German well by the D125, just outside Gibercy.**

Now drive back through Gibercy and return to the main road, the D905. Turn left; after approximately one kilometre turn right in the direction of Crépion. After fifty metres stop (carefully! this can be a busy road) at the side of the road and look to the left. Built into the side of the ridge, several concrete pillboxes can be seen. This is the site of the **Crépion German gun battery (8)** (N49°18.924′ E005°24.030′). Hundreds of gun emplacements were built in 1915 in the German hinterland in preparation for the Battle of Verdun. However, the concrete structures that remain today on this site were built in 1917/1918 as part of the Etzel Line defences and were used for sheltering gun crews. The bunkers are built on private property and are not accessible.

Turn around where it is safe to do so and drive back to the D905; turn right. After three kilometres, take a left turn onto the D65a in the direction of Chaumont-devant-Damvillers. Once within the village limits, turn left at the T-junction. Just before you reach the church, turn right. After fifty metres you come to a fork in the road; keep left. After forty metres, turn right onto a farm track. The track is in a bad state but with a bit of care it is perfectly drivable unless the weather has been very poor. If you should

*Above*: German
shelters in a field
near Crépion and
Moiry.

*Right*: A German
heavy gun in action.

decide against this, it takes you ten minutes on foot from the village to
reach the **Henry Gunther Monument (9)** (N49°18.928′ E005°25.749′)
that stands on the top of the ridge.

The memorial renders homage to the 79th Division and Henry
Gunther and his comrades, whose actions here pushed the American
advance in the Verdun sector to its furthest extent. On the American right

wing, the final assault was carried out by the 26th and 79th Divisions. By 8 November the Germans were pushed back from the Meuse Heights and had retreated to a line running from Damvillers to Romagne-sous-les-Côtes to Ville-Devant-Chaumont. They were ordered to hold the Kriemhild Line at all costs. On 10 November 1918 the village of Chaumont-devant-Damvillers and the surrounding hills were liberated by the 314th, 315th and 316th Regiments.

During the night of 10 November, the 313th Regiment was called up from Death Valley and was marched to Ormont Hill at Crépion. The First Battalion of the 313th Regiment, including Co. A, Gunther's company, was then ordered to advance east from Ville-devant-Chaumont in the direction of Azannes, an important German

**The Henry Gunther Monument at Chaumont.**

logistical centre. At 10.59 am, when Co. A moved towards Thil Wood, the German front line on 11 November, Gunther was killed by a machine-gun burst that struck him in the left temple. General Pershing's Order of the Day recorded Henry Nicholas Gunther as the last American soldier to die in the First World War. For more information on Henry Gunther, see page 214.

Return to the D905 and turn left. Take the first exit to the right and pass through Ville-devant-Chaumont. **Ville-devant-Chaumont German Cemetery (10)** (N49°17.529′ E005°25.470′) lies a few hundred metres beyond the village. As for many others on the left bank, this German cemetery was started soon after the start of the Battle of Verdun (21 February 1916). Wooden barracks to accommodate field hospitals and dressing stations were quickly erected and by the end of March already 6,000 wounded had been treated here. Those who died of their wounds are buried here, along with the dead who were retrieved from the battlefield. The last casualties in the cemetery buried here during the war date from the autumn of 1917, when the French launched their major counter offensive to regain the lost ground from 1916.

However, the cemetery also holds graves dating before and after 1916 and 1917. The reason for this is that after the war the French used the cemetery as a concentration cemetery; German field graves

THIL WOOD

The field where Gunther was killed.

Ville devant Chaumont

*Inset*: Henry Nicholas Gunther (1895-1918).

that were scattered around the battlefield were reburied here. In total, 1,766 soldiers are buried in Ville-devant-Chaumont; 1,517 soldiers have an individual grave, eight-two of these remain unknown. The mass grave holds 249 bodies; 193 are unknown.

Drive back via Ville-devant-Chaumont to the T-junction D905/D65; turn right. After a few hundred metres, just before you reach Thil Wood, a narrow farm road starts on your right. This track runs parallel with the edge of the wood; park as soon as you can. Henry Gunther was killed in the field on the right of the woods. Follow this track for about ten metres and enter the wood. You can clearly make out the banks in between which were the railway tracks. Follow the banks for fifty metres until you come to the large concrete bunker that was once part of **Feldbahnhof Frosch (11)** (N49°17.890′ E005°26.605′). This narrow gauge railway station was built in 1918. Three 60 cm wide light railway lines joined here and the station was used to unload ammunition, building material and troops. In the centre of the front wall one can still admire the name that the

151

**Ville-devant-Chaumont German Cemetery.**

German Engineers gave to the station's central shelter: white pebbles set into the concrete read: *Frosch* [Frog] *1918*. The four entrances lead to a central hallway. The four rooms are in a bad state and are flooded. However, at your own risk, one can have a peak inside via the far left entrance by standing on the rubble created by an explosion that partially destroyed the far left shelter. Outside the shelter, several flooded shell holes can be seen, a likely testimony of the intense American barrage that preceded the Armistice; whilst various earth works in the vicinity also are suggestive of its logistics purpose.

Walk back to your car and continue to Azannes-et-Soumazannes. At the crossroads where the D65 is crossed by the D66, turn right on to a farm road. After about a hundred metres you reach the entrance of **Azannes-et-Soumazannes German Cemetery (12)** (N49°17.576′ E005°27.841′). The cemetery is of French origin (the original 16th century gate and several pre-war French graves are at the back) and dates from before the First World War when Soumazannes was an independent village.

The Germans started to bury their dead in Soumazannes at the end of February 1916. The number of German soldiers that were killed during the opening stages of the Battle of Verdun was so appalling that there was an urgent need for cemeteries. According to the German War

**The German shelter at Frosch Station.**

**The central hallway of the shelter.**

Graves Commission, most of the 817 men buried here date back to the first three months of the battle, of whom many were killed in the Fort Douaumont area (taken on 25 February 1916 by the 24th Brandenburger Regiment). The boundary between the original French civilian cemetery and the German war cemetery is marked by an original war time German monument, dedicated in 1916 to the fallen of the Königliches Bayerische Armierungs Battalion X. This was one of many pioneer units that were responsible for the construction of trenches, narrow gauge railway lines, bridges and roads. In Verdun these men operated immediately behind the first lines, hence the high number of casualties. During the war, Armierungs Battalion X was mostly deployed in the Verdun /Argonne area but also at various other locations on the Western Front (Lille, for example), which are listed, along with dates that they were there, on the memorial. The motto 'Getreu bis zum Tode' means 'Faithful unto death'.

After the war, the French authorities added twenty-eight German graves from Gremilly to the cemetery. From 1926 to 1930, basic landscaping projects were undertaken; trees were planted and grass was sown. German cemeteries of the First World War were modernized from

154

1966, when major landscaping took place. The original wooden crosses were replaced after 1976 by more permanent and uniform grave markers. Several of those named on the pioneer memorial are buried here.

Return to your car and take the first turn to the left. Follow the Rue Haute and keep going straight until you come to the main road, the D65. Turn right and continue in the direction of Gremilly. After a kilometre there is a farm on the right; this is La Gare Farm. Continue along the D65 and enter the woods. After a few hundred metres turn left on to a narrow road that takes you into the woods. After a mere fifty metres,

**Azannes I German Cemetery at Azannes-et-Soumazannes.**

155

*Above*: **The Bavarian Services of Supply monument.**

*Left*: **The 16th century gate of the French civilian cemetery.**

turn left again. This road leads to Gremily Cemetery. From here the road changes into a farm track and takes you to the Côte de Ramon. This is serviceable for most cars, with care, until you reach the edge of the forest. However, in wet conditions, continue on foot. From here, the track is in a pretty bad state in some places, but perfectly accessible for four-wheel drive cars. You will find the **Josef Becker Grave Monument (13)** (N49°17.147′ E005°28.559′) next to the track where the wood ends. The inscription reads in translation: Here rests comrade Gefreiter der Reserve (during World War One the Gefreiter rank was considered a transition rank for promotion and from which number replacements were selected as Unteroffizier (Corporal; a British equivalent would be lance corporal) Josef Becker, 10 Company, RIR 98 (reserve infantry regiment 98), killed 13 June 1915. The RIR 98 was part of the 33rd Division. Becker was born in Mulheim am Rhein near Köln.

At the beginning of the war the 33rd Division, with the 34th Division, formed XVI Corps, based in Metz. Reservists began arriving on 29 July 1914. At the outbreak of the hostilities the 33rd Division was part of Fifth Army under the command of the German Crown Prince. On 1 September

*Above left*: **Josef Becker's original grave monument on Côte Ramon, near Gremilly.**

1914 it crossed the River Meuse at Sivry; the division later took up the line in the Argonne. On 24 September the 98th Regiment was reduced from the original 2,000 men to thirteen officers and 982 men. It remained in the Verdun sector until after the Battle of Verdun in 1916. On 15 December the regiment was transferred to the east of Beaumont-Hamel, on the Somme, and did not leave until 8 February 1917. Unfortunately, it is not known under what circumstances Becker died. Facing the monument, there are several German bunkers to be seen in the field to the left of the track. They are part of the northern extension of the Michel Zone (see St. Mihiel in this series), an impressive defense system that was designed as a definitive stop line, between Germany and France.

After the war Becker's grave was removed to Azannes II German Cemetery; he lies buried in Block 7 Grave 587. The grave marker is easy to find; it is located in the back row, just in front of a white sandstone monument. To reach the cemetery (see **13a** on the map) drive back to Azannes-Soumazannes along the D65. Just outside the village, turn right onto the D66, direction Romagne-sous-les-Côtes. After a kilometre, Azannes II German Cemetery is on the left, beautifully situated on rising ground.

# Car Tour 3

# The sector of the 5ᵗʰ and 32ⁿᵈ Divisions

*Duration: A full day's tour*
*Distance: Fifty kilometres*
*Map: IGN 3111 SB Stenay*

This non-circular tour starts near Vilosnes and ends at Lion-devant-Dun.
Both villages are situated close to the D964, the main road between
Stenay and Verdun. There are no shops, cafés or petrol stations along
the way, so be sure you bring everything you need for a picnic. Walking
boots are not needed; most of the stops can be easily reached by car or
after a short walk. Should you want to visit the interior of the concrete
shelters (at your own risk!) mentioned in this tour, make sure you bring
a torch. In July and August a good brand of insect repellent is essential
in wooded areas. To reach the start of the tour, follow the D964 in the
direction of Vilosnes; this takes about twenty minutes, coming from
either Stenay or Verdun.

The first part of the tour takes you to points of interest along the
Kriemhild Line. This is done to get a better understanding of the lie
of the land and why the German defences were built where they are.
It continues to the logistical area between Bréhéville and Peuvillers
(liberated by the 32ⁿᵈ Division); the tour ends in the 5ᵗʰ Division's sector,
north-east of the Meuse.

### GPS coordinates for Car Tour 3

|  |  |  |
| --- | --- | --- |
| (1) | Bunker Ravin du Trou de Mesnil | (N49°20.505' E005°15.351') |
| (2) | Bunkers Haraumont | (N49°20.789' E005°16.357') |
| (3) | Panoramic view | (N49°20.826' E005°16.620') |
| (4) | Kriemhild Line shelters | (N49°20.827' E005°18.131') |
| (5) | Peuvillers German water tower | (N49°21.730' E005°23.258') |
| (6) | German officers' quarters | (N49°22.193' E005°23.633') |
| (7) | German shelter | (N49°22.186' E005°23.656') |
| (8) | Peuvillers German Cemetery | (N49°22.200' E005°23.684') |
| (9) | German Memorial | (N49°22.918' E005°23.674') |
| (10) | Lissey German Cemetery | (N49°23.297' E005°22.375') |

159

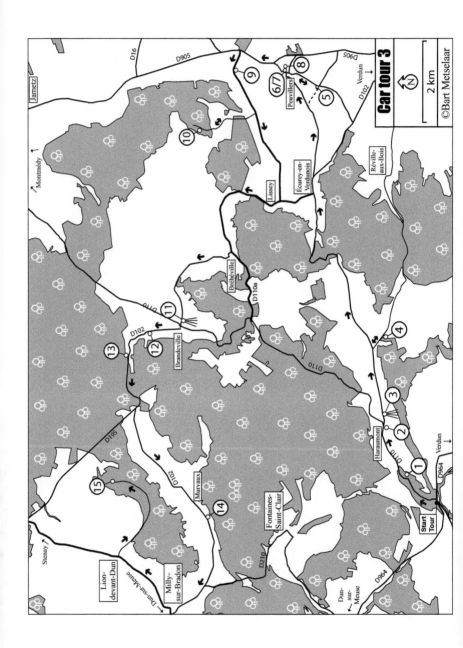

Car tour 3

N

2 km

©Bart Metselaar

| | |
|---|---|
| (11) Brandeville railway centre, then and now | (N49°23.656' E005°18.383') |
| (12) Brandeville Necropole Nationale | (N49°24.128' E005°18.243') |
| (13) Maginot Line bunker | (N49°24.406' E005°17.723') |
| (14) Frank Luke Memorial | (N49°17.909' E005°07.031') |
| (15) 5$^{th}$ Division Monument Côte St. Germain | (N49°24.620' E005°15.143') |

When you reach the junction of the D964, D123b and the D110 near Vilosnes, take the D110 in the direction of Haraumont. Just as you leave the woods a track starts on your right; park here, but do not block the road (there is space off the road by the track). Follow the edge of the wood on your right for about a hundred metres until you see a substantial amount of concrete on your right and just inside the wood; this is the site of the **Ravin du Trou de Mesnil Bunker (1)** (N49°20.505' E005°15.351'). This shelter forms part of the last major German defence line, the Kriemhild Line.

From the second half of 1917 until September 1918, the Germans carried out a comprehensive building programme all along the Western Front. The line became popularly known as the Hindenburg Line. In the Meuse-Argonne five lines (which together formed one ten kilometre deep defensive zone) were planned. The last and most powerful lines were called the Giselher and the Kriemhild Line, but in reality these too were more like defensive zones than lines. On the Left Bank, in

**A German Kriemhild Line shelter near Vilosnes.**

Romagne, the Kriemhild Zone was successfully breached on 14 October by the 32nd Division. However, on the right bank the Americans only managed to reach the Volker Line, the third line, on 20 October. The defences of the Giselher and Kriemhild Lines beyond the Volker Line proved too formidable to overcome without serious reinforcements.

Almost a fortnight later, on 3 November, the 5th Division was finally ordered to cross the Meuse and attack the Germans from behind. At the same time, the 79th Division launched attack after attack at the Giselher Line (Grande Montagne, Cornwilly Hill). This line was finally reached on 7 November 1918. However, the Kriemhild Line was still unattainable and was only occupied after the German retreat.

Return to your car and carry on to Haraumont; drive past the church and continue straight in the direction of Écurey. Just before you reach the last houses of Haraumont there are two **bunkers (2)** (N49°20.789′ E005°16.357′); one on each side of the road. The one on the left is a typical example of a late-war (1918) German shelter. It was built to provide secure accommodation for observers who used the bell tower of the church as an observation post. Inside the shelter there is only one room, which measures two by four metres. Next to the entrance you can see the metal I-beam supports that once held the wooden platform of the fire step; the metal rungs provide an easy access to the roof. Unfortunately the site is currently used as a rubbish dump; the bunker is not accessible.

On the other side of the road stands a second concrete structure. Interestingly, the entrance is facing west and the aperture east instead of the other way around, as might be expected from a German First World War bunker. Unfortunately, no additional information could be found

**La Grande Montagne**

**Sivry Wood**

**316th Memorial**

**Le Long Bois**

**Cha**

**One of the two bunkers at Haraumont.**

but it is likely to be a French fieldwork that was part of the second line of defence of the French Maginot Line. This fortified zone was built in the 1930s to protect France against a possible German invasion. The bunker was used for both observation and, given its large aperture, as a machine gun or 25mm gun position, widely used by the French army at that time. It presumably guarded the Meuse bridges between Vilosnes and Sivry. The shelter is made from reinforced concrete and the outside is lined with natural stone for camouflage purposes. There are still numerous small field works to be found between Vilosnes and Sedan that date back to the Second World War. In the area between Montmédy and Brandeville eighteen major works (see Stand 13) were planned, but because of significant budget cuts only two were built.

Leave the village and carry on for a few hundred metres until you come to the concrete water reservoir that stands on the left of the road. The reservoir provides an excellent platform for a **panoramic view (3)** (N49°20.826′ E005°16.620′) across the Meuse-Argonne battlefield. Use the photograph in the book as a reference. The most important

**View from the Kriemhild Line towards the Giselher Line.**

thing to take from this site are the commanding views; every valley in this vicinity held German artillery batteries and there were countless observation posts. From this elevated position, it is easy to appreciate that the combination of artillery, almost unlimited observation and air supremacy proved a lethal combination, as Pershing, his commanders and certainly the ground troops painfully experienced. The mistake of not attacking both banks at the same time can not be appreciated better than from this spot.

Continue along the D110 in the direction of Écurey; after 1,500 metres turn right on to a metalled track. Just after you have passed a wood on your right, stop. In the field on the right you can see two low-lying **Kriemhild Line shelters (4)** (N49°20.827′ E005°18.131′), which might be obscured in the early summer months by crops. Neither shelter is accessible. Shelters like this would normally be occupied by machine gun-crews and observers. If you look beyond the shelters, you can see the line of trees that mark the 316th Memorial (see Car Tour 2 Stand 3), which is built in the former Giselher Line.

Return to your car and continue along the D102 to Écurey. Once you have passed through Écurey take the first exit on the left on to a relatively narrow road. The exit is marked with a rather faded sign for Peuvillers. When you enter Peuvillers you come to a T-junction; turn right here. After two hundred metres the tarmac road changes into a gravel road. When you reach the line of trees take the right fork; follow this for

**Two German shelters in a field near Solferino Farm. Note the line of trees of the 316th monument in the distance on the left; the woods in the far distance mark the German Third Line, the *Volker Stellung*.**

**One of three water towers at *Bahnhof* Peuvillers, dating from 1915.**

about fifty metres until you see the **Peuvillers German water tower (5)** (N49°21.730′ E005°23.258′).

In preparation for the Battle of Verdun, which started on 21 February 1916, hundreds of artillery pieces were positioned to the north and west of Verdun. To assure a steady supply of ammunition, troops, building material and other supplies for the build up around Verdun, the Germans constructed several strategic railway lines. The lines, as well as the approach roads were, as far as possible, camouflaged. Consequently, warehouses and munition dumps were built in numerous places, as well as railheads and railway stations. Peuvillers Station measures approximately 1,600 metres in length and is fifty metres wide; the railway tracks were protected by two five metre high embankments. Other important logistical centres, amongst others, were Damvillers, Azannes, Dun-sur-Meuse and here at Peuvillers. What makes the rail head at Peuvillers stand out are the three water towers dating from 1915. With approximately forty ammunition trains arriving daily at its peak at *Bahnhof* Peuvillers, it was essential that the boilers of the steam engines could be replenished as soon as possible to make way for the next train.

Peuvillers then and now. Left: the former officers' quarters (1915-2020).

German graffiti on the back wall of one of the former officers' quarters: *Zur Mühle Stube* (To the Mill Bar).

166

The line, which was a branch line starting from Metz, then continued to Brandeville (see Stand 11) and Dun-sur-Meuse, where the Germans also built a bridge across the river. During the inter war years the line was repaired by French army engineers and connected from Dun-sur-Meuse to the main line at Vouziers. This was done to assure a steady flow of soldiers, weapons and other supplies to the Maginot Line.

Drive back to Peuvillers and enter the village; follow the main road. Before you cross the bridge, park your car on the left side of the road. The two houses in front of you are former **German officers quarters (6)** (N49°22.193' E005°23.633'). On 27 August 1914, the village (then 140 inhabitants, today fifty-five) was occupied by the German 14th Artillery Regiment, which quickly established a field hospital in the small church. The soldiers who died here were buried in an orchard across the road.

Just across the bridge (note the *lavoir* to the right as you cross), on the right, stands a **German bunker (7)** (N49°22.186' E005°23.656'). This was used to provide shelter from air raids; however, the village passed the war unscathed – so the church has an interesting medieval architectural history. It is in fact one of only three villages in the Meuse Department that have no war memorial because none of the civilian population nor soldiers that were born in Peuvillers were killed in battle or as a result of both the First and Second World Wars. The *Peuvillois* believe that they were protected by St. Gertrude, the patroness of the village. A statue dedicated to her stands in front of the town hall, and each year a procession is dedicated in her name. If you have some time to spare, it is worth the time to take a look at the beautiful parish church, which is dedicated to St. Gertrude. The first phase of this building dates to the 12th century; the bell tower was finally added in the 18th century. The first records of this charming village date from 1040. You can reach the entrance to the church from where you have parked your car. The key of the church can only be obtained at the Mairie, which is situated next to the church, on Friday afternoon. Inside the church, immediately on the left, there is a beautiful stained glass window dedicated to eight *Peuvillois* men who were imprisoned in camps in Germany in the Second World War; it is believed that they were safely guided through their ordeal by St. Gertrude.

Return to your car, cross the bridge and stop at **Peuvillers German Cemetery (8)** (N49°22.200' E005°23.684'). The first soldiers who died of wounds at the improvised hospital in the church were buried in a nearby orchard. The fighting at the Meuse crossings between the end of August and the start of September 1914 took a heavy toll for both the German and French armies. Another improvised cemetery was quickly started next to the communal cemetery. Later, these bodies were

A German shelter in Peuvillers.

exhumed and reburied in the orchard. However, most of the soldiers that are buried here died from wounds or disease during the battle of Verdun that raged in 1916; another wave of burials occurred in August and September 1917, when the French launched a major offensive to regain lost ground of the Verdun Offensive. After 1917 the cemetery fell out of use.

Neglected since the end of the war, the cemetery was in a bad state when in 1926 the German War Graves Commission started to raise funds for a formal entrance and a memorial. The monument is built according to the style that was in vogue at that time in southern Germany and depicts a mourning woman. Before new individual grave markers to replace the wooden crosses could be made, the world financial crisis of 1929 started. The events that ultimately led to the outbreak of the Second World War did not help progress either; work on the cemetery did not restart until 1969. In 1973 a major landscaping project turned the cemetery into what we see today; the final resting place of 967 German soldiers.

Go back to your car and leave Peuvillers; turn left onto the D905. After two kilometres, turn left onto an unnamed road in the direction of Lissey. After a few hundred metres you come to a large **German Memorial Stone (9)** (N49°22.918′ E005°23.674′) on the left. It is

*Above left*: Hauptmann Müller's headstone in Peuvillers German Cemetery.

*Above right*: Müller's original headstone was found in a heap of rubble near the church. After a period of training in November and December 1915, his regiment entrained on 25 December for the Verdun front. At the beginning of January 1916 the 13th Reserve Division, to which Müller's 39th Reserve Infantry Regiment belonged, was concentrated in the Damvillers area. In spite of the terrible winter conditions, it spent January and February in preparations for the attack. From 21 February to 10 March the division was heavily engaged in the Samogneux area. The fighting was so intense that the 13th lost fifty-one per cent of its infantry. Hauptmann Arthur Müller was seriously wounded in the first days of the offensive. Mortally wounded, he was evacuated from the battlefield to the *feldlazarett*, the field hospital at Peuvillers. He died on 23 February 1916. Müller was awarded both the Iron Cross first and second class. The headstone has now been donated to a museum.

possible to make a quick stop here, but beware of the traffic; although the road is very narrow it is very busy.

During the first half of the 1960s, young German volunteers from the German province of Hesse assisted the German War Graves Commission to build a stone wall around Lissey German Cemetery. On 17 July 1962 disaster struck as, on the way from Damvillers to the cemetery, their transport vehicle missed the bridge and crashed into the creek. Klaus Borg, 18 years old, and Volker Mang, 16 years old, were killed and sixteen other young people were injured in the crash. This memorial was erected to remember the two young men who were killed in the tragic accident. It is made from the same Vosges sandstone as that used in the cemetery.

About two kilometres from the latter monument, there is a signpost on the right side of the road that indicates **Lissey German Cemetery (10)** (N49°23.297′ E005°22.375′). At one point you enter a farm yard; do not worry, just follow the signs. After 400 metres you arrive at the gate of the cemetery.

**Memorial for Klaus Borg and Volker Mang, two young volunteers for the German War Graves Commission who died in a vehicle crash on 17 July 1962. NB! This small country road can be surprisingly busy.**

Because of the successful French counter-attack in the Verdun area in August/September 1917, German casualty clearing stations had to be moved away from the front. To be able to bury the men that were killed in the fighting and the men that succumbed of wounds in the field hospitals, a new cemetery was started. When you enter the cemetery, which is beautifully situated on the edge of Bois de Lissey, roughly the first half of the cemetery is dedicated to soldiers who died during this period. The cemetery is organized in such a way that men from the same unit or who died on the same date lie buried together.

In the centre of the cemetery the German War Graves Commission erected a round chapel made from sandstone imported from the Vosges. A heavy bronze gate provides access to the building. Inside the chapel eleven oak panels, bearing the names of (most) of the soldiers who lie buried here, are fixed to the wall. Interestingly, the names of soldiers that were found after the war and were reburied here are recorded at the bottom of (facing the door from inside the chapel) the left panel. The design of the chapel dates from 1926 when there were not yet uniform regulations for the lay out of German war cemeteries and is therefore unique on the Western Front.

The northern section of the cemetery is dedicated to the fallen of the Meuse-Argonne Offensive and the fighting on the right bank between September and November 1918. So far as the author knows, this cemetery likely has the largest number of burials that date from this period. Lissey German Cemetery holds 922 war dead, including nine Austrian-Hungarian soldiers and one Askari.

Before the war started, Camconobhza Nonoba, a young askari soldier from the German colony of German South-West Africa, accompanied his old commanding officer to Germany. When the war broke out, he became batman to this German officer and before long they were moved to the Western Front. When in 1915 the colony was lost to South Africa, Private Nonoba decided to continue to fight for his former colonial masters. Nonoba was killed on the battlefield of Verdun, presumably in October 1917. His unit remains unknown.

171

*Above and left*: The chapel at Lissey German Cemetery.

*Opposite, left*: Two German soldiers killed towards the end of the war.

*Opposite, right*: Camconobhza Nonoba, a young askari who fought with the Germans at Verdun.

As a black German soldier, there was no hope of returning to his fatherland that was now under South African rule (South Africa, since 1910 one of the dominions of the UK, fought on the allied side during the First World War. The best known of the actions of the troops that fought in Europe as the South African Brigade was at Delville Wood, on the Somme). After the war, former German South-West Africa came under the control of the UK and then was made a South African League of Nations mandate. The colony developed relatively peacefully under South African control rule, until the 70s and 80s, when there was a substantial independence movement, some of it armed. In 1990 the mandated territory became independent as Namibia. In total, 40,000 *Reichsneger* were drafted into the Imperial German Army to fight in the German African colonies; it remains unknown how many black soldiers made it to the Western Front nor how many were killed. Interestingly enough, Nonoba's name does not appear on the oak boards in the chapel.

Return to the main road and turn right in the direction of Lissey; from here, follow the D102 to Bréhéville and eventually to Brandeville. On entering the latter village, stop after you have passed the first house on the left; on the opposite side of the road stands a shed with a white corrugated iron roof. From here, you have a good then and now view of the site of the former **Brandeville Railway Centre (11)** (N49°23.656′ E005°18.383′). Apart from trees, gardens and a few new houses, the village and the church have not changed. For more information on the German railway system, see Stand 5.

The massive German railhead and logistical centre at Brandeville, then and now. The wartime photograph was probably taken from a high structure, such as a water tower.

Continue along the D102 until you come to a crossing; turn (second) right, in the direction of Murvaux. Just a kilometre from Brandeville, on the left side of the road, you see **Brandeville Necropole Nationale (12)** (N49°24.128′ E005°18.243′).

On the night of 27 August 1914 the garrison of Montmédy, about 2,700 strong, was ordered by General Joffre to retreat to Verdun to help with the defence of the city. The fortress of Montmédy was abandoned at nightfall, but only after supplies and armament were rendered useless to the enemy. Unfortunately, there were no suitable guides to lead the way and consequently about half of the garrison got separated from the rest and became lost. The next morning, most of the dispersed men took shelter in the wooded area between Mouzay and Damvillers; it was impossible to cross the Meuse, as the bridges between Dun and Mouzay were already in German hands.

To escape captivity, the French turned south to try to reach Verdun via Brandeville and Sivry. Alas, during the night of 28-29 August the French came across a large contingent of Germans in the woods near Brandeville. The French quickly decided to attack the Germans at first daylight to create an escape route to the south. At first, due to the element of surprise, the French inflicted serious losses on the Germans. However, they quickly recovered from the first shock and started to reorganize their troops and hit back. Before long, the action turned into disaster for the French; 600 were killed and the remaining 850 men were taken away to a work camp in Ingolstad, Germany. Only a few of the soldiers managed to reach Verdun.

The cemetery was originally started by the Germans, who buried the French in a mass grave. Today, 516 men lie buried here. The Battle of Brandeville, as it became known after the war, is commemorated each year on the last Sunday of August. The memorial was inaugurated on 30 August 1936; in the church of Brandeville, a stained glass window is dedicated to the tragic events that happened here.

Proceed along the D102; just before the road disappears into the forest, you see a **Maginot Line bunker (13)** (N49°20.505′ E005°15.351′) close to the right side of the road. Unfortunately, the bunker is not accessible; it stands on private property.

The Maginot Line, named after a French Minister of War, André Maginot, was a line of concrete fortifications, obstacles and weapon installations built by the French between 1929 and 1939 to deter invasion by Germany and force them to move around the fortifications. It was designed to protect France's borders with Italy, Switzerland, Germany, and Luxembourg.

**Brandeville Necropole Nationale.**

After the massive building program near the borders came to an end, the French Ministry of Defence decided in October 1939 (following German rearmament, the annexation of Austria and culminating in the invasion of Poland on 1 September 1939) that a second line of defences should be developed. Originally, nineteen self contained mini-fortresses were planned but only a few were built. The sub-zero temperatures during the winter of 1939-1940, material shortages and financial cut backs were the reason that only a few bunkers were built. None were finished before the German invasion of France on 10 May 1940.

Carry on along the D102 in the direction of Murvaux. Just a hundred metres after you have left that village there is an ornate crucifix atop a pedestal on the left of the road; at the time of writing there are two houses behind the monument, a pink and a yellow one. This is the site of the **Frank Luke Memorial (14)** (N49°17.909′ E005°07.031′), erected in honour of the American flying ace Frank Luke, who flew sorties during both the St. Mihiel and the Meuse-Argonne Offensives. His flying feats earned him the Medal of Honor and the Distinguished Service Cross. Between 12 and 29 September 1918, Frank 'the Arizona Balloon Buster' Luke was credited with shooting down fourteen balloons and four aircraft. However, on 29 September his luck ran out when he was shot down by the Germans.

French Maginot Line bunker dating from 1939.

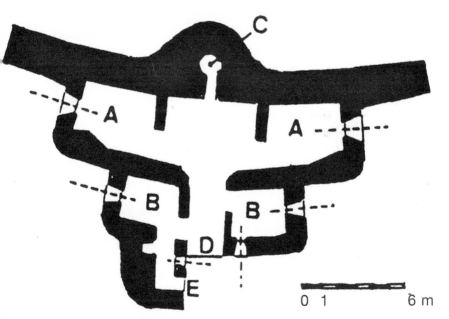

Schematic plan for this type of bunker: A. An aperture for a 25mm anti-tank gun; B. Machine gun; C. Observation post; D. Entrance for guns; E. Entrance for personnel

'September 29: Soon after Luke's commanding officer grounded him, Luke took off and headed for three balloons near Dun-sur-Meuse. As he headed towards the American Balloon Headquarters, he dropped a message that read: 'Watch three Hun balloons over the Meuse. Luke.' Minutes later a red glow filled the sky. Luke had downed the first balloon. What happened to Luke after that is still unknown. But he would never return from this mission.'

Luke was listed as missing in action. However, in January 1919, a body in an unmarked grave was exhumed after it had been buried by the Germans in an orchard opposite Murvaux Communal Cemetery on 30 September. From the inspection of the grave and interviews held with the locals of the town, it quickly became clear that this had to be Luke's grave.

'The undersigned, living in Murvaux, Department of the Meuse, certify to having seen on the 29th of September, 1918, toward evening an American aviator followed by an escadrille of Germans in the direction of Liny, descend suddenly and vertically toward the earth, then straighten out close to the ground and fly in the direction of Briers Farm, where he found a German captive balloon, which he burned. Then he flew toward Milly, where he found another balloon which he also burned in spite of incessant fire directed toward his machine. There he apparently was wounded by [ground fire]. From there he came back over Murvaux and still with his guns he killed six German soldiers and wounded as many more. Following this he landed and got out of his machine, undoubtedly to quench his thirst at the stream. [In fact, Frank Luke had been shot down by German machine gun fire from the ground, his plane was badly damaged and a bullet had pierced his lungs.] He had gone fifty yards when he saw the Germans come toward him. He still had the strength to draw his revolver to defend himself. [He fired a few shots.] A moment after, he fell dead following a serious wound he received in the chest. [He succumbed to wounds inflicted by the machine gun and had been forced to land.] Certify equally to having seen the German commandant of the village refuse to have straw placed in the cart carrying the dead aviator to the village cemetery. This same officer drove away some women bringing a sheet to serve as a shroud for the hero, and said, kicking the body: 'Get that out of my way as quickly as possible.' The next day the Germans took away the aeroplane, and the inhabitants also saw another American aviator fly very low over the town, apparently looking for the disappeared aviator.'

*Above left*: **The Frank Luke Memorial at Murvaux.**

*Above right*: **Luke's headstone in the Meuse-Argonne American Cemetery at Romagne.**

**Frank Luke in front of his fighter plane.**

179

It is also reported that the Germans took his shoes, leggings and money, and left his grave unmarked. The body at Murvaux was exhumed and Luke's remains were re-interred in Romagne. Between 12 and 29 September 1918, Frank Luke was credited with shooting down fourteen balloons and four planes. He flew sorties during the St. Mihiel Offensive as well as during the Meuse-Argonne Offensive. On 3 May 1919, Frank Luke Jr. was posthumously awarded the Medal of Honor. After the Second World World, Luke Air Force Base, located just west of Glendale, Maricopa County, Arizona, a major training base for the U.S. Air Force Air Education and Training Command, was named in his honour. Today, his grave can be found at the Meuse-Argonne American Cemetery, Plot A, Row 26, Grave 13, Romagne-sous-Montfaucon.

Continue along the D102 to Milly-sur-Bradon. When you reach the centre of the village, turn left onto the D102c and carry on to Lion-devant-Dun. Just before you enter the village, a rustic oak sign indicates *'Côte St Germain'*. Follow the signs and drive uphill. The road can be a little rough but is perfectly navigable in dry weather. At a certain point, you come to a fork (the only one along the route) in the road; turn left here. After a kilometre you arrive at a clearing. Park your car near the trees. On the site there are several picnic benches from where you can enjoy both your lunch and the magnificent view. In the middle of the clearing stands a **5ᵗʰ Division Monument (15)** (N49°24.620' E005°15.143'). Before and during the Great War there were no trees on Côte St Germain but after the war the hill was reforested. Today, we owe the clearing where the monument stands to the approximately 1,000 hang glider and delta wing clubs that come to this place from all over France to take off from this spur.

The impressive, four metres high, monument made from natural stone differs from the other memorials of the division, which are made from

concrete and are significantly smaller in size. The monument marks the capture of the Côte St Germain by 9 Infantry Brigade (60th and 61st Regiment and the 14th Machine Gun Battalion), commanded by Brigade General LJC Castner. The hill was wrested from the Germans after two days of fighting. When the German garrison was threatened by encirclement on 7 November, they retreated east.

From this point, which is also known as Hill 350, the Germans had commanding views ranging from the Argonne in the west to the Ardennes in the east. The hill is also marked on maps as the *Camp des Romains*; if you look over the edge of the plateau the earthworks that were part of the Roman defences can still be seen.

**The impressive, four metres high, 5th Division Memorial marker on Côte St. Germain.**

Drive back via Lion and Milly; from here it is easy to return to the main road, the D964 between Stenay and Verdun.

**The magnificent view looking north-west from Côte St. Germain.**

# Car Tour 4

# The Meuse Crossings: The 5th Division

*Duration: A full day's tour*
*Distance: Forty kilometres*
*Map: IGN 3111 SB Stenay*

This circular tour concentrates on the exploits of the US 5th Division, commanded by Major General Hanson E. Ely. From 12 October the division was engaged in heavy fighting around Cunel, Bantheville and Forêt Wood, north-east of Brieulles. In late October orders were received to prepare for the crossing of the River Meuse between Brieulles and Dun-sur-Meuse. On 3 November the first, albeit modest, crossing was made. The following days saw the rapid expansion of bridgeheads on the right bank. In this tour, we follow in the footsteps of the 5th Division and visit the various bridgeheads marked with a white stone obelisk-type monument. It has been said by cynics that a monument was placed at each spot where General Ely stopped to relieve himself; there are twenty-eight divisional markers in the Meuse, by a country mile far more monuments than any other division that was involved in the Meuse-Argonne Offensive. Eight of them are included in this tour. Unfortunately the literature, as well as contemporary maps, are not always conclusive about the exact locations of the crossings. Over time several of the markers have been moved to make way for road development and building projects. The most recent marker that was relocated (2015) is the one in Cléry-le-Petit.

There is a small supermarket/bakery in the centre of Brieulles. There are currently restaurants, a supermarket and a petrol station in Dun. Apart from the restaurants (open between 12.00 and 2.00 pm), there are no public toilets along the route. Bottled water, binoculars, a torch and sturdy boots are recommended.

## GPS coordinates for Car Tour 4

(1) 5th Division Monument l'Herminette    (N49°19.630′ E005°12.293′)
(2) 5th Division Monument Brieulles    (N49°20.123′ E005°11.211′)
(3) 10th Brigade Crossing    (N49°20.056′ E005°11.417′)

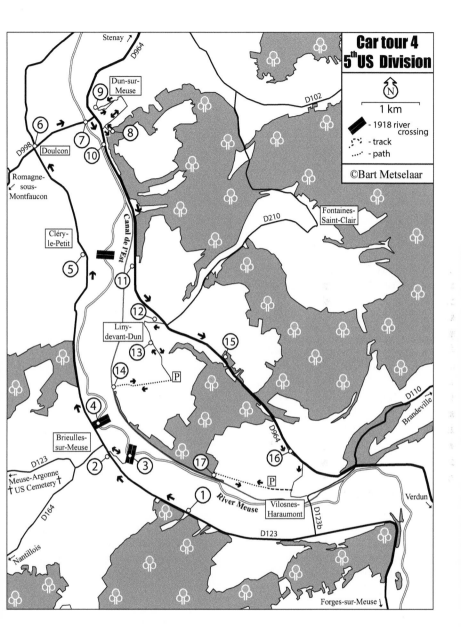

(4)  The first crossing            (N49°20.332′ E005°11.039′)
(5)  5th Division Monument Cléry-le-Petit  (N49°21.925′ E005°10.862′)
(6)  5th Division Monument Doulcon    (N49°22.871′ E005°10.153′)

| (7) | Pershing Memorial Bridge | (N49°23.120′ E005°10.969′) |
| (8) | Dun German Cemetery | (N49°23.010′ E005°11.180′) |
| (9) | Dun church panorama | (N49°23.195′ E005°11.020′) |
| (10) | 5th Division Monument | (N49°22.871′ E005°11.135′) |
| (11) | 5th Division Monument | (N49°21.803′ E005°11.589′) |
| (12) | Mairie, Liny, then and now | (N49°21.320′ E005°11.834′) |
| (13) | Liny-devant-Dun German Cemetery | (N49°21.140′ E005°11.799′) |
| (14) | Meuse crossing | (N49°20.710′ E005°11.260′) |
| (15) | 5th Division Monument Châtillon Wood | (N49°20.970′ E005°12.833′) |
| (16) | 5th Division Monument Vilosnes | (N49°20.140′ E005°13.802′) |
| (17) | Bunkers Kriemhild Line, Vilosnes/ Canal de l'Est | (N49°19.980′ E005°12.679′) |

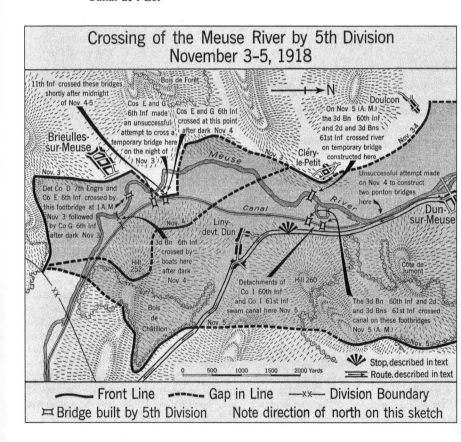

Crossing of the Meuse River by 5th Division
November 3–5, 1918

The tour starts at the **5ᵗʰ Division Monument at l'Herminette (1)** (N49°19.630' E005°12.293'), located along the busy D123 road between Vilosnes and Brieulles. The safest place to park your car is on the farm track that starts next to the monument. From here you have a great view across the plains of the Meuse towards the Meuse River and the Canal de l'Est behind it. Situated on the far side of these water channels and exactly opposite this memorial, the Kriemhilde Line continues on the right bank. Obscured by the trees of Châtillon Wood, two concrete shelters for machine-gun crews stand guard over the Meuse (see also stand 17). The 5ᵗʰ Division monument marks the right flank of 10 Brigade, a point reached on 1 November 1918. It is the southern boundary of the 5ᵗʰ Division and it also marks the boundary between the US 5ᵗʰ and the French 15ᵗʰ Colonial Divisions.

Turn your car on the farm track (there is more than enough space in front of the house) and turn right onto the D123, direction Brieulles. After two kilometres you enter the limits of Brieulles village; on your right there is a huge wholesale shop for combustibles – wood, fuel etc. On the left there is a lone, large willow tree. In front of this tree stands another **5ᵗʰ Division Monument (2)** (N49°20.123' E005°11.211'). You can park in front of the monument. This marker commemorates the fact that at dawn on 4 November 1918, opposite this point, the 6ᵗʰ Regiment was the first to reach the right bank.

Return to your car and continue on the D123 further into Brieulles for about fifty metres. Turn right at the sign 'Humblet, Scierie'. Cross the railroad and follow the road until you come to a T-junction (see map at the start of this tour). Park here and walk to the river. This is one of the sites of **10 Brigade's crossing (3)** (N49°20.056' E005°11.417') referred to on the 5ᵗʰ Division marker of stand (2). A second bridge was built some hundred metres to the left.

**The 5ᵗʰ Division boundary marker at L'Herminette, Brieulles.**

*Left*: The 5th Division marker (for 4 November), Brieulles.

*Opposite*: The crossing point opposite the quarry.

*Below*: The site where 10 Brigade made the crossing of the Meuse; the quarry is right opposite this point.

BRIEULLES    CLÉRY

CROSSINGS

On 4 November, after several other attempts had previously failed, the 3$^{rd}$ Battalion, assisted by a detachment of the 7$^{th}$ Engineers, crossed the river and the canal by ferrying the troops over in French pontoons found in Brieulles and by using rafts, comprising telegraph poles that were lashed together. A large abandoned quarry (see photo on p.101) on the right bank of the canal provided shelter for the troops. By 8.00 pm the entire battalion, some 1,100 men, were on the east side of the canal. The Germans were caught off guard and taken completely by surprise by the achievement. The bridgehead was quickly expanded in the direction of Châtillon Wood, visible on the right.

**The bend in the river at Brieulles, where the first successful crossing of the Meuse was made.**

Drive back to the D123 and turn right in the direction of Cléry. Just as you leave Brieulles, opposite the Brieulles campsite, are two very large, colourful flower pots; park on the side of the road, walk up the improvised stairs across the railway and follow the trail. This is the site where, on 3 November 1918, at 12.00 am, twenty men of the 7$^{th}$ Engineers made the **first successful attempt to cross the Meuse (4)**(N49°20.332′ E005°11.039′). A footbridge was constructed quickly and Company E, 6$^{th}$ Engineers, 3$^{rd}$ Division, were brought in to transport bridging equipment across the water plain to the Canal de l'Est some 200 metres further on. When the Germans discovered what was going on, a heavy barrage forced the engineers to withdraw. It was painfully obvious that during daylight any attempt was destined to fail. Later that day a reconnaissance patrol discovered a much safer place to bridge the canal a few hundred metres upstream. It was decided to await darkness before another attempt was made.

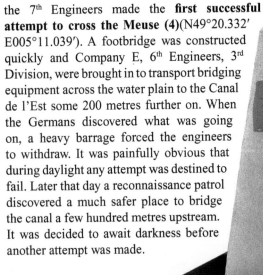

**The 5$^{th}$ Division marker in Cléry.**

Walk back to your car and carry on until you are at Cléry-le-Petit. The **5ᵗʰ Division Monument (5)** (N49°21.925′ E005°10.862′) stands next to the first house on the right of the road. The driveway that leads to the house doubles as a farm track, so there is no problem parking your car here; but be sure not to block the track. Walk along the track, past the wood piles until you see the river on the right, below you.

Cléry was liberated on 2 November by the 60ᵗʰ Regiment, 9 Brigade, 5ᵗʰ Division. On 4 November the Regiment was ordered to cross the Meuse at Cléry. The first attempt was made at Warinvaux Lock, northeast of Cléry, but the engineers were literally blown out of the water by the German defenders, who overlooked the proceedings from the Meuse Heights. It was decided to move back about a kilometre to the south (where you are now standing), where it was hoped they could make another attempt at building a bridge, this time out of the direct observation of the German gunners.

The 5ᵗʰ Division marker is built on a ridge that is roughly aligned northeast. The river flows at the far eastern tip of the ridge. At dawn on 5 November a footbridge was thrown across the river, protected from observation by the overhanging ridge. Companies of both the 60ᵗʰ and the 61ˢᵗ Regiments successfully went across it but were soon discovered by the Germans.

Captain Edward C. Allworth (1895-1966) of the 60ᵗʰ saw his company before him struggling to complete the crossing of the canal. Lieutenant Morrison was leading two platoons against the fortified slopes of Hill 260; the rest of the company was west of the canal facing the half-sunken bridges and a tornado of bullets. To save the day Captain Allworth mounted the canal bank and rallied the ranks. Calling on his men to follow, he plunged into the water, swam to the opposite shore and then dashed up the hill to the head of his company. Under the inspiration of his dynamic leadership, his men and some men of the 61ˢᵗ captured the broad, northern base of Hill 260 and seized over a kilometre of line

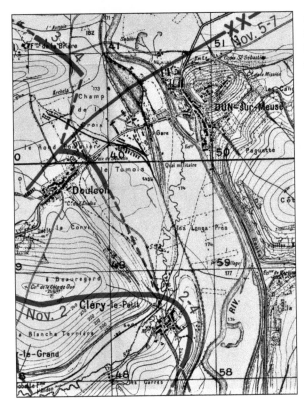

A contemporary map of the Cléry, Doulcon and Dun area.

from the enemy. In the process they overcame a profusion of machine-gun posts and took numerous prisoners, more than he had men in his command. In 1919 Allworth received the Medal of Honor, leaving the army in 1922 as a major.

After the German machine-gun positions were eliminated, the bridgehead was reinforced and the bridges repaired.

Return to your car, pass through Cléry (note the cheese factory that dominates the village; this is the factory where the world famous cheese, *La vache qui rit,* the smiling cow, is processed) and proceed along the D123 to Doulcon. Just as you enter Doulcon you come to a T-junction. Turn right onto the D998. As soon as you are on the D998 you will see the Mairie, the town hall, come up on your left; park here. Sandwiched between two minor but busy roads stands the Doulcon War Memorial; the **5th Division Monument (6)** (N49°22.871′ E005°10.153′) is located a few metres behind it. On this marker, the capture of Doulcon by Co C, 61st Regiment, is remembered. With the capture of this village on 3 November 1918, the Germans were pushed back to Dun. Once

190

across the Meuse the Germans dynamited the bridges and Pershing's hope of capturing them intact was gone. During the night of 5-6 November, the 7th Engineers, 5th Division, finished work on a heavy pontoon bridge that was suitable for artillery columns. As the American infantry on the right bank moved faster than the supply trains (or columns) – the fighting in the Meuse-Argonne on the left of the river had priority over operations on the right bank – there was a great shortage of artillery support, food, ammunition and medical supplies in the front line. Now, with armistice negotiations underway, it became very important to the American High Command to maintain the pressure on the Germans.

**Captain EC Allworth, Medal of Honor.**

Continue along the D998 in the direction of Dun. The third bridge along this road is the **Pershing Memorial Bridge (7)** (N49°23.120′ E005°10.969′). There is a parking space on the left, just after you have crossed the bridge and just before the (often very busy) T-junction. General Pershing characterized the crossing of the Meuse River in Dun on 4 and 5 November 1918 as 'one of the most brilliant military exploits by American forces during the war'. For what it is worth, the crossing of

**Doulcon War Memorial and the 5th Division marker.**

the Meuse was indeed an historical milestone for the AEF and therefore the *Society of the Fifth Division* funded the conversion of the bridge into a rather impressive memorial, which was dedicated on 4 July 1931. The bridge has since been destroyed twice, in 1940 by the French and in 1945 by the Germans; on both occasions the Society of the Fifth Division funded its renovation. On each side of the bridge there is a bronze plaque, one in French and one in English, that commemorate the exploits of the 5th Division.

Return to your car; at the T-junction, take a right turn onto the D964, direction Verdun. After about a hundred metres, take a left turn onto the Rue sous Vaux. After fifty metres you see the **Dun German Cemetery (8)** (N49°23.010′ E005°11.180′) sign on your right; turn onto the Chemin de Jumont and park in front of the cemetery.

This German cemetery was established as early as December 1914 and continued to be in use until September 1918, the start of the Meuse-Argonne Offensive. In September 1914, because of its extensive railway connections and loading docks, Dun was turned into a large field hospital. Between 25 September and 30 November 1914, more than 12,000 sick and wounded soldiers were treated here, casualties of the fighting in the Argonne Forest and at the Meuse crossings. With such a number

**The Pershing Memorial Bridge in Dun-sur-Meuse.**

**Dun German Cemetery.**

of men treated in the field hospitals in and around the village, a cemetery was soon needed. An extension was built when,  on 21 February 1916, the Germans started the Battle of Verdun. The huge influx of wounded that were treated during this ten month period means that more than half of the Germans that lie buried here date from the battle. A third wave of burials occurred in August and September 1917, when a massive, but localised, French counter offensive forced the Germans to retreat from Hill 304 and the Mort Homme. In 1926, the first horticultural works were started but the financial world crisis of 1929 brought that work to an end. The cemetery was finally finished between 1966 and 1971. There are 1,664 individual burials, including three Jewish (actually a surprisingly small number), two Austro-Hungarian and twenty-six unknown graves.

Head back to the Chemin de Jumont and turn right; follow this road until you come to a T-junction. Turn left and continue up hill to Dun Haut. Park (N49°23.219′ E005°11.071′) next to the fortress church, Notre Dame de Bonne Garde, dating from 1346, which was built over the foundations of a much older, tenth-century church. If you have time to spare, it is

*Above and below*: The Meuse crossing at Dun-sur-Meuse, then (note the pontoon bridge) and now, 1918-2020.

worthwhile to walk around the medieval ramparts and visit the church, which, more or less, survived the war. *Opening hours of the church: July and August, 14.00-18.00 pm.* To appreciate the **Dun Meuse crossing panorama (9)** (N49°23.195′ E005°11.020′), walk to the front of the church and follow the railing to the left up to where the large information panels stand. From here you have a magnificent view across the Meuse Valley. Look to the left at the river below; nearly all of the 5th Division Meuse crossings were made in this area. The first crossing at Dun was made a little to the south of where the Canal de l'Est and the Meuse join, see the 'then' picture on page 196. Brieulles is on the far left in this photograph; the television mast near Montfaucon is visible in the centre. Below the church you can see the three bridges of Dun and the D998 that runs to Doulcon, see Stand 6; this is the main road to Romagne, Varennes and the Argonne Forest.

Drive back, via a one way street, to the D964 and turn left in the direction of Verdun. After fifty metres you will come to a **5th Division Monument (10)** (N49°22.871′ E005°11.135′), which stands in front of the local police station, the Gendarmerie Nationale. You can park in front of it. This marker recalls the building of a heavy pontoon bridge by the 7th Engineers that was used by various artillery and supply trains, starting from 6 November. See also Stand (6) and the photograph at Stand (9).

About two kilometres further along the D964, on the right side of the road and behind a railing, stands another **5th Division Monument (11)** (N49°21.803′ E005°11.589′). You cannot park here, but on the other side of the road there is private road that leads to a transformer station; you can briefly park here. You are opposite Stand (5). See the photograph on page 196.

A kilometre further along the D964 lies Liny-devant-Dun. Once within the village limits, take the first road on the right. After fifty metres, you will come to the **Mairie (12)** (N49°21.320′ E005°11.834′) of Liny on your right and across the little stream that flows through the village. Take a look at the then and now photographs in the book (p.197). During the war German officers occupied the building.

Proceed along this road and turn left as soon as you see the *Deutsches Friedhof* sign. Drive up hill and park in

A Signals Corpsman at work running telephone wires across the River Meuse; note the pontoon bridge behind him. The fortified church (dating from 1346) of Dun-sur-Meuse stands on top of the high ground in the background. It was a quite remarkable survivor of the fighting. See p.194 for the reverse view, taken from outside the church.

front of **Liny-devant-Dun German Cemetery (13)** (N49°21.140′ E005°11.799′). On 30 August 1914, after being spotted by a French observation team that had taken up position in the bell tower of the church at Montfaucon, French batteries opened fire on German batteries and infantry that were massing in the valleys surrounding Liny. The German gunners moved their guns into position and before

196

*Above and below*: **The Mairie of Liny, then and now, 1916-2020.**

long a serious artillery battle started. The French had prepared a gun line on the heights north of Brieulles running from Forêt Wood in the direction of Nantillois and Cunel. The German 12th Division, ordered to take Cunel, Nantillois and Montfaucon, was consequently literally shot to pieces. On 31 August fresh and heavier artillery units arrived. The next days were the scene of bloody artillery battles and heavy clashes between the French and German artillery and infantry. Eventually the French retreated south and gave up Montfaucon, but the Germans would never reach Verdun.

197

The cemetery, which holds 449 graves, was begun in February 1916 at the start of the Battle of Verdun. Like Dun, the village was turned into a large casualty clearing station. Consequently, the bulk of the burials here date from that period, although there are also some headstones dating from the start of the Meuse-Argonne Offensive.

Interestingly, this cemetery was designed by architect Robert Tischler and was to serve as a blueprint for all German war cemeteries in France. This perhaps explains why to some it has an unusually 'complete' feel about it for a German cemetery. Every design and feature had to be run through a French building commission: the width and height of buildings, symbols that were allowed to be used, building material etc; it seemingly took forever to come to a mutual agreement before work on Liny German Cemetery was finished. The shortage of foreign exchange in 1933 put an early end to the project. Meanwhile, work had also started on Romagne German Cemetery, but, apart from the memorial building, it has never been completed the way it was intended. After the Second Word War, and with hundreds of thousands more soldiers to be buried, a much more sober design was chosen.

Facing the entrance of the cemetery, follow the track that runs along its left for about 500 metres uphill until you come to a T-junction. Take a right turn and follow this track as long as it is serviceable and you have room to turn your car. Do not drive on the farmer's field. In wet conditions, go on foot and continue to the edge of the Canal de l'Est. It is not possible to reach the canal by car. Here, in the early morning of 4 November, at the bottom of Moyenvaux Ravine, the canal was crossed for the first time, making it the first successful crossing to the right bank by the 5th Division. The quarries, now rather eroded, are visible to the left and right on this side of the canal and were used to stock ammunition and, naturally, for shelter.

Take a look at the then and now **Meuse crossing/footbridge (14)** (N49°20.710' E005°11.260') photograph (p.201); the remains of the iron footbridge that was blown by the Germans are clearly visible in the 'then' photograph. On the other side of the canal, a platform that led to the pontoon bridges is still visible. Although the facing of the canal on this side has been replaced, you can still see that the canal has been

Deutscher Soldatenfriedhof 1914-18
LINY - DEVANT - DUN
Cimetière Militaire Allemand

*Above*: **Liny German Cemetery.**

*Right*: **The German eagle stands guard at the entrance.**

widened here; this was done before the war to create a small harbour to load limestone into barges. An anonymous eyewitness explains the problems that the Americans faced:

'One bridge was completed shortly after midnight and the other was finished about 2.00 am. A patrol of eight men was just about to across to the German side when the Boche woke up. From both flanks and from two nests directly in front burst forth a terrific fire, sweeping the bridges and combing the canal bank. The party on the bridge was forced back by the hail of bullets and efforts were concentrated on silencing the resistance. Stokes mortars dropped their explosives on the hill and rifle grenades were directed towards strongholds. The entire ammunition supply was finally exhausted, yet the machine guns had not been silenced; their emplacements could not be accurately spotted in the darkness. More Stokes ammunition was sent for but did not arrive in time. All the rifle grenades in the support companies were collected and sent forward, with extra rifle and Chauchat ammunition. Lieutenant Colonel Hodges crossed the river and took command of the firing line to make one last supreme effort before daylight. The canal bank was suddenly manned and a terrific fire brought to bear on the enemy with every weapon at hand. By this time the enemy was fully aware of what was going on and all his forces were concentrated on the defence of the canal. The bridge was so constantly and thoroughly covered that crossing was utterly impossible.'

Just as on the previous day, the remainder of that day was spent hugging the canal bank. One of the two bridges was destroyed and sunk by German artillery fire, the other damaged. At dusk on 4 November, obscured by fog and after a terrific but short American bombardment, the east bank was taken and the machine guns in the quarries silenced.

Walk back to your car and return to the main road, the D964 in Liny. Once here take a right turn in the direction of Verdun, Vilosnes and Consenvoye. After a kilometre, you will see a parking space on the left. Park at the **5th Division Monument (15)** (N49°20.970′ E005°12.833′). This monument marks the establishment of a bridgehead that was started on 4 November at the canal, see Stand (14) and the liberation of Châtillon Wood. This marker stands directly opposite the 5th Division marker described at Stand (1) that marks the divisional boundary between the US 5th and the French 15th Colonial Divisions. However, the American attack had been so successful that the Americans started for Vilosnes in the French sector, two kilometres south of this point, to assist the French to establish a bridgehead of their own.

Return to your car and continue to Vilosnes. Just before Vilosnes, turn right into a parking area. This little stretch of road is the original road to Verdun before it was replaced by the current one. Therefore, it is one of the rare **5th Division Monuments (16)** (N49°20.140′ E005°13.802′) that stands on its original 1919 location. The marker commemorates the attack on the German garrison in Vilosnes on 6 November by the 6th Regiment, 10 Brigade, thereby permitting the French finally to cross

*Above and below*: The Meuse crossing at Liny, then and now, 1918-2020.

the Meuse and establish a bridgehead. From here, you have an excellent view across the Meuse Valley. Vilosnes church steeple and the bridge across the river and canal are clearly visible. The wooded ridge on the other side is La Ville Wood. These woods were used by the Germans for billeting, and numerous barrack camps were built in them.

When you are back on the D964, turn right after fifty metres in the direction of Vilosnes. When you come to the fork in the road turn right. From here, you take the second track (Rue Haute) on the right. The approximately one kilometre long track is only accessible for 4x4 cars with a high clearance. When you come to the end of the track, look to your left. This is where the Germans built two **Kriemhild Line shelters** (17) (N49°19.980′ E005°12.679′) in 1917 for the machine gunners that were guarding approaches to the Meuse and the canal. The bunkers are each of a simple design; two entrances lead to a small 3x3 metre chamber.

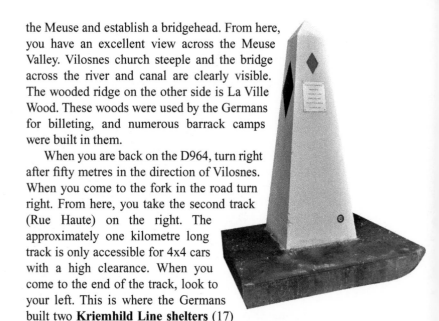

**View from the right bank to the left bank at Vilosnes; note the church steeple and bridges.**

**A Kriemhilde Line bunker near Vilosnes.**

They are accessible, but at your own risk. If there are cows in the field where the shelters are built (it is an old chalk quarry) do not enter; in this part of France there is invariably a bull present among the cows.

Once back in your car, turn around and, back to the village, turn right. When you come to the canal, turn left and continue to a main road, the D123b. A left turn takes you to Sivry, Consenvoye and Verdun, a right turn over the river and back to Brieulles, the starting point of this tour.

# Walk 1

# The 26th and 79th Divisions: Ormont Hill

*Duration: A full morning's tour.*
*Distance: 6 kilometres*
*Map: IGN 3112 ET Verdun*

This circular walk concentrates on Ormont Hill, or Hill 360, as the Americans called it. Defended by the 1st Landwehr Division, Ormont Hill held out until 9 November. By that time, it had been under attack by the French 18th Division, the US 26th Division and finally the US 79th Division. This walk is not designed as an in-depth study of the fighting that took place on the hill but to get a good understanding of the conditions of the terrain; a wooded hilly area crammed with observation posts, bunkers, trenches, shell holes and mud. It shows the nightmarish conditions in which the French, Americans and Germans were fighting.

Should you be in need of fuel or provisions, Damvillers is only a few kilometres away from the starting point; Crépion, a tiny village, a hamlet, is at the foot of Hill 360. There are no public restrooms along the route. As usual, walking boots, binoculars and a bottle of water are recommended. Ticks, the possible carriers of Lyme's Disease, are common in forested areas; it is advisable to wear long trousers and to check yourself for ticks when you are back in your accommodation. Be aware of rusted metal and do not pick up anything that even remotely looks like an explosive. After all, you are visiting a major former war zone and accidents still happen. In summer, a good brand of insect repellent is indispensable.

**A NOTE ON FOOTWARE:** Even in summer, Ormont Wood can be muddy; in the autumn, winter and spring it is extremely muddy. Therefore it is strongly recommended that you wear rubber boots.

**A NOTE ON GPS:** This walk can best be made with the aid of a GPS device; points 6 to 13 in particular are difficult to find without one, most notably in summer, when most of the sites are obscured by foliage.

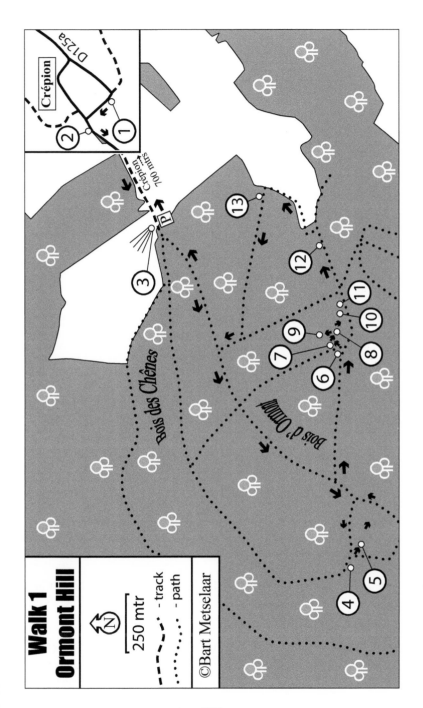

# GPS coordinates for Walk 1.

| | | |
|---|---|---|
| (1) | Crépion pillbox | (N49°18.482′ E005°23.395′) |
| (2) | Crépion German stone stairs | (N49°18.515′ E005°23.295′) |
| (3) | Panorama Molleville Farm | (N49°18.161′ E005°22.444′) |
| (4) | German well/troughs | (N49°17.718′ E005°21.419′) |
| (5) | Ormont Farm ruins | (N49°17.683′ E005°21.143′) |
| (6) | Destroyed pillbox/trenches | (N49°17.734′ E005°21.978′) |
| (7) | Trenches/fire step/ wire | (N49°17.748′ E005°21.980′) |
| (8) | Masonry trench walls | (N49°17.734′ E005°22.077′) |
| (9) | Observation platform | (N49°17.766′ E005°22.052′) |
| (10) | Observation Post 1 | (N49°17.721′ E005°22.182′) |
| (11) | Observation Post 2 | (N49°17.729′ E005°22.221′) |
| (12) | Remains of concrete shelter | (N49°17.772′ E005°22.422′) |
| (13) | German cemetery | (N49°17.919′ E005°22.576′) |

This tour starts at Crépion, a hamlet with about forty inhabitants; the first two points of interest are situated in the village and can be visited by car. The only way to reach Crépion is via the D905, which runs from Damvillers to Azannes. From the D905 you continue onto the D125a to Crépion. When you reach the village, do not be intimidated by the road sign with the blue and white arrow that points to the right; keep driving straight on, as it is not a one way street. After a hundred metres follow the road to the right and stop at the water troughs. On the right side of the troughs you can see the **Crépion pillbox (1)** (N49°18.482′ E005°23.395′). According to the locals, this concrete shelter was used by the officers who were billeted nearby to shelter against air raids and incoming gunfire. Facing the troughs, you can already see the impressive Hill 360 in the distance.

**Troughs and bunker in Crépion.**

**Entrance to the former German cemetery in Crépion.**

Proceed in the same direction; when you come to the church turn left. After a mere thirty metres, you see the stone stairs of a **former German cemetery (2)** (N49°18.515′ E005°23.295′) on your right. After the war the graves were removed by the French and the good quality Teutonic masonry stairs are all that is left to indicate its existence.

Follow the farm track until you reach the forest. You are now at Ormont Wood, or Hill 360, as it became popularly known among American soldiers. Park your car in front of the barrier (N49°18.154′ E005°22.449′).

Just where the farm track reaches the woods, the track forks. From this track you have a magnificent view of **Molleville Farm (3)** (N49°18.161′ E005°22.444′). The farm buildings can be seen at the bottom of a clearing that is surrounded by woods. Take a look at the photograph in the book. As you can see, the American right flank was threatened by the Germans and artillery fire from Hill 360, which could hit them from behind. Because of the stubborn German resistance on hills like these, and the gun batteries that sheltered behind them, the American attack quickly became bogged down. The Molleville Ravine/ Clearing stayed under German control until the beginning of November.

Go back to the barrier and walk along the chalk track for about 1.5 kilometres. At a certain point (use the map or GPS) a trail starts on your right. When you follow this trail for about sixty metres down hill, the path is crossed by a little stream. Go left and follow the stream until you are at the **German trough (4)** (N49°17.718′ E005°21.419′). Behind the trough are several artificial water basins; these were used to refill canteens, for washing clothes and bathing.

Walk back through the wood, parallel with the track you followed to reach the trough. After about forty metres and roughly on the same alignment with the trough are the ruins of **Ormont Farm (5)** (N49°17.683′ E005°21.143′). Apart from large piles of overgrown rubble, only one battered wall of the farm remains. In German possession for most of the war, the farm and barns were totally destroyed by artillery fire during the Battle of Verdun in 1916.

Now return to the main chalk track; this can easiest be reached by the path that leads to the German trough. Once back on the main track turn left

**A German-built trough near Ormont Farm.**

208

**All that remains of Ormont Farm today (2020).**

**Ormont Farm under German occupation (*Collection Wim Degrande*).**

and continue for 200 metres until a ten metres wide track starts on your right hand. It is easy to identify by the large concrete gutter that is built across it to prevent erosion of the main track. **NOTE:** Use your GPS device to find the next stands. All points of interest are on the LEFT side of the track.

*Above left*: **A destroyed dugout, Ormont Wood.**

*Above right*: **The remains of a trench with a concrete parapet and fire step.**

*Above left*: **Detail of shrapnel holes in a so-called Heinrich corrugated iron plate.**

*Above right*: **Remains of a masonry trench.**

After 600 metres, (a tree bearing a green/white square '14' sign on the right side of the track), enter the trench for five metres and go right. This is the site of one of the many **destroyed pillboxes /trenches (6)** (N49°17.734′ E005°21.978′). Continue along this trench for another twenty-five metres until you are at a **concrete fire step (7)** (N49°17.748' E005°21.980'). From the trench floor you can get up onto the fire step, originally a two feet high ledge built out from the trench wall, used to fire a rifle over the parapet.

Take a good look at the trees; although the wood has been reforested twice since the war, the loggers have avoided cutting the surviving trees from the war. The simple reason for this is the shrapnel that is embedded in the trees. Even today, strands of wire hang from the trees. A little further along this trench a twisted 'Heinrich' corrugated metal sheet can be seen, riddled by shrapnel. These sheets were used all along the front line to build shelters but were also used as formwork to construct bunkers. If you would like, it is possible to follow the trench system for some distance, however, note that the author (without the aid of GPS) lost his way twice while preparing this walk.

Return to the main track and turn left; after 170 metres, leave the track and turn left. Follow the trench system until you come to a **masonry trench (8)** (N49°17.734′ E005°22.077′). As you can see, the trench has a parapet that is built from stone, collected when the Germans were digging the trenches. Originally the trenches were fitted with wooden walls, duckboards, deep shelters and concrete observation posts.

About fifty metres further on, on roughly on the same alignment as the masonry trench, you will find the remains of an extremely rare German **observation platform (9)** (N49°17.766′ E005°22.052′). The platform was built by connecting two trees with iron girders that were then bolted together to create the basis for a wooden observation platform. Of course, the wooden platform has long gone, but the trees, although toppled over by a major storm in 2006, are still there. Incredibly, one of the trees still has metal steps attached to it. During the war there were many observation posts like this, sometimes even with multiple storeys; but, naturally, few have survived today.

Return to the main track and turn left. After some 170 metres, there is concrete **observation post 1 (10)** (N49°17.721′ E005°22.182′) hidden

**The toppled observation post in January 2020.**

**Observation post nr 1, with its roof blown off.**

in the side of the trench that runs parallel with the track. This side of Ormont Hill (or Hill 360) looks down on Death Valley and was a regular target of the American artillery.

A few dozen metres further along the same trench stands **observation post 2 (11)** (N49°17.729′ E005°22.221′). The bunker is still intact and has room for one man only. There is a doorway at the back and this is connected to a deep trench. Its elevated position guarantees a magnificent

*Above*: **A German concrete shelter on the edge of Ormont Wood (Stand 12).**

*Left*: **Observation post nr 2.**

212

view across the battlefield in the direction of Death Valley, Haumont Wood and Haumont-près-Samogneux. Of course during the war there were no trees blocking the view and the observation post was heavily camouflaged.

Proceed along the track for another 300 metres; hidden in the trench are the remains of a **concrete shelter (12)** (N49°17.772′ E005°22.422′). Especially in summer, profuse undergrowth makes it hard to identify or reach the bunker. Save for the outer walls, the structure has been completely destroyed.

Now continue along the track until you reach the edge of the forest; turn left and follow its edge for about 500 metres until a trail starts on your left. Please make sure that you do not damage the farmer's crops. Walk on for fifty metres; a former **German cemetery (13)** (N49°17.919′ E005°22.576′) is on your right. In between the trenches and dugouts lie two German headstones with their backs on the ground. The bodies were removed by the Germans before the end of the war but some of the headstones were left behind. They are barely legible and therefore the engraving on the stones are included in full here.

The left stone reads: *Hier ruht ein unser Kamerad, Unuffz. Wilhelm Tielz, Gefallen 23-2-16, 103 G.P.?* and the right stone reads: *Hier ruht in Frieden unser lieber Kamerad Bruno Zeidler, IR 155, 23-2-16.*

The 7th West Prussian Infantry Regiment No. 155th was part of the 10th Reserve Division and stayed in the Meuse area from the start of the war until the end of 1917. In February 1916 the 155th was held in reserve but in spite of this a few battalions were engaged during the first phase of the Battle of Verdun that started on the ice cold and snowy 21 February 1916. Tielz and Zeidler, both of 10 Company, were killed only two days after the battle started. Unfortunately, and in spite of intensive research, almost no additional information could be found, except that Zeidler was born in Althöfchen, Schwerin, and Tielz in Hörde, near Dortmund. The names are not recorded in the archives of the German War Grave Organization, the *Volksbund Deutsche Kriegsgräberfürsorge.*

Go back to the trail, turn right and walk on until you reach the chalk track. Turn right and walk back to your car.

**The grave marker of Wilhelm Tielz, January 2020.**

# Henry Gunther Tour

# The last American soldier killed in the war

*Duration: Approximately two hours*
*Distance: Ten kilometres*
*Map: IGN 3112 ET Verdun*

Before the start of this tour it needs to be made clear that the
monument erected on the Côte de Chaumont in 2008 does
**not** mark the spot where Gunther was killed; it commemorates
the fact that he is officially described as the last American soldier
to be killed in action in the Great War. It also remembers the fact that the
314th Regiment, 79th Division, made the deepest thrust into the German
line on the entire front east of the Meuse. In addition, there has been
much speculation, which continues today, especially on line, about how
and why Gunther died. One popularly held opinion is that he willingly
sacrificed himself to prove his loyalty to his country. This sounds very
noble; but the truth is that no one knows what was going through his
mind on that fateful November morning.

The tour starts at the Henry Gunther Memorial on the Côte de
Chaumont ridge, beyond Chaumont-devant-Damvillers. From here,
there are stunning views that show the final positions of the 79th Division
on the last day of the war. The last two points of interest of the tour are
visited by car and take you to the approximate spot where Gunther was
killed.

Except for Damvillers, which is about six kilometres from Chaumont-
devant-Damvillers, there are no toilets or restaurants along the way. A
pair of binoculars and a bottle of water are useful additions to your visit.
In summer, it is advisable to use a good brand of insect repellant.

### GPS coordinates for the Henry Gunther Tour.

| | |
|---|---|
| (1) Henry Gunther Monument | (N49°18.928′ E005°25.749′) |
| (2) Panorama Côte de Morimont | (N49°18.928′ E005°25.749′) |
| (3) Panorama Meuse Heights | (N49°18.928′ E005°25.749′) |
| (4) Panorama Côte de Romagne | (N49°18.947′ E005°26.366′) |

(5) Bunkers and trenches Hill 328     (N49°18.919′ E005°25.449′)
(6) The field where Gunther was killed     (N49°17.729′ E005°25.957′)
(7) German front line at Thil Wood     (N49°17.881′ E005°26.520′)

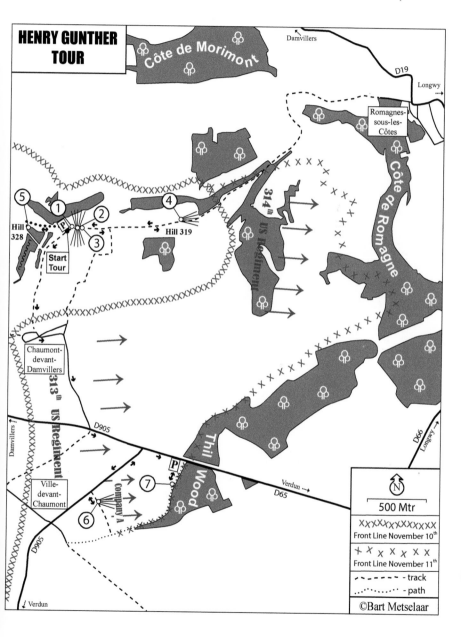

### Sergeant Henry Gunther (1895–1918)

Henry Nicholas Gunther was born on 6 June 1895 in Baltimore, Maryland. Aged 23 and of German origin, Gunther worked as a book keeper and clerk at the National Bank of Baltimore. Drafted into the army (313th Regiment, 79th Division) in September 1917, he was quickly promoted to supply sergeant, responsible for clothing. The 313th arrived in France in July 1918. Gunther was to marry his girlfriend Olga Grueb when he returned home. Following the censor's interception of a letter critical of army life, in which he reported on the miserable conditions at the front

**Henry Gunther (1895-1918).**

and advised a friend to try anything to avoid being drafted, Gunther was reduced to a private. His company (Co A) participated in the capture of Montfaucon (27 September) and Nantillois (28 September) during the first phase of the Meuse-Argonne Offensive. As bad luck would have it, he was killed on the last day of the war near Ville-devant-Chaumont and became known as the last American to die in World War One.

It is striking that, in spite of ignoring direct orders from his commanding officer, Gunther was posthumously restored to his former rank of sergeant and awarded both the Distinguished Service Cross and a Divisional Citation for Gallantry in Action. In France, he is remembered with a memorial constructed near the place where he was killed. Gunther was one of 320 Americans killed and more than 3,240 seriously wounded in the last hours of the war. It has

been estimated that there were about 11,000 fatalities (a large number of soldiers, almost certainly the great majority, died from the Spanish Flu) on the Western Front on 11 November 1918. In 1923, Gunther's body was returned to Baltimore and buried in Section W of the Holy Redeemer Cemetery.

### Friday 8 and Saturday 9 November

On Friday 8 November, the 15th French Colonial Division cleared the area between Sivry and Étraye of the last German resistance. To the east, the Germans had retreated to a line beyond the Thinte Creek. This meant that the 79th Division had no enemy to the north and could turn to the east after establishing liaison with the French 15th Colonial Division. Therefore, the 79th Division was ordered by General Claudel, Commander of II French Corps, to 'exercise its pressure' in the direction of Wavrille, Étraye, Réville and Écurey. The night of 7-8 November was used to move the troops to their new positions. At noon the leading battalions started the advance. Patrols sent out before the attack started

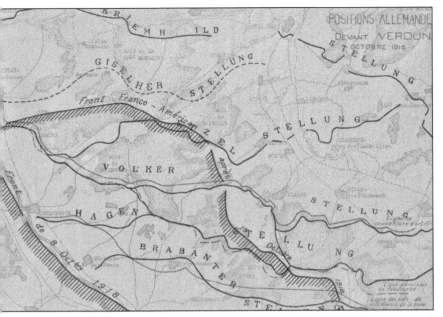

**German defences on the right bank, October-November 1918.**

reported the area in front of the division deserted by the Germans. Apart from occasional shelling and without much opposition, the line Écurey, Réville, Étraye, Wavrille Wood, Bélieu Wood and Ormont Wood was reached; the Meuse Heights in this sector were almost cleared of Germans and their artillery. However, the Etzel and Kriemhield Lines, running from Étraye, Damvillers and Chaumont to Romagne-sous-les-Côtes, had still to be dealt with.

During the night of 8-9 November new orders were issued to the 314th Regiment, 79th Division, to launch an attack in the general direction of Romagne-sous-les-Côtes. The left flank boundary was the line Étraye-Côte d'Horgne (often misspelt in American books as Côte d'Orne), the right flank Ormont Wood, Moirey (exclusive) and Azannes. Night patrols which slipped down in the unknown valleys ahead reported that there was no sign of the enemy on the west bank of the Thinte Creek. At 6.00 am, the 314th Regiment attacked; little opposition was encountered and by 10.15 am Crépion and Wavrille were occupied, including the heavily contested Ormont Hill/Hill 360. When the advance continued onto the Woëvre Plains, resistance stiffened; German shell fire once more made it impossible to continue the advance. With nightfall, defensive positions west of the Thinte Creek were taken up.

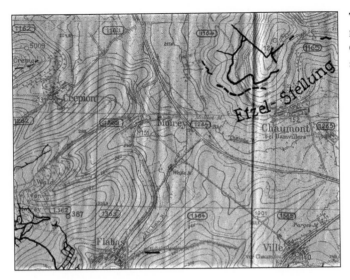

**Trench map of the Chaumont area, 1918.**

In his dugout near Molleville Farm, General Kuhn sent out the following report to General Claudel:

'My infantry held up at close of operations today in front of Côte 361 and Côte 328. The troops progressed halfway up the western slope of Côte 328; unable to proceed any further. These hills are strongly defended by wire, machine guns, some 77mm guns and the equivalent of 37mm canon. Probably defended by comparatively few men. I do not believe the hill can be taken by frontal attack. Possibly a concentric attack from the north, west and south might succeed.'

### Sunday 10 November, the attack on Hill 328 and Hill 319.

At 4.00 am the 52nd Field Artillery Brigade started a two hour preliminary barrage on Hill 328; at 6.00 am Second Battalion/314th stormed up the slope, followed by the First Battalion in support. Twenty-five minutes later, greatly assisted by heavy fog, Hill 328 was taken without opposition. Three bewildered Germans were captured in a dugout; according to their information all four companies, some 200 men, of the 31st Regiment, 1st Landwehr Division, had fled during the bombardment and apparently they were the only ones left. The attack was pressed east towards Hill 319, but this was held up by machine-gun fire from Chaumont and Hill 319 (Côte de Chaumont). They were also fired upon from Hill 356, the Côte de Horgne. Unfortunately, the 26th Division, which was supposed to take Chaumont-devant-Damvillers, a village a

Observers on Hill 328 watching the fire in Ville-devant-Chaumont.

View from Chaumont towards Hill 328 (left) and Hill 319 (right).

**View of Main Street, Chaumont, after the battle. The German sign reads:** *Kap der guten Hoffung,* **Cape of Good Hope.**

little south of the ridge between Hill 328 and Hill 319, was stopped at Ville-devant-Chaumont by an intense German barrage. No help could be expected from the 26th Division. Therefore, several platoons of the First and Second Battalion, 79th Division, were sent out to outflank the German positions on Hill 319 and in the process they mopped up the German resistance in the village of Chaumont-devant-Damvillers; but heavy machine-gun fire from Hill 319 forced them to evacuate the village. Meanwhile, the situation on the ridge became untenable; the Americans were fired upon from three sides and strafed by German planes. Without the help of artillery and Allied planes to drive off the German aviators it proved impossible to take Hill 319. Finally, at 3.50 pm, a thirty minute concentration of 'heavies' on the German strong points did the trick; as the artillery barrage lifted, eight companies of the 314th Regiment rushed Hill 319 'and found that the resistance had been literally blown away'. At about 7.45 pm, the hill was taken; the Americans prepared for the worst and dug in. Suppressing fire on the hills (d'Horgne, Morimont, Côte de Romagne) surrounding the 314th continued throughout the night.

### Monday 11 November.

On the American right wing, the final assault of the war in this sector was carried out by the 26th and 79th Divisions. The Germans were pushed back from the Meuse Heights and retreated to a line running from Damvillers to Romagne-sous-les-Côtes. They were ordered to hold the Kriemhild Line at all costs.

During the night of 11 November, the 313th Regiment was called up from Death Valley and was marched to Ormont Hill at Crépion to reinforce the 314th, 315th and 316th Regiments, 79th Division. The First Battalion of the 313th Regiment, including Company A, in which Gunther served, was ordered to advance east from Ville-devant-Chaumont in the direction of Azannes, an important German logistics centre. The 313th was sandwiched between the 314th Regiment on the left and the 26th Division on the right. Earlier that morning, Chaumont-devant-Damvillers and Ville-devant-Chaumont were mopped up and the attack continued towards Côte de Romagne (the 314th) and Azannes (the 313th). When Company A advanced across a field on the right side along the D65 to Thil Wood, a heavy German barrage was put down but fortunately, according to several eye-witnesses, 'the marshy ground absorbed much of the impact of the explosions'.

Emerging from a bank of fog, descending a rise in the field that they were in, Company A, including Private Gunther and his friend Sergeant Ernest Powell, were suddenly surprised by German machine gunners who were entrenched in the edge of Thil Wood. Gunther fired a few rounds but the Germans held their fire; instead, they tried to wave him off. Gunther continued his advance in spite of Sergeant Powell's orders to stay put. At 10.59 am, although it is very unlikely that anyone under the chaotic circumstances at the time looked at his watch, one of the gunners opened fire; Gunther was struck in the left temple and died instantly. Popular stories about Germans shouting at Gunther to warn him should be regarded with some suspicion; according to many eyewitness accounts, the noise here during the last thirty minutes of the war was ear-shattering. Another thing that must be taken into consideration is the fact that the average American soldier was oblivious to the day, let alone the hour, of the Armistice.

Corporal Oscar Lubchansky, Co G, a clerk with the 2nd Battalion, 313th Regiment and grandfather of Gene Fax (author of the excellent book on the 79th Division, *With their bare hands*), noted on his copy of the Armistice order that he had received the document at 10.30 am. He then guided and accompanied Captain Burgwin to the advance PC before Moirey and noted: ... *our artillery was raising hell all the while. At 11.00 am on the dot firing ceased.* With both German and American shelling reaching a crescendo, it was simply impossible to reach Sergeant Powells' Company A to inform him of the imminent armistice in time.

General Pershing's Order of the Day recorded Henry Nicholas Gunther as the last American soldier to die in the First World War. Despite records of Americans being killed after 11.00 am, Gunther is still officially credited as the last soldier killed during this conflict.

**The tour.**
The tour starts at the rural village of Chaumont-devant-Damvillers. When you reach Chaumont via the D65a, turn left at the T-junction and continue on Main Street. Just before you reach the church, turn right. After fifty metres you come at a fork in the road; keep left. After forty metres, turn right onto a farm track. The track sometimes is in a bad condition but if you mind your car's clearance, it is perfectly negotiable. Otherwise, it takes you fifteen minutes on foot to reach the **Henry Gunther Monument (1)** (N49°18.928′ E005°25.749′) that stands on the top of the spur between Hill 328 and Hill 319. The monument describes the history of the 79th Division and was unveiled in 2008.

Standing on the same place, look at the wooded ridge behind the monument; this is the **Côte de Morimont (2)** (N49°18.928′ E005°25.749′). The German artillery was placed behind the ridge and German troops were well-entrenched. On 11 November 1918, Morimont Hill, or Hill 361, was the objective of the 315th Regiment. They made it to the bottom of the valley in front of you, but were shot to pieces by the German artillery. The attack continued until the Armistice came into effect.

If you turn around, standing with your back towards the monument, you have an excellent view towards the **Meuse Heights (3)** (N49°18.928′ E005°25.749′). On the morning of 11 November, the valley that lies in front of you was the scene of heavy explosions and hundreds of soldiers from the 313th could be

**The Henry Gunther Monument at Chaumont.**

**View of the German positions of 11 November 1918.**

Ville-devant-Chaum

The field where Gunther was killed

Thil Wood

View of the Meuse Heights.

seen advancing in a southern (left) direction towards Thil Wood. The field where Gunther was killed is clearly visible; look at the photograph in this book for further details.

Face the monument and turn right; take the right fork and continue for about 200 metres until you reach the highest point; you are now on Hill 319. From this point, you have a great view towards the **Côte de Romagne (4)** (N49°18.947′ E005°26.366′). This wooded ridge was the focus for the attack by the 314th Regiment. Some platoons managed to reach the base of the ridge but before anything could develop from there the war had ended.

Return to the monument and continue straight on; at the fork in the track close by, turn right and walk uphill. When you reach the summit, walk through the field alongside the wire fence (mind the crops!) and carry on to the edge of the woods. On entering the woods you immediately see the remains of the **bunkers and trenches on Hill 328 (5)** (N49°18.919′ E005°25.449′). The German defences here were utterly destroyed by the heavy American bombardment of 10 November prior to the storming of the hill by the 314th Regiment. The German garrison fled their positions and the hill was taken without opposition.

Return to your car and drive back to Chaumont and from here to the main road, the D905. When you have reached the D905, turn left in the direction of Ville-devant-Chaumont. Take the first exit on the right and carry on for about a kilometre. Opposite the first farm on the right,

**View from Hill 319 of Côte de Romagne.**

225

*Left*: Remains of one of the concrete observation posts on Hill 238.

*Below*: Company A's view of Thil Wood

The German view of Company A.

a farm track starts. Park here and walk along the track for about fifty metres. Look across the field toward the woods; this is **the field where Henry Gunther was killed (6)** (N49°17.729′ E005°25.957′).

When you stand in the lower end of the field and look toward the woods, there is a wide field and then Thil Wood. The field looks flat but it is not; tt has a slight rise in the middle of it. Should the crop conditions allow and you can walk across it, crouching low, you cannot see the edge of the wood. The machine gunners were tucked down along the edge of the wood and Gunther and Sergeant Powell did not see them before it was too late. In any case, it was extremely foggy that morning. When they emerged from behind the rise, they suddenly found themselves very close to the German line. In spite of being ordered by Powell to stay put, Gunther fired a few rounds at the German line upon which the Germans, still some distance away, waved at him to indicate to stop shooting.

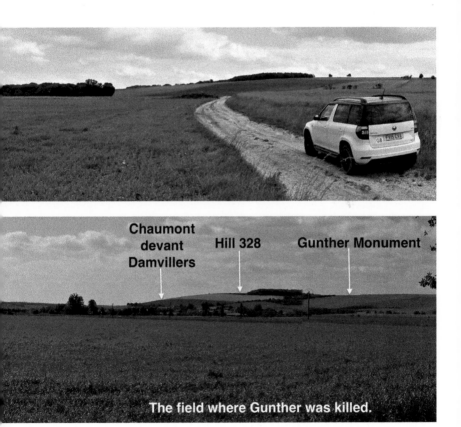

The field where Gunther was killed.

A shell hole large enough to fit a small van in it on the edge of Thil Wood, 2020.

*Above*: A small dump of German *Kugelhandgranaten* Model 1915, Thil Wood, 2020.

*Left*: A German 10.5 cm dud and broken German stoneware found on the edge of Thil Wood, 2020.

The noise of exploding shells and the crackling of machine guns all around was deafening. Gunther fired off another few rounds. A machine gun opened up and Gunther was fatally hit.

Return to your car and drive back to the D905/D65 T-junction; turn right onto the D65. When you come to the edge of Thil Wood, there is a narrow track on the right; park here. Walk along the edge of the wood for about a hundred metres and look across the field towards Ville-devant-Chaumont, see the panorama photograph in this book (p.226). This is the approximate spot from where the Germans watched the Americans come out of the fog, often referred to as the German road block. In fact it is the **German front line (7)** (N49°17.881′ E005°26.520′) of 10-11 November 1918. From here you can clearly see the rise in the field from the German perspective. Gunther's Company A moved towards the edge of the wood from the direction of Ville-devant-Chaumont, seen in the background on the left.

## Fell In Last Battle With 313th

*HENRY N. GUNTHER*

*CHARLES FISHER*

That "Baltimore's Own," the Three Hundred and Thirteenth Infantry, was in action up to the last hour before the signing of the armistice is shown by the names that have recently appeared in the casualty list. Mr. and Mrs. George Gunther, 3011 Eastern avenue, have received notification from the War Department that their son, Private Gunther, was killed in action on November 11, probably in the early hours of Peace Day. He was a member of Company A. Private Fisher, of Company G, Three Hundred and Thirteenth, was killed in action on November 5 and his name appeared in the casualty list yesterday.

**A newspaper clipping from *The Baltimore Sun*, dated 14 December 1918.**

# Appendix 1

# Order of Battle for the Right Bank operations

**First (American) Army: General John J Pershing.**
**From 16 October: General Hunter Liggett.**
**Chief of Staff: Major General Hugh Drum.**

XVII Army Corps, commanded by General Henri Édouard Claudel.

II (Colonial) Corps, commanded by General Henri Édouard Claudel (from 6 November).

### 5th Infantry Division.
Major General John E. McMahon

9 Infantry Brigade
    60th Infantry Regiment
    61st Infantry Regiment
    14th Machine Gun Battalion
10 Infantry Brigade
    6th Infantry Regiment
    11th Infantry Regiment
    15th Machine Gun Battalion
5th Field Artillery Brigade
    19th Field Artillery Regiment (75 mm)
    20th Field Artillery Regiment (75 mm)
    21st Field Artillery Regiment (155 mm)
    5th Trench Mortar Battery
    13th Machine Gun Battalion

7th Engineer Regiment
9th Field Signal Battalion
Headquarters Troop, 5th Division
5th Train Headquarters and Military Police
5th Ammunition Train
5th Supply Train
5th Engineer Train
5th Sanitary Train
17th, 25th, 29th, and 30th Ambulance Companies and Field Hospitals

## 26th Infantry Division.

Major General Clarence C. Edwards, (relieved 26 October 1918).
Brigade General Frank E. Bamford.

51 Infantry Brigade
    101st Infantry Regiment
    102nd Infantry Regiment
    102nd Machine Gun Battalion
52 Infantry Brigade
    103rd Infantry Regiment
    104th Infantry Regiment
    103rd Machine Gun Battalion
51st Field Artillery Brigade
    101st Field Artillery Regiment (75 mm)
    102nd Field Artillery Regiment (75 mm)
    103rd Field Artillery Regiment (155 mm)
    101st Trench Mortar Battery
    101st Machine Gun Battalion

101st Engineer Regiment
101st Field Signal Battalion
Headquarters Troop, 26th Division
101st Train Headquarters and Military Police
101st Ammunition Train
101st Supply Train
101st Engineer Train
101st Sanitary Train
101st, 102nd, 103rd, and 104th Ambulance Companies and Field Hospitals

## 29th Infantry Division.

Major General Charles G. Morton

57 Infantry Brigade
    113th Infantry Regiment
    114th Infantry Regiment
    111th Machine Gun Battalion
58 Infantry Brigade
    115th Infantry Regiment
    116th Infantry Regiment
    112th Machine Gun Battalion
54 Field Artillery Brigade
    110th Field Artillery Regiment (75 mm)
    111th Field Artillery Regiment (75 mm)
    112th Field Artillery Regiment (155 mm)

104th Trench Mortar Battery
110th Machine Gun Battalion

104th Engineer Regiment
104th Field Signal Battalion
Headquarters Troop, 29th Division
104th Train Headquarters and Military Police
104th Ammunition Train
104th Supply Train
104th Engineer Train
104th Sanitary Train
113th, 114th, 115th, and 116th Ambulance Companies and Field
Hospitals

## 32nd **Infantry Division.**
### Major General William G. Haan
63 Infantry Brigade
    125th Infantry Regiment
    126th Infantry Regiment
    119rd Machine Gun Battalion
64 Infantry Brigade
    127th Infantry Regiment
    128th Infantry Regiment
    120th Machine Gun Battalion
57th Field Artillery Brigade
    119th Field Artillery Regiment (75mm)
    120th Field Artillery Regiment (155mm)
    121st Field Artillery Regiment (75mm)
    107th Trench Mortar Battery
    121st Machine Gun Battalion

107th Engineer Regiment
107th Field Signal Battalion
Headquarters Troop, 33rd Division
107th Train Headquarters & Military Police
107th Ammunition Train
107th Supply Train
107th Engineer Train
107th Sanitary Train
125th, 126th, 127th, and 128th Ambulance Companies and Field
Hospitals

### 33rd Division
Major General George Bell Jr

65 Infantry Brigade
    129th Infantry Regiment
    130th Infantry Regiment
    123rd Machine Gun Battalion
66 Infantry Brigade
    131st Infantry Regiment
    132nd Infantry Regiment
    124th Machine Gun Battalion
58th Field Artillery Brigade
    122nd Field Artillery Regiment (75mm)
    123rd Field Artillery Regiment (155mm)
    124th Field Artillery Regiment (75mm)
    108th Trench Mortar Battery
    122nd Machine Gun Battalion

108th Engineer Regiment
108th Field Signal Battalion
Headquarters Troop, 33rd Division
108th Train Headquarters & Military Police
108th Ammunition Train
108th Supply Train
108th Engineer Train
108th Sanitary Train
129th, 130th, 131st, and 132nd Ambulance Companies and Field Hospitals

### 79th Infantry Division
Major General Joseph H. Kuhn

157 Infantry Brigade
    313th Infantry Regiment
    314th Infantry Regiment
    311th Machine Gun Battalion
158 Infantry Brigade
    315th Infantry Regiment
    316th Infantry Regiment
    312th Machine Gun Battalion
154th Field Artillery Brigade
    310th Field Artillery Regiment (75 mm)
    311th Field Artillery Regiment (75 mm)
    312th Field Artillery Regiment (155 mm)

304th Trench Mortar Battery
310th Machine Gun Battalion

304th Engineer Regiment
304th Field Signal Battalion
Headquarters Troop, 79th Division
304th Train Headquarters and Military Police
304th Ammunition Train
304th Supply Train
304th Engineer Train
304th Sanitary Train
313th, 314th, 315th, and 316th Ambulance Companies and Field Hospitals

# Appendix 2

# The French Divisions employed in the Right Bank operations

### The 15th Colonial Infantry Division.
The 15th Colonial Division was commanded by General Étienne Guérin. On 5 July 1915 the division was first deployed in the Argonne sector. Later, it fought in the Champagne, on the Somme, the Chemin des Dames, in Picardy and at Verdun. Rested between 10 August and 5 September 1918, the division moved to Lorraine and came under American command for the rest of 1918. From 12 to 16 September it participated in the elimination of the St. Mihiel Salient. From 20 October it occupied the Meuse Heights on the right bank, north of Verdun. It relieved the American 33rd Division, captured Vilosnes and Sivry and advanced east to Damvillers on 7 November.

### The 18th Division.
The 18th Infantry Division was commanded by General Joseph Andelauer. An active division in 1914, from 11 August 1914 it participated in the fighting around the Franco-German border in the Nancy area. The division was deployed on the Western Front until it was pulled out of the line on 4 August 1918 to occupy the quiet Damloup-Beaumont area, north of Verdun. As part of the American-led Meuse-Argonne Offensive, from 8 October it attacked Cote 344 and Samogneux and eventually took Haumont Wood and Ormont Farm. It protected the left flank of the American 29th Division and paved the way for the 26th and 79th Divisions to continue the push north.

### The 26th Division.
The 26th Division was commanded by General Jean de Belenet. Active in 1914, it fought on the Franco-German border (Battle of the Frontiers), the Somme, Oise, Flanders, Picardy and Verdun. On 12 September 1918, under American command, it participated in the St. Mihiel Offensive and advanced to Hattonchâtel. Soon after the Germans were removed from the St. Mihiel Salient the 26th Division was moved to Caures Wood, north of Verdun. Under American command, it was placed on the fight flank

of the French XVII Corps, where it acted as the pivot around which the attack on the right bank moved to the north and to the east. Its task was to hold fast and keep contact with its neighbouring divisions. It therefore only made a limited advance.

The achievements of the 18th and 26th French divisions on the right flank of the American positions were not as spectacular as those of the 33rd, 29th and 79th Divisions but were equally important. It is only fair to say that the defensive positions of the Austro-Hungarian and German divisions were formidable in this region. The topography worked solely in favour of the defenders. A quick look at the map shows that the 18th Division's attack was not a frontal attack but rather ran parallel to the KuK-German front. Therefore, the strong defensive positions and stubborn opposition that was met on the right flank of XVII Corps (the French 18th and 26th Divisions) should not be measured in square miles gained but be regarded as being as difficult as the problems faced by the US 33rd and 29th Divisions on the left flank. Seen in this light, it is understandable that the French divisions did not make the same progress as American divisions.

# Appendix 3

# Composition of an average American infantry division on arrival in France. 28,000 officers and men

| Platoon | 65 men | Lieutenant |
|---------|--------|------------|
| Company | 250 men | Captain |
| Battalion | 1,000 men | Major or Lieutenant Colonel |
| Regiment | 4,000 men | Colonel |
| Brigade | 8.000 men | Brigadier General |
| Division | 28,000 men | Major General |

### *Division*

A division's establishment provided for two infantry brigades, each with two regiments, with four battalions per regiment, and four companies per battalion. A company had six officers and 250 men, and the strength of a regiment was 112 officers and 3720 men. All told, a fully established division had 17,666 riflemen, 260 machine guns, and seventy-two guns (forty-eight 75mm and twenty-four 155mm).

In addition there were various units for headquarters, engineering, communications, and supply, which brings the total to some 28,000 men.

By the autumn of 1918 and after the enormous casualties of the Spring Offensive, an American division was roughly equivalent to at least two, usually three and in the last month or two, up to four German divisions. The only formations in France roughly comparable in size to the Americans were the four divisions of the Canadian Corps; but even these had several thousand men fewer.

The size of the American major formations (ie division, corps and army) provided a significant command problem and, taking into account all the circumstances, was more a negative than a positive in their performance in the battle. Indeed, it is doubtful if any of the other combatants would have wanted a division of much more than 12,000 men, with battalions of 700; the fire power of individual soldiers and platoons had increased so much in the course of the war that command and control issues became more complex. The challenge facing General Pershing was that he had too few qualified officers to staff these formations and, inevitably, many of them lacked battle experience and even fewer had experience of command in battle in France and at that level.

### Corps
An American Corps comprised from two to six divisions – usually three; it had under command a number of artillery, engineering, signal, and supply units to support its divisions.

### Army
An American army consisted of from three to five Corps. It had specialist units under command. The American First army was created in August 1918. In mid October the American Second Army was created, followed by a Third Army just as the war was ending.

# Appendix 4

# Some Facts and Figures

**The average American divisional strength in numbers, September 1918.**
The maximum authorized strength was 991 officers and 27,114 men. The *effective strength in the field* was 16,000 rifles, divided over four regiments.

| | | | |
|---|---|---|---|
| Division: | 16,000 men | = 2 Brigades | = 4 Regiments |
| Brigade: | 9,000 men | = 2 Regiments | |
| Regiment: | 4,400 men | = 4 Battalions | |
| Battalion: | 1,100 men | = 4 Companies | |
| Company: | 275 men | = 4 squads | |
| Squad: | 70 men | | |

| | |
|---|---|
| Companies A, B, C and D | = 1st Battalion |
| Companies E, F, G and H | = 2nd Battalion |
| Companies I, J, K and L | = 3rd Battalion |

Also included were three machine-gun battalions, each one attached to an infantry regiment. Each individual machine-gun battalion was made up of four companies.

**Total number of soldiers committed on the right bank.**

| | |
|---|---|
| – 165,000 Americans | – 6 divisions |
| – 45,000 French | – 3 divisions |
| – at most 100,000 Germans and KuK | – 11 divisions |

**Losses/casualties 26 September to 11 November in the Meuse-Argonne.**
The estimated American losses were 122,063 killed, wounded and missing. A little less than one fifth, 26,277 men, were killed or died of wounds, of whom 14,246 are buried in Romagne American Cemetery in France. American losses were worsened by the inexperience of many of

the troops and officers and the tactics used during the early phases of the operation, combined with the widespread onset of the global influenza outbreak known as the Spanish Flu.

## Approximate American losses during the First World War.

There is no exact number of First World War casualties; at best, most numbers are good approximations. The numbers in books and on internet sites usually vary; but most sources that I have checked agree on the numbers below, taken from 'American Armies and Battlefields in Europe', published in 1938.

The Americans lost 116,516 dead and 202,628 wounded, a total of 319,144 of the 4.7 million men who served, a 'modest' total when compared to those of other belligerent nations (French: 1,300,000, British 700,000, Germans 1,773,000). An interesting fact is that more American military personnel were killed by disease, usually Spanish Flu (63,114), than by acts of war (53,402). By applying the lessons and triage techniques that had been learnt by European doctors and surgeons earlier in the war, American doctors were able to reduce the number of deaths caused by shrapnel, infected gunshot wounds and gas.

German losses at the Meuse Heights remain unknown, but an estimated 20,000 were taken prisoner. Pressured on all fronts, the German administrative system, including casualty records, buckled under the strain of the scale of operations from March 1918, particularly from August onwards.

## General Pershing's view of the actions on the right bank:

'In the First Army, an attack by the III Corps to the east across the Meuse, south of Dun-sur-Meuse, in conjunction with the northward movement by the French XVII Corps, was prepared as a preliminary to a new line of advance to the east. On November 3rd, 4th and 5th, the 5th Division of the III Corps, in a brilliant manoeuvre on a wide front, effected crossings of the Meuse and established bridgeheads south of Dun-sur-Meuse. The heights of the Meuse were gradually cleared by the III Corps and the French II Colonial Corps, which had relieved the French XVII Corps. Now, for the first time since 1914, the French positions around Verdun were completely free from the menace of these heights. In these operations, the 5th Division, assisted by a regiment of the 32nd, on November 5th had captured Milly and established its line from there south to the Bois de Châtillon. By night of the 9th, it had advanced to Remoiville and north of Mouzay. Our front of attack was also extended to the south and by November 10th an excellent line of departure was secured for an offensive in the direction of Montmédy.'

This is about all that could be found about the right bank offensive in Volume 2 of his memoirs; it is painfully clear that this battlefield was not his main concern. Notice that the only AEF division to receive a mention was the 5th: Pershing was a regular and it would not be particularly controversial to note that he had a bias towards the regular army and regular army formations.

# Appendix 5

# The German and KuK outline Order of Battle for the Right Bank operations

The information in this appendix is largely taken from *Histories of 251 Divisions of the German Army which participated in the War (1914-1918)*, first published in 1920 but which was prepared by the American intelligence staff, based on a variety of sources, in mid-1918.

In 1918, the German Army on the Western Front was organized in four army groups; one of these was **Army Group Gallwitz,** or *Heeresgruppe Gallwitz,* commanded by General der Artillerie Max von Gallwitz.

Army Group Gallwitz was organized into two Armies:

| | |
|---|---|
| **Fifth Army**: | Cavalry General Georg von der Marwitz. |
| | *The Meuse-Argonne Sector.* |
| **Armee Abteilung C**: | Lieutenant General Georg Fuchs. |
| | *The Metz and St. Mihiel Sectors.* |

*Maas Gruppe West, Maas Gruppe Ost, Gruppe Ornes* **and** *Gruppe Beaumont* were part of **Fifth Army** and under the command of von der Marwitz. There were ten *Gruppen* or corps attached to **Army Group Gallwitz.** However, only the four corps involved in the fighting on the right bank are included here. The average strength of a German division in 1914 was approximately 15,000 men. By 1918 this number had dwindled to 8,000 – 9,000 men at best, sometimes reduced to not much more than half that number.

**Maas Gruppe West: General Ernst von Oven**
7th Reserve Division:     Major General Wilhelm Ribbentrop

**Maas Gruppe Ost: General Franz Ludwig Freiherr von Soden.**
1st KuK Division:     Field Marshal Josef Metzger
15th Division:     Lieutenant General Gerhard Tappen

**Gruppe Ornes or KuK XVIII Corps: Field Marshal Ludwig Goiginer**
33rd Division:     Major General Wilhelm Groener
192nd Division:     Lieutenant General Max Leuthold

Between 8 and 15 October 1918, the sector was reorganized and reinforced by fresh divisions.

## Maas Gruppe Ost: General Franz Ludwig Freiherr von Soden.

| | |
|---|---|
| 106th KuK Division: | Field Marshal Karl Kratky |
| 7th Reserve Division: | Major General Wilhelm Ribbentrop |
| 228th Division: | Major General Paul von der Heyde |

## Gruppe Beaumont: Lieutenant General Karl Dieffenbach

| | |
|---|---|
| 32nd Division: | Major General Maximilian von Scheel |
| 1st Landwehr Division: | General Albano von Jacobi |
| 15th Division: | Lieutenant General Gerhard Tappen |

## Gruppe Ornes or KuK XVIII Corps: Field Marshal Ludwig Goiginer

| | |
|---|---|
| 33rd Division: | Major General Wilhelm Groener |
| 27th Division: | Major General Heinrich von Maur |
| 192 Division: | Lieutenant General Max Leuthold |

## Maas Gruppe West: 8 October
### 7th Reserve Division

The division was activated on 2 August 1914 and was composed of reserve troops from Prussia. One week later, it left for Belgium and was first engaged in the Battle of the Marne, where on 6 and 7 September it suffered heavy losses. The division stayed in France until the end of the war and was engaged in many battles, including the Battle of Verdun (June 1916) and the Battle of the Somme (September 1916).

During the last days of March 1918 the 7th Reserve Division took part in the German Spring offensive but suffered such heavy losses that is was hastily relieved. On 8 September, after the division had been rested and trained in Laon, it was transferred to the Meuse-Argonne sector, where it was moved into the front line between Brieulles and Forges.

When the Americans started the attack on the right bank on 26 September it was caught by surprise and completely swamped, offering little resistance worth noting. The remainder of the 7th Reserve Division was withdrawn to the right bank only two days later, where it was rested and kept in reserve. However, on 9 October the remains of the division were used to bolster the hard-pressed 1st KuK Division, which was on the brink of collapse. The last troops of the 7th were finally withdrawn on 25 October. The losses in the Argonne had been horrible and are estimated at 3,500. By the time of the Armistice it had been almost annihilated. By 15 October, Maas Gruppe West had been entirely moved to the left bank and the sector was taken over by Maas Gruppe Ost.

## Maas Gruppe Ost: 8 October
### 1<sup>st</sup> KuK Division

The 1<sup>st</sup> KuK (Kaiserlich und Königlich) Division had participated in many battles on the Italian front prior to its transfer to the Western Front. It was regarded as a first rate division, and its commander, Field Marshal Josef Metzger, was a highly respected officer, even by the Germans. At the start of 1918, under pressure from the German High Command, the Emperor Charles agreed that four Austro-Hungarian Divisions would be transferred to the Western Front. In July 1918, 234 boxcars were needed to transfer the 1<sup>st</sup>, 35<sup>th</sup> and 37<sup>th</sup> Divisions, along with the 106<sup>th</sup> Division and heavy artillery units, to the Verdun Front. The 1<sup>st</sup> and 35<sup>th</sup> Divisions, as well as some heavy artillery, were assigned to Army Group Gallwitz; the 1<sup>st</sup> Division to the German Fifth Army, east of the Meuse, while the 35<sup>th</sup> Division joined Army Detachment C. In August 1918, the division numbered 8,400 men.

In mid-August 1918, the 1<sup>st</sup> KuK Division replaced the worn out 232<sup>nd</sup> Division on the right bank and became part of Maas Gruppe Ost. It occupied the Brabant Sector, a seven kilometres length of front stretching from Brabant-sur-Meuse to Sivry, adjacent to the River Meuse. The line offered excellent natural defensive positions. From 1 to 7 October, the division was in a state of readiness. On the next day they were vigorously shelled and attacked all along their front line. Although the Americans did not break through their defences, they were forced to withdraw and suffered heavy losses. On 9 October they were reinforced by the German 228<sup>th</sup> Division. By that point the combat strength of the division had been almost completely exhausted; the 1<sup>st</sup> KuK had suffered a casualty rate of 80 per cent and was relieved by the 228<sup>th</sup> Division on 10 October. Several battalions of the division, like the *Sturmbattalion 106,* were later used as replacements.

### 15<sup>th</sup> Division

The Prussian 15<sup>th</sup> Division was originally formed in September 1818. The recruits were from the populous Rhine provinces. During the Franco-Prussian War of 1870-1871 the Division fought with distinction at Mars la Tour, Gravelotte, Metz, Péronne, Amiens and St. Quentin. Upon mobilization in August 1914 it was moved into Luxembourg before entering France. It crossed the Meuse at Sedan and participated in the Battle of the Marne (6-12 September 1914). The 15<sup>th</sup> Division participated in almost every important battle on the Western Front but also briefly served in Russia and Rumania.

September 1918 found the division on the right bank of the Meuse, between Damvillers and Flabas. It had suffered heavy losses during previous battles earlier in the year and needed rest and re-equipping. On 26 September, they were back on active duty in the Bois de Caures sector, famous for Colonel Driant's heroic actions in the opening of the Battle of Verdun, to prepare for the allied attack. It continued to hold this reasonably quiet sector until the cessation of the fighting. The division was rated as second class, but it had sustained such heavy losses in 1918 that by September it was but a shadow of its former self.

## Maas Gruppe Ost: 15 October to 11 November
### 106th KuK Division

The 106th KuK Division, under the command of Field Marshal Karl Kratky, arrived in Montmédy in September 1918. The division was made up from Landsturm members, a third-line reserve formation made up of older men, originally intended to perform home defence duties. In spite of this, it had previously seen service in Russia and Italy. Under pressure from the German High Command, the division was transferred to German service.

On 19 September the 106th was transferred to the command of Gruppe Ornes to act as security detachments in the Volker and Kriemhild Lines, thereby freeing up German troops for front line service. On 29 September two units, the 25th Regiment and the 106th Sturmbattalion of the Division, were redeployed to the area around Sivry to bolster the crumbling German 7th Division. Its composite units were under the command of the KuK 1st Division, KuK XVIII Corps. On 9 October the 25th Regiment and the 106th Sturmbattalion formally took over half of the 7th Division's front line sector. The remaining three regiments of the Division remained as labour and security detachments for Gruppe Ornes and witnessed no combat. It was never deployed on the Western Front as a whole division.

### 7th Reserve Division
*See Maas Gruppe West, 8 October.*

### 228th Division

The 228th Division was a composite division made up of regiments from other divisions. It was formed in Sedan in May 1917 and was commanded by Major General Paul von der Heyde. Between 20 and 24 August 1917 it was involved in what the French call the Second Battle of Verdun, during which it lost heavily. Relieved on 24 August, it was sent to the Meuse Heights, where it occupied a quiet sector of the front line and received 900 replacements.

Engaged in several battles in 1918, it is worth noting that it was also engaged near Le Hamel towards the end of the opening German Spring Offensive of March 1918. Four months later, on 4 July, the American 33rd Division was part of the combined Australian/British force that liberated the village. The German 228th Division and the American 33rd would be adversaries again on 9 October on the Meuse Heights.

On 12 September the 228th Division was transported by train from the Somme to Spincourt, a back area of the Meuse Heights. On 28 September it marched via Dun to Romagne after the American breakthrough at Montfaucon. From 28 September to 8 October it was engaged between Nantillois and Cunel, after which the division was shifted to the relatively quieter right bank of the Meuse to become part of Maas Gruppe Ost, where it first supported and then later relieved the 1st KuK Division. It stayed in line until 5 November but was withdrawn to Fontaine and Écurey after that date. The 228th Division was rated as a third class division but stayed in the line until the armistice.

### Gruppe Ornes (or KuK XVIII Corps): 8 October
### 33rd Division

The division was formed on 1 April 1887 and was stationed at Strasbourg; three years later it was moved to *Festung* Metz, Fortress Metz. The division was tasked with guarding the new Franco-German border. Since France had lost the Franco-Prussian War of 1870-1871, most of the former French provinces of Alsace and Lorraine were now German territory. At the beginning of the war the 33rd Division, under the command of Major General Wilhelm Groener, quickly crossed the French border and was deployed in the Verdun/Argonne sector. It was involved in the taking of Montfaucon on 3 September 1914, an important French observation position. The Division stayed in this sector until the spring of 1918.

The 33rd Divison was regarded as a first class division. During the German Spring Offensives of 1918 it was used as a shock division on the Somme and, later, on the Aisne. However, the division was greatly disorganized by its losses in the retreat from the Marne and never recovered from them. With its offensive power depleted, it was deployed is a third rate reserve formation in a quiet sector of the front.

On 15 August it was withdrawn from the front line and rested at Stenay, Meuse. Here, it received replacements from the dissolved 33rd Reserve Division. By the end of that same month it was moved into the line in the Ornes Sector, Gruppe Ornes, and was placed under Austro-Hungarian Command. A shadow of its former self, it remained in this sector until the end of the war.

**192ⁿᵈ Division**

In 1915 this division had started as 192 Brigade and only became the 192ⁿᵈ Division in June 1916, towards the end of the reorganisation of the German army into three battalion regiments. It was a composite division, made up of troops originating from Saxony, Bavaria and Westphalia. The Division spent a lot of time in the Champagne region until it was deployed to the Verdun Front in March 1916, where it suffered heavy losses in the fighting around Avocourt. In September it was engaged in the fierce fighting at Fleury and Douaumont. At about the end of October replacements were drafted into the Division to bring it up to something like full strength; but now the members of the division were all Saxon. Due to the mediocre quality of the troops, the 192ⁿᵈ spent 1917 in a calm sector (Bezonvaux) of the Verdun Front. After 'resting', the division entered the line at the tip of the Salient on 26 August 1918. Despite being assaulted by the French on three sides, it managed to extract itself from the front line and retreated to the Michel Zone.

On 22 September, when the St. Mihiel Sector had stabilised, the 192ⁿᵈ was taken out of the line. It was stationed on the right bank of the Meuse, close to Étraye, between Consenvoye and Damvillers. Although it did well at St. Mihiel, it was rated as a third class division. Therefore, it was moved to the right flank of Gruppe Ornes, a quiet sector, for the remainder of the war.

**Gruppe Ornes or KuK XVIII Corps: 15 October to 11 November**
**33ʳᵈ Division**
*See Gruppe Ornes, 8 October*
**27ᵗʰ Division**
*Played no significant part in the fighting*
**192 Division**
*See Gruppe Ornes, 8 October*

**Gruppe Beaumont: 15 October to 11 November**
**32ⁿᵈ Division**
This division was formed on 1 April 1887 in Bautzen, a hill top town in eastern Saxony, located on the River Spree. On the night of 2 August 1914 the Division entrained for Luxemburg to act as reserve troops. It crossed the Meuse near Dinant and by the end of August it went into action in France. Besides serving six months in Flanders (Ypres/Messines), it fought battles all along the French front.

One entry in the divisional history mentions that 'in June 1917, the morale of the division was very low because of the losses suffered in

May 1917 at Mont Haut [Nivelle Offensive, Champagne]. However, from May to June 1917, there were only two desertions.'

During the German Spring offensives of 1918 the division suffered such heavy losses that it was moved to the quiet Lorraine sector. It arrived in Spincourt, on the right bank, on 4 July, where it received 1,500 replacements. Regarded as a third class division, they were moved into the quiet Bezonvaux Sector, about ten kilometres north-east of Verdun. On 1 October the 32nd Division was marched to the rear, where it was rested until 5 October. On 9 October, however, it came into line in the Écurey-Étraye-Moirey sector and was heavily engaged in Moirey Wood. Losses were such that some companies (a theoretical 120 men) were reduced to fifteen men. Taken out of the line on 24 October, the Division reappeared in its former quiet sector of Bezonvaux, freeing the rested 106th KuK Division to be deployed elsewhere. The remains of the 32nd Division held this sector until the Armistice.

### 1st Landwehr Division

The 1st Landwehr Division, made up of older men serving in second-rate reserve regiments, was established in August 1914. Shortly after the outbreak of war it was sent to the Eastern Front, where it participated in the Battle of Tannenberg and the Battle of the Masurian Lakes, among others.

After the Armistice with Russia (17 December 1917), the 1st Landwehr Division was transported by rail to Belgium. Here it received replacements from the dissolved 9th and 20th Landwehr Regiments. These regiments had been largely destroyed during the autumn fighting in Flanders and the remainder of the troops were used to bolster the 1st Landwehr. Unsurprisingly, it was regarded as a third rate formation with little military value, although it did receive some praise after the Battle of the Lys in April 1918.

Notwithstanding its problems, after a short period of rest, it was deployed to several places in Belgium (Hooge, heavy losses) before it was moved to the Meuse region in France. On 16 October it held the front line in Flabas, where they lost scores of men during the heavy fighting. Incredibly, they held their sector until the end of the war.

### 15th Division

*See Maas Gruppe Ost, 8 October*

### German losses

During the Meuse-Argonne Offensive, the Germans lost about 126,000 men, of whom approximately 28,000 were killed. It is unknown how many were killed or wounded in the fighting on the right bank.

Cavalry General von der Marwitz and his aide-de-camp somewhere on the Western Front in 1917. They are obviously close to the front, as they have both very clearly kept their gasmasks handy.

# Advice to travellers and useful addresses

The Meuse/Woëvre region is not very densely populated; it is an area dotted with small villages. Most people make their living from agriculture. To do the weekly shop, people normally go to one of the larger towns e.g. Verdun, Stenay or Étain. On the former battlefield, an area of thirty square kilometres, there are only a few places where you can fill your petrol tank, buy snacks to take with you on your battlefield tour and have a cup of coffee. However, the area can easily be reached from Verdun; from there, it is only a fifteen minutes drive to the heart of the battlefield.

The car tours are all accessible – at least as of the date of publication – in a standard saloon car and in many cases in a small minibus. However, if planning a tour in a vehicle bigger than a car/camper van, it is advisable to check out the route beforehand. Naturally, the car tour stops are all accessible to those touring by mountain or electric bike.

### Gas/Petrol stations
Consenvoye, Damvillers, Dun-sur-Meuse, Stenay, Verdun.

### Supermarkets
Dun-sur-Meuse, Stenay, Verdun.

### Cafés and/or lunch facilities
Consenvoye, Damvillers, Dun-sur-Meuse, Stenay, Verdun.

### Countryside Code
When you are walking in the countryside, and especially when you are crossing over farmland, please follow the Countryside Code – leave gates and property as you find them and please take your litter home with you. Do not obstruct farm tracks with your vehicle (or, if you do, stay close by so that you can move it quickly if necessary). It might sound obvious, but do not walk through fields where there are crops growing – there are plenty of other places, e.g the sides of roads and tracks, from which there are excellent panoramic views. The roads in the area are generally well maintained – however, they are often narrow, so please walk along them taking due care. Heavy traffic tends to be tractors but often there are

forestry trucks, large, long, often unwieldy and not infrequently driven too fast for the road conditions.

### *Where to stay*
There are numerous B&Bs in the Meuse-Argonne area; search on Google on 'Chambres d'hotes', 'Gites de France', www.booking.com. or www.tripadvisor.com Many B&Bs have a restaurant licence and offer good quality three course dinners at a reasonable price. This saves you considerable time on arrival, as you do not have to go out searching for a restaurant; whilst it is also very handy during the rest of your stay. Some well-known English speaking possibilities are:
Montfaucon: www.14-18 Meuse-Argonne.com
Vauquois: www.lemontcigale.fr
Dun-sur-Meuse: www.bikersbedsfrance.uk
Verdun: www.tourisme-meuse.com
Verdun (hotel): www.lesjardinsdumess.fr

### *Guided tours*
For guided tours in English, French, Dutch and German, contact museum19141918@gmail.com or www.meuse-argonne-battlefield-tours.com

### *Museum*
Montfaucon: www.14-18 Meuse-Argonne.com
5 Rue de l'Argonne
55270
Montfaucon d'Argonne
03 29 86 19 87

### *Ordnance and relics of the war*
The bomb disposal unit in the Meuse (Lorraine) consists of ten men who, day in and day out, put their lives at risk to clear the former battlefields of the deadly heritage of (mainly) the First World War. Every year these men collect some hundred tons of shells of all types – gas, shrapnel and high explosive – as well as hand grenades. Gas shells have the potential to be particularly hazardous and one out of three shells fired during the 1918 campaigns contained gas. However, they only collect shells when there is immediate danger to the public; this means that the forests etc have not been cleared. Advice to travellers - do **NOT** pick anything up off the ground that looks suspect. Use your common sense and leave such things well alone. Munitions are designed to kill and sometimes they still do. In summer 2018, a tourist was killed by an unexploded shell. Rusty metal is also an ideal breeding ground for tetanus.

**A typical find on the battlefields: a pile of shells waiting for destruction by the bomb disposal squad, June 2020.**

### Metal detectors

The use of metal detectors is prohibited, even with permission from the owner of the land. Fines can be as high as 7000 euros; whilst the impounding of the offender's vehicle is a standard procedure.

### Maps

Some supermarkets, like the Leclerc at Verdun, carry a range of maps, as does the museum at Fleury. If you want to study the area in more detail, the maps in the IGN Série Bleue are highly recommended. Maps 3111 SB (Stenay), 3112 ET (Verdun) and 3212 SB (Étain) cover the whole area as described in this book. They are available on: (https:// ignrando.fr/boutique/cartes/randonnee-france.html) Once you are on the homepage of the site use the search (*rechercher par mots cles*; search on key words) button top right. This will immediately take you to the map you desire.

Should you be interested in the history of Verdun and surroundings, the *Battleground Europe* map*, Verdun* by Bart Metselaar is a must-have. Hundreds of points of interest, ie memorials, forts, bunkers and monuments, are clearly indicated on this handy map. Available on www. pen-and-sword.co.uk or on Amazon and in various of the museums in the area.

### Driving in France

In France motorists drive on the right hand side of the road; all car passengers must wear seat belts. The roads in the Meuse-Argonne area are mostly well maintained. The maximum speed in villages, towns and cities is 50 km/h, on national roads (N and D roads, i.e. N209, D15) it is 80 km/h and on motorways 130 km/h unless indicated otherwise (for example, 110 km/h in rain).

Priorité à droite. Give way to traffic coming from your right. If you are driving along a road, anyone joining that road from your right hand side has right of way – usually, but not always, also indicated by a sign with an 'X'. If you happen to be on a road that has a yellow diamond sign, then anyone on that road has priority. There are variations, but the wisest course is to assume priority from the right. Most intersections are marked by white bollards with a red stripe towards the top.

Drivers must also carry a luminous yellow vest in the car, in an easily accessible place; should you have a breakdown in France, you have to wear the highly visible jacket when you are getting out of your car. There should also be such jackets (*gilets jaunes*) for any passengers. A warning triangle is also essential and this must be readily accessible in your boot. You should also have a first aid kit and breathalyser – the law on the latter is hazy, but better to be safe than sorry. Nowadays, you are required to have a sticker on your windscreen that indicates the emissions category of your vehicle. Failure to comply can result in on the spot fines, usually between €45 and €90.

### The weather

In summer it can be very hot in this area. As regards the rest of the year, the weather is usually quite good but from time to time you may need wellington (rubber) boots – though good quality walking boots should suffice, even in winter, and should be a minimum footwear requirement year round; have protective wet weather gear against rain and possibly an umbrella. Tip for a pleasant trip into the forest: apply a good brand of insect repellent. Since ticks, the possible carriers of Lyme's Disease, are particularly common in forest areas, it is advisable to cover up by wearing long trousers whenever you visit a forest and roll down the sleeves of your shirt.

### Water

It is quite safe to drink tap water in France, which is continually monitored for its quality. Some of the walks can be lengthy, so be sure to bring a supply of bottled water with you.

***Pharmacies***
There are numerous pharmacies and one can usually be found in the bigger towns in the area, such as Damvillers, Dun-sur-Meuse, Stenay and Verdun.

***Hospital***
Should you require medical aid, there is a hospital in Verdun as well as in St. Mihiel. Most doctors and specialists speak English or at least the basics.

Hôpital Saint Nicolas,
2 Rue d'Anthouard
55100 VERDUN
03 29 83 84 85

# Acknowledgements

My sincere thanks go to Bart Metselaar, who once again delivered the superb maps for the tour section; Didi, my wife, for her patience and test-driving and walking the tours with me; the American Battlefield and Monuments Commission (ABMC); the National Archives and Records Administration (NARA), Washington, DC, who supplied me with great quantities of much yet unpublished photographic material; the University of Texas for their freely accessible and brilliant Perry-Castañeda Library Map Collection; Christina Holstein; Gene Fax; Matthew Young; Jacques and Thibault Mansy for sharing their research on the 5th Division; Suzanne van Baarsen for allowing me the use of her super fast internet connection, Eric Mueller for his support and test walking; Paul Osman; Wim Degrande; Jan Cornelis de Mik for his research on German soldiers; Maarten 'Duke' Elsendoorn; Alfons & Janine Postma.

The black and white American photos used for this book are from the National Archives, Washington, DC; all other photographic material is from my personal collection, unless indicated otherwise.

As usual, a special thanks goes to the people who put the book together: Matt Jones, Jon Wilkinson and Dom Allen.

Doubtless there are others: you know who you are and I am very grateful. All errors in this book are solely my responsibility.

Nantillois, August 2020.

# Selective Bibliography

33rd Division A.E.F., Frederic L Huydekooper, Gustave Soupert, Luxembourg, 1919.

Abschied vom Doppeladler, Anton Graf Bossi-Fedrigotti, Verlagsgemeinschaft Berg, Abteilung Türmer Verlag, Berg am See, 1990.

A History of the 90th Division, Major George White, The 90th Division Association, 1920.

American Armies and Battlefields in Europe, American Battle Monuments Commission, Government Printing Office, Washington D.C., 1938.

Battleground Europe 14-18 Map of Verdun, B. Metselaar, Pen & Sword, Barnsley, South Yorkshire, UK, 2020.

Histories of 251 Divisions of the German Army which participated in the War (1914-1918), War Department, Government Printing Office, Washington, DC, 1920.

History of the 89th Division, George H. English Jr., The War Society of the 89th Division, Smith-Brooks Printing Company, Denver, Colorado, 1920.

History of the 90th Division, Major George Wythe, The 90th Division Association, The De Vinne Press, New York City, New York, 1920.

History of the Yankee Division, Harry H. Benwell, The Cornhill Company, Boston, Massachusetts, 1919.

Illinois in the World War, Volume One, unknown, State Publications Society, Chicago, Illinois, 1920.

Le prix d'une alliance, Jean-Claude Laparra, Ysec éditions, Louviers, 2002.

Le secteur fortifié de Montmédy 1935-1940, Stéphane Gaber, Editions Serpenoise, Metz, 2000.

Les États-Unis dans la Grande Guerre, Léon Abily, Marines Éditions, Rennes, France, 2010.

Medals of Honor of the Meuse-Argonne, Maarten Otte, Exposure, Rosmalen, The Netherlands, 2016

Meuse-Argonne: Breaking the Line, Maarten Otte, Pen & Sword, Barnsley, England, 2018.

My Experiences in the World War, Volume II, John J. Pershing, Frederick A. Stokes Company, New York, 1931.

New England in France 1917-1919, a History of the Twenty-Sixth Division USA, Emerson Gifford Taylor, The Riverside Press, Cambridge, USA, 1920.

Pour la France, A guide to the formations and units of the land forces of France, Michael Cox and Graham Watson, Helion and Company Ltd, Solihull, West-Midlands, 2012.

Summary of Operations in the World War of the 5th, 26th, 28th, 32nd, 33rd, 79th, and 90th Divisions, ABMC, United States Government Printing Office, Washington D.C., 1943 to 1948.

The 32nd Division in the World War, Wisconsin War History Commission, Michigan War History Commission, 32nd Division Historical Detail, Wisconsin Printing Company, Milwaukee, Wisconsin, 1920.

The Austro-Hungarian Divisions on the Western Front, Ian Jones, The Ohio State University, accessed on line, 2019.

The Fifth U.S. Division in the World War 1917-1919, Society of the Fifth Division, Wykoop Hallenbeck Crawford Co, New York, NY, 1919.

The Stand: The final flight of Lt. Frank Luke, Jr, Stephen Skinner, Schiffer Publishing Ltd, Pennsylvania, 2008.

The Iron Division in the World War, H.G. Proctor, The John C. Winston Co, Philadelphia, 1919.

Under the Lorraine Cross, Arthur H. Joel, Columbia University, New York, NY, 1921.

United States Army in the World War 1917-1919, Military Operations of the American Expeditionary Forces, Volume 9, Center of Military History, United States Army, Washington, D.C., 1990.

# Selective Index

Aisne-Marne, xiv, 5

**American Army**
First Army, v, xix, 3, 5, 7, 10, 16,
    17, 38, 66, 71, 73, 86, 90, 96,
    238, 240

**Corps:**
I, 8, 16, 61
III, 11, 20, 26, 73, 90, 95, 96, 103,
    240
V, 8, 9, 89, 90
XVII, xix, 10, 27, 28, 36, 38, 46,
    54, 56–8, 63, 70, 71, 73, 77,
    85, 86, 90, 230, 236, 240

**Brigades:**
9th, 95, 96
10th, 96, 182
51st, 67
52nd, 32, 63, 218
58th, 28, 29, 46, 71, 78
63rd, 89, 232
64th, 89, 232
65th, 233
66th, 21, 35, 233
157th, 71, 74, 81, 233
158th, 71, 73, 74, 76–8, 81, 233
158th FA, 39

**Divisions:**
3rd, 188
5th, v, 73, 76, 86, 88–91, 95–7,
    100, 102, 103, 105–108, 142,
    159, 161, 162, 180–8, 195,
    198, 200, 230, 240
26th, v, xxi, 9, 15, 17, 20, 28,
    57–72, 78, 81, 83, 85, 89, 131,
    137, 150, 204, 218, 220, 221,
    231, 232, 235, 236, 257
29th, v, xxi, 15, 20, 26, 28, 32,
    34–41, 43, 46–8, 50–60, 63,
    65, 71, 110–12, 117, 122–4,
    128, 129, 131, 133, 134, 178,
    230–3, 235, 236
32nd, v, xxi, 17, 54, 60, 70,
    89–94, 105, 107, 113, 159,
    162, 232, 233, 240, 243, 244
33rd, v, xxi, 11, 15, 20–43, 46–8,
    54, 55, 110, 112, 113, 117,
    128, 129, 136, 140, 157, 232,
    233, 235, 236
79th, v, xxi, 17, 21, 34, 52, 60,
    69–73, 76–8, 81, 82, 84–7, 96,
    127, 131, 133, 137, 141–3,
    145, 149, 150, 162, 204, 214,
    216, 217, 220–2, 233–6
80th, 20, 21, 24, 26, 71, 95
90th, 8, 73, 95, 107, 109

**Regiments:**
6th, 101–103, 105, 107, 185, 200
11th, 95, 98, 103, 105, 107, 108
60th, 95, 96, 102, 105, 106, 109,
    181, 189, 230
61st, 95, 96, 100, 102, 105, 106,
    181, 189, 190, 230
101st, 61, 63, 65–8, 85, 87–9, 231

102nd, 61, 63, 65, 67, 85, 88, 231
103rd, 61, 63, 64, 89, 231
104th, 57, 61, 63, 78, 231
108th Eng., 32, 33, 113
113th, 37, 47–9, 51–5, 57–9, 231, 232
114th, 37, 54, 59, 60, 231, 232
115th, 29, 37, 39, 41, 43, 46, 48, 51–3, 55, 58, 59, 123, 231
116th, 29, 37, 39, 43, 45, 48, 49, 51–3, 55, 56, 58, 59, 123, 231
125th, 89, 92, 232
126th, 89, 232
127th, 89, 92, 232
128th, 89–92, 105, 107, 232
129th, 20, 26, 35, 233
130th, 20, 26, 35, 233
131st, 20, 21, 26, 32, 34, 233
132nd, 20, 21, 26, 28, 29, 31, 33, 34, 113, 233
313th, 70, 71, 74, 83, 84, 150, 216, 221–3, 233
314th, 70, 71, 74, 78, 79, 81–3, 127, 150, 214, 217, 218, 221, 225, 233
315th, 70, 71, 74, 76, 83, 150, 221, 223, 233
316th, 70, 71, 74, 76, 78, 81, 83, 133, 137, 139–42, 150, 164, 221, 233
320th, 26

**Battalions:**
111th MG, 47, 58, 74, 231
124th MG, 21, 29, 31, 233
312th MG, 74, 233

Amiens, Battle of, 2, 3, 244
Anderson, 1st Sgt, J.S., 31, 32
Argonne, Forest, xvii, xix, 4, 6, 10, 15, 34, 116, 192, 195

Austro-Hungarian, 11, 29, 32, 35, 36, 39, 40, 43, 45, 111, 114, 116, 117, 121, 122, 130, 145, 193, 236, 244, 246
Azannes-et-Soumazannes, 69, 78, 83, 86, 87, 89, 150, 153, 165, 206, 217, 221
Azannes-et-Soumazannes German Cemetery, 137, 153, 155, 158

Bamford, Brig Gen F.E., 66, 231
Barbären Brunnen, 137, 145, 146
Barnabé, Père, 110, 117–20
Barricourt Heights, 73
Beaumont, 29, 85
Beaumont-Hamel, Somme, 158
Becker, 137, 157, 158
Belenet, Gen J. de, 235
Bélieu Wood, 57–60, 65–8, 71, 74, 78, 217
Bell Jr., Maj Gen G., 20, 233
Belleau Wood, xv
Bonne Espérance Ridge, 89
Borg, Klaus, 170
Bourvaux Ravine, 46
Boussières Ravine, 45
Brabant Line, 33, 39, 40, 123
Brabant-sur-Meuse, xxi, 28, 29, 32, 33, 39, 48, 54, 59, 113, 123, 128, 244
Brabant Wood, 29, 45
Brandeville, 73, 90–2, 103, 105, 107, 163, 167, 173–5
Brandeville Necropole Nationale, 107, 175, 176
Bréhéville, 90, 107, 159, 173
Brieulles-sur-Meuse, 25, 26, 73, 77, 90, 91, 95, 96, 98, 99, 102, 105, 139, 142, 182, 185–8, 195, 197, 203, 243
Brieulles Wood, 26

Buck, Gen B.B., 42
Buisson Chaumont Wood, 79, 81
Bultroy Wood, 52, 55–7, 59,
   66, 133
Bundy, Maj Gen O., 46

Caldwell, Brig Gen V.A., 39
Canal de l'Est, 184, 185, 188, 195
Caures Wood, 46, 87, 235, 245
Château Thierry, xiv, 61, 89
Châtillon Wood, 102, 103, 184,
   185, 187, 200, 240
Chaume Wood, 25, 29, 32–6, 46,
   74, 76, 113, 129, 142
Chaumont-devant-Damvillers,
   xxi, 83, 85, 148, 150, 214, 218,
   220–2
Chênes Wood, 57, 58, 63, 65, 66,
   71, 127
Claudel, Gen, H.E., 10, 11, 27,
   47, 70, 77, 216, 218, 230
Cléry-le-Petit, xxi, 96, 100–103,
   109, 182, 183, 188–90
Coassinvaux Ravine, 49, 54, 58,
   63, 125
   see also Death Valley
Consenvoye, xviii, xxi, 15, 25, 28,
   29, 32, 33, 39, 41, 43, 52, 110,
   112–15, 134, 139, 200, 203,
   247, 250
Consenvoye German Cemetery,
   110, 114, 116, 117
Consenvoye Wood, 29, 32, 34, 36,
   39, 41, 45–7, 51, 131, 135, 137
Costin, Pte H.G., 42
Côte Dame Marie, 89
Côte de Morimont, 83, 214,
   221, 223
Côte de Poivre, 63
Côte de Romagne, 81, 83, 84,
   214, 221, 225
Côte des Roches, 49, 54

Côte d'Horgne, 78, 83, 217,
   218, 221
Côte Laimont Wood, 26, 102
Côte St. Germain, 103, 105, 106,
   161, 180, 181
Crépion, 79, 138, 148–50, 204,
   206, 207, 217, 221
Croix de Guerre, 55, 123
Cul de la Vaux Ravine, 78
Cunel, 15, 34, 36, 95, 182,
   197, 246

Damvillers, xxi, 83, 84, 87, 92,
   137, 143, 144, 145, 150, 165,
   169, 170, 175, 204, 206, 214,
   217, 221, 235, 244, 247, 250
Damvillers German Cemetery,
   137, 144, 146
Dannevoux, 20, 24, 26
Death Valley, 49, 63, 64, 71,
   80, 112, 125, 127, 150, 212,
   213, 221
   see also Coassinvaux Ravine
Distinguished Dervice Cross, 45,
   55, 176, 216
Doulcon, xxi, 96, 100, 183, 190,
   191, 195
Drillancourt, 20
Drum, Maj Gen H., 230
Dun-sur-Meuse, xx, xxi, 73, 77,
   90, 96, 102, 104, 105, 142,
   165, 167, 175, 178, 182, 184,
   190–2, 194, 197, 240, 246, 250
Dun-sur-Meuse German
   Cemetery, 184, 192, 193

Écurey-en-Verdunnois, 73, 78, 90,
   91, 162, 164, 216, 217, 246,
   248
Edwards, Maj Gen C.R., 61,
   66, 231
Ely, Maj Gen H.E., 95, 182

Étraye, 41, 43, 52, 73, 78, 216, 217, 247, 248
Étraye Wood, 57, 59, 60, 71, 78, 133, 217
Etzel Line, 14, 20, 29, 46, 48, 53, 142, 148, 217

Flabas, 69, 72, 86. 244, 248
Foch, Marshal F., xvii, 1, 2, 4–7
Fontaines-Saint-Clair, 105, 107
Forges, 20, 21, 25, 33, 243
Forges Creek, 20, 21
Forges Wood, 20, 21, 23

**French Army**

**Corps:**
XVII, xix, 10, 27, 28, 36, 38, 46, 54, 56–8, 63, 70, 71, 73, 77, 85, 86, 90, 230, 236, 240
II Colonial, 77, 78, 240

**Divisions:**
10th Colonial, 85
15th Colonial, 17, 37, 58, 72, 73, 76, 81, 90, 91, 96, 105, 107, 129, 185, 200, 216, 235
18th, 28, 29, 32, 34–8, 38, 46–8, 51, 57, 60, 63, 124, 204, 235, 236
26th, 28, 63, 72, 85, 235, 236

**Regiments:**
66th, 54

Freya Line, 73, 96
Frosch, Feldbahnhof, 137, 151, 153
Fuchs, Cav Gen G., 242

**German Army**
XVI Corps, 157
XVIII Corps, 242, 243, 245–7

**Divisions:**
1st Austro-Hungarian, 29, 32, 46
1st Landwehr, 204, 218, 243, 248
7th Res Div, 29, 157, 242, 243, 245
15th Div, 242–4, 248
27th, 243, 247
32nd, 29, 33, 34, 46, 247, 248
33rd, 242, 243, 246, 247
106th Austro-Hungarian, 243, 244–6, 248
192nd, 60, 65, 242, 247
228th, 29, 36, 53, 133, 243–6

**Regiments:**
5th KuK, 33
61st KuK, 29
102nd, 34
112th KuK, 41
177th, 34
232nd Res. KuK, 34, 244
177th, 34

**Battalions:**
105th KuK Sturm Bat., 34

Gallwitz, General M. von, xix, xx, 12, 242, 244
Gibercy, 83, 145–8
Giselher Line, 15, 34, 54, 73, 74, 76, 78, 79, 133, 143, 161–4
Goiginer, Field Marshal L., 242, 243
Grande Montagne, 34, 54, 140, 141, 162
Grande Montagne Wood, 35, 52, 54–9, 73, 74, 76, 77, 133, 142
Gregory, Sgt E.D., 45, 46
Grémilly, 137, 154, 155, 157
Groener, Maj Gen W., 242, 243, 246
Gruppe Beaumont, 232, 242, 243, 247

Gruppe Ornes, 242, 243, 245–7
Guérin, Gen, 235
Gunther, H.N., v, xxi, 84, 85, 137, 149–51, 214–16, 221–3, 225, 227, 229

Haan, Maj Gen, W.G., 89, 232
Hagen Line, 14, 20, 23, 33, 39, 41, 123, 136
Haraumont, 73, 77, 78, 129, 159, 161–3
Haumont-près-Samogneux, 29, 40, 67, 80, 112, 121, 123–5, 127, 213
Haumont Wood, 29, 43, 49, 63, 65, 124, 213, 235
Hill 252, 102
Hill 319, 81, 83, 85, 218–22, 225
Hill 328, 79, 81–3, 85, 215, 218–20, 222, 225
Hill 350, 181
Hill 360, 65–7, 79, 181, 204, 206, 207, 212, 217
    see also Ormont Hill
Hill 370, 52, 73, 75
Hill 378, 73–6, 140
Hindenburg Line or Zone, 2, 9, 11, 14–17, 34, 70, 73, 83, 89, 90, 96, 161
Hindenburg, Field Marshal P. von, 3
Houppy Wood, 59, 65
Hundred Days' Offensive, 1, 2

Jacobi, Gen A. von, 243
Jametz, 92, 108
Joel, 2nd Lt A.H., 71, 72, 79, 81, 83, 127
Johnston, Capt E., 45
Juanahandy, Capt, P., 111, 123, 146

Kriemhild Line, xv, 16, 27, 54, 78, 93, 142–4, 150, 159, 161–4, 184, 185, 202, 203, 221, 245
Kühler, Sgt H., 31
Kuhn, Maj Gen J.H., 70, 218, 233

Lady, 2nd Lt I., 75
l'Andon Creek, 109,
Leuthold, Lt Gen M., 242, 243
l'Herminette, 96, 182, 185
Liggett, Gen H., 16, 17, 66, 73, 230
Liny-devant-Dun, 98, 99, 103–105, 178, 184, 195, 196, 197, 200, 201
Liny-devant-Dun German Cemetery, 198, 199
Lion-devant-Dun, 105–107, 159, 180, 181
Lissey, 107, 159, 168, 173
Lissey German Cemetery, 169–72
Lissey Wood, 92, 171
Loison Creek, 108
Loman, Pte B.H., 33
Longuyon, xx, 96, 108
Long Wood, 73
Louppy-sur-Loison, 106, 108, 109
Ludendorff, Lt Gen E. von, 3, 7
Luke, Frank, 161, 176, 178–80

Maas Gruppe Ost, xix, 11, 29, 46, 242–6, 248
Maas Gruppe West, 242, 243, 245
Maginot Line, 118, 161, 163, 167, 175, 177
Mallon, Capt G.H., 23
Mang, Volker, 170
Malbrouck Hill, 29, 39, 40, 41–3, 45, 112, 123, 129, 130
Marne, xiv, 1, 4, 5, 61, 243, 244, 246
Marwitz, von, xx, 11, 46, 242, 249
Maur, Maj Gen H. von, 243
McMahon, Maj Gen J.E., 230

Medal of Honor, 23, 24, 31–3, 42, 43, 45, 46, 68, 176, 180, 190, 191

Metz, 4, 5, 10, 157, 167, 242, 244, 246

Metzger, Field Marsal J., 242, 244

Meuse-Argonne American Cemetery, xi, 83, 179, 180, 239

Meuse, Heights, xvii, xviii, xix, 11, 14, 15, 21, 27, 28, 46, 47, 78, 87, 96, 109, 122, 141, 150, 189, 214, 217, 221, 223, 224, 235, 240, 245, 246

Meuse, River, xix, 34, 38, 41, 96, 112, 120, 185, 191

Michael, Operation, 1

Michel Zone, 5, 7–9, 158, 247

Milly-sur-Bradon, 102, 103, 105, 178, 180, 181, 240

Moirey, 69, 78, 79, 86, 87, 217, 222, 248

Moirey Wood, 59, 60, 85, 248

Molleville Farm, 36, 47, 48, 52, 58, 59, 71, 133, 134, 137, 206, 207, 218

Molleville Ravine, 47, 53, 55, 56, 59, 63, 65, 112, 130, 131, 133, 134, 207

Molleville Wood, 46, 48, 49, 52, 53, 55, 59, 132

Montfaucon, xi, xix, 14, 69, 70, 71, 112, 141, 142, 180, 195–7, 216, 246

Morton, Maj Gen C.G., 37, 47, 53, 54, 231

Mouzay, 105, 108, 175, 240

Moyenvaux, gully, 98, 99, 101, 103, 198

Murvaux, 102, 103, 105, 175, 176, 178–80

Museum Meuse-Argonne 1918, 251

Nantillois, 26, 71, 197, 216, 246, 251, 255

Neufchâteau, 5, 61

Opie, Maj, 55

Ormont Farm, 29, 32, 49, 54, 63, 206, 208, 209, 235

Ormont Hill, v, xxi, 29, 57, 60, 66, 67, 72, 78–80, 150, 204, 212, 217
    *see also* Hill 360

Ormont Wood, 35, 36, 47, 49, 51, 54, 56–9, 65, 68, 72, 74, 78, 204, 207, 210, 212, 217

Oven, Gen E. von, 242

Paris, 1, 4, 5, 118

Perkins, Pte 1st Class M.J., 68

Pershing, Gen J.J., xxi, xiv, 1, 3–9, 17, 66, 142, 150, 165, 184, 191, 192, 222, 230, 237, 240, 241

Peuvillers, 73, 93, 159, 164–9

Peuvillers German Cemetery, 159, 167, 169

Plat Chêne Wood, 34, 35, 47, 52, 53, 56, 142

Quartière, La, 49

Regan, 2nd Lt P.J., 42, 43

Reine Wood, La, 49, 54, 59, 65

Remoiville, 82, 108

Réville-aux-Bois, 77, 78, 143, 144, 216, 217,

Réville Wood, 57

Ribbentrop, Maj Gen W., 242, 243

Richene Hill, 47, 48, 71

Romagne-sous-les-Côtes, 78, 81, 150, 158, 217, 221

Romagne-sous-Montfaucon, 15, 16, 34, 54, 75, 83, 89, 162, 179, 180, 195, 239, 246

Romagne-sous-Montfaucon German Cemetery, 198

Sandlin, Sgt W.B., 23, 24
Samogneux, 15, 29, 33, 39, 42, 71, 96, 110, 112, 117–23, 127, 169, 213, 235
Sedan, xv, xx, 163, 244, 245
Sivry-sur-Meuse, xviii, 24, 26, 28-30, 34, 35, 57, 73, 74, 76, 77, 107, 129, 137–41, 158, 163, 175, 203, 216, 235, 244, 245
Slack, Pte C.K., 31
Soden, Gen F.L. Freiherr von, 11, 12, 33, 242, 243
Spring Offensive, xiv, xxi, 1, 2, 41, 61, 237, 243, 246, 248
Stenay, xi, 24, 73, 96, 107, 112, 137, 138, 159, 181, 182, 246, 250, 252, 254
St. Mihiel, xvi, xix, xxi, 3–10, 12, 15, 17, 20, 61, 62, 95, 158, 176, 180, 235, 242, 247
St. Panthealon Chapel, 137, 139
Stone, Capt, 45

Tappen, Lt Gen G, 242, 243
Theriault, 2nd Lt J.E., 41
Thil Wood, 83, 150, 151, 215, 221, 225, 226–9

Thinte Creek, 28, 79, 92, 93, 216, 217
Tielz, Wilhelm, 213
Tischler, Robert, 198

Vaux de Mille Mais Ravine, 35, 74
Vaux de St. Martin Ravine, 52
Ville, de, Wood, 87
Ville-devant-Chaumont, 83, 87, 150, 151, 216, 219–21, 225, 229
Ville-devant-Chaumont German Cemetery, 137, 150, 152
Villeneuve Farm, 34, 35
Vilosnes, 73, 77, 96, 103, 105, 107, 129, 159, 161, 163, 184, 185, 200, 202, 203, 235,
Volker Line, 39, 43, 46, 142, 162, 164, 245
Vosges, 12, 95, 116, 170, 171

Wavrille, 73, 78, 216, 217
Wavrille Wood, 71, 74, 78, 79, 217
Wiesenschlenken Line, 20, 21
Wilson, Pres., xii, xiii
Woëvre Plains, 74, 79, 87, 217, 250
Wolf, Brig Gen, 35
Woodcock, Capt, 55

Zeidler, Bruno, 213